LOG OF THE UNION

LOG OF THE UNION

JOHN BOIT'S REMARKABLE VOYAGE

To the Northwest Coast and Around the World

1794-1796

edited by

EDMUND HAYES

F.R.G.S.

O H S

MCMLXXXI

To
S.E.M.
alias Olaf, the deckhand,
whose inspiration is largely responsible
for this publication.

LOG OF THE UNION

specially illustrated by
HEWITT R. JACKSON

Title page:
The *Union*: Stern view with sweeps used to aid navigation. (Hewitt Jackson)

North Pacific Studies No. 6

Contents

Foreword

    Thomas Vaughan   xi

Preface

    Edmund Hayes   xiv

Introduction

    Edmund Hayes   xvii

Editorial Principles

    Bruce T. Hamilton   xxxvii

Journal and Remarks of a Voyage Around the World

1794-1796

Newport, Rhode Island
to the
Falkland Islands

29 August 1794 to 21 January 1795   3

The Falkland Islands
to Columbia's Cove,
Vancouver Island

22 January to 16 May 1795   25

Trading
on the
Northwest Coast

17 May to 11 September 1795   41

The Hawaiian Islands
to
Canton, China

18 October 1795 to 10 January 1796   80

Columbia's Cove
to the
Hawaiian Islands

12 September 1795 to 17 October 1795   66

Canton
to
Boston, Massachusetts

11 January to 8 July 1796   93

Notes

Edmund Hayes   121

Research on the Sloop *Union*

Hewitt R. Jackson   127

Illustrations

The *Union*: Stern view with sweeps.
(Hewitt Jackson)   Title page

The *Union*: Full profile. (Hewitt Jackson)   xvi

Map: Boston, 1775.   xix

John Boit, Sr.   xxvii

John Boit, Jr.   xxvii

Sarah Brown Boit   xxvii

The *Union* entering Boston Harbor,
drawn by John Boit, Jr.   xxix

Map: World Chart with *Union*'s course.
(Hewitt Jackson)   xxxii-xxxiii

The *Union* at Columbia's Cove, September
1795. (Hewitt Jackson)   Frontis

Log of the *Union*: John Boit, Jr's. manuscript
title page (part one).   5

Log of the *Union*: Original entries for 6-9
September 1794.   6

The *Union*: Cross section at main hatch.
(Hewitt Jackson)   12

The *Union*: Inboard profile; Quarter board and
bulwark details. (Hewitt Jackson)   19

Profile of Jasons Isles, drawn by John Boit, Jr.   21

Map: West Falkland Island, drawn by
John Boit, Jr.   22

Map: States Bay, drawn by John Boit, Jr.   23

Profile of Staten Island, drawn by John Boit, Jr.   27

The *Union*: Cross section at 3. (Hewitt Jackson)   32

The *Union*: Cross section at L. (Hewitt Jackson)   33

Map: Northwest Coast with *Union*'s course.
(Hewitt Jackson)   38-39

Log of the *Union*: Original entries for 30 May–
2 June 1795.   44

The *Union* and Nootkan canoe near Nootka Sound.
(Hewitt Jackson)   46

The *Union* at Nootka Sound, drawn by
John Boit, Jr. 48

The *Union*'s battle with Indians at Barrell's Sound,
21 June 1795. (Hewitt Jackson) 51

The *Union* arriving off the mouth of the Columbia
River, 12 July 1795. (Hewitt Jackson) 54

Log of the *Union*: Original entries for 5-8
August 1795. 58

Map: Bulfinch Sound (Nasparti Inlet),
drawn by John Boit, Jr. 60

Map: Queen Charlotte Islands. (Hewitt Jackson) 62

Log of the *Union*: John Boit, Jr's. manuscript
title page (part two). 68

The *Union*: Rudder details. (Hewitt Jackson) 69

Log of the *Union*: Original 16 October
1795 entry. 71

The *Union*: Deck details, ground tackle and
armament. (Hewitt Jackson) 73

The *Union*: Deck structure and details.
(Hewitt Jackson) 75

The *Union*: Jib stay details. (Hewitt Jackson) 76

The *Union*: Windlass and cable details. (Hewitt
Jackson) 77

The *Union*: Longboat details and plans. (Hewitt
Jackson) 78

The *Union*: Cross section at 12. (Hewitt Jackson) 82

The *Union*: Cross section at F. (Hewitt Jackson) 83

Map: Pearl River Delta, Canton and Macao with
Union's course. (Hewitt Jackson) 84

Map: Canton detail. (Hewitt Jackson) 85

Map: Macao detail. (Hewittt Jackson) 85

The *Union* nearing the Boca Tigris and the Pearl
River, 4 December 1795. (Hewitt Jackson) 89

Map: South China Sea and Sunda Strait with
Union's course. (Hewitt Jackson) 96

Map: Straits of Bangka and Sunda and *Union*'s
course. (Hewitt Jackson) 97

The *Union*, with sails reefed, rounding Cape of Good
Hope, April 1796. (Hewitt Jackson) 107

Map: Boston and environs, late eighteenth century. 116

The *Union* entering Boston Harbor, 8 July 1796.
(Hewitt Jackson) 118

Preliminary study for the reconstruction of the sloop
Union. (Hewitt Jackson) 128

Preliminary study of the *Union* at Barrell's Sound.
(Hewitt Jackson) 131

Foreword

At last blue-water sailors have reinterpreted this mariner's classic story, laid down in the dawn of America's greatness. This is heady reading in our time, when the maritime towns of legendary fame are laced with empty and shoaled-up wharves boasting flea markets and tennis clubs. For the moment it would appear that youthful exploits, along with maritime opportunity, have vanished to the dark side of the moon. Not so for the late 18th century. We are captured, as John Boit, Jr., 19 years old and already a merchant captain, blithely enters in his Log on August 1, 1794, "Adieu to the pretty girls of Newport."

Down Narragansett Bay, Boit sailed his own ship, the long-limbed *Union* (89 tons burthen), bound for the Northwest Coast with a bone in her teeth; off on a voyage with 22 young men, 10 carriage guns and lots of other armament for natives and Chinese pirates; bent on a global voyage, which chairbound sailors today study with awe; around the Horn around the world, and most profitably too for Boit's counting-house backers. No novice here, but a young argonaut who earlier trained with Robert Gray, sailing around the world (the first by an American merchant captain) in the *Columbia Rediviva* as Gray's fifth mate.

It was Boit who at 17 wrote the memorable description of that laconic Boston trader's most famous discovery of May 12, 1792. Perhaps the stripling did not write every word, but the description is in his Journal of the *Columbia Rediviva*, and we think he did go to the Boston Latin School:

"This day saw an appearance of a spacious harbour abrest the Ship haul'd our wind for itt, observ'd two sand bars making off, with a passage between them to a fine river. . . . the River extended to the N.E. as far as eye cou'd reach, . . . we directed our course up this noble river in search of a Village. The beach

was lin'd with Natives, who ran along shore following the Ship." Later [18 May 1792] Boit stated: "Vast many Canoes full of Indians . . . were constantly along side. Capt. Grays [sic] named this river Columbia's and the North entrance Cape Hancock, and the South Point Adams."* Boit subsequently wrote the only complete narrative of this audacious voyage around the world.

When the *Columbia Rediviva* at last returned home to Boston from the Northwest Coast and Canton via the Cape, Boit signed almost immediately for Virginia and Dublin as mate in the *Eliza*. When Boit sailed the *Union* as captain we know that a half-owner in the sturdy sloop was his brother-in-law Caleb Hatch. But we need be under no illusion. Boit was chosen because (even in his late teens) he was a proven master of an unforgiving profession in command at sea.

When Boit and his zestful young men arrived in Columbia's Cove, Bulfinch Sound (Nasparti Inlet) on the treacherous west coast of Vancouver Island, they were 260 days out from Newport and more than ready for the trade that made Boston men (any American) famous and sometimes notorious on the Coast. What a ring it gives his story to have the natives come swarming out, and then to recognize him and to inquire of his companions from the *Columbia*.

Hair-raising is his account of later being attacked by several hundred Indians off the south tip of the Queen Charlotte Islands. A murderous flotilla that would only retreat after cannons and swivel guns had killed 40 or more outraged or rapacious natives and their war leader. There were no casualties in the *Union* but Boit again appears as a no-nonsense man, whom one might see as bold, resourceful and maybe fair.

---

*Frederic W. Howay, *Voyages of the "Columbia" to the Northwest Coast* (Boston, 1941), pp. 397-98.

And so he appeared to be throughout his life as a mariner (as he was so listed a year before his death in Boston at 55 years in 1829). One way or another this captain always returned to the sea.

Edmund Hayes, a friend of many years, has carefully analyzed and edited this remarkable story. It was Mr. Hayes who encouraged Mr. Hewitt Jackson to provide the illustrations for this volume. To have been involved in some small way in the publication of this voyage has given me much pleasure. Because, as Boit encircled the globe, his account drew a sterling circle for me. The man who first urged Edmund Hayes to undertake this demanding editorial job was his old friend and sailing companion Samuel Eliot Morison. "Sam" served as cook and part-time crew for Edmund and Anna Hayes in the mid-1930s, sailing the rough sea passage between the Columbia capes and Nootka—bound for Columbia's Cove.

I was first directed to these North Pacific voyages by a great historian, Fulmer Mood, who long ago served as professor Morison's first graduate assistant at Harvard. And it was Walter Muir Whitehill, another old Boston friend of Samuel Morison and of the Oregon Historical Society, who further urged that this publication be undertaken. He understood the rock-ribbed associations between Boston and Oregon. (After all our Portland on the Columbia was named Boston but for the errant turn of a flipped coin.) Walter followed through on this publication with the Massachusetts Historical Society, when he flew home from our Oregon visit to his beloved Boston—just a few days before his sudden death. We are all grateful to that Society's executive director Stephen Riley and Len Tucker for their fine scholarly interest and spirit of cooperation.

When Boit began his long voyage home from the fur markets of Canton and Whampoa in January 1796, he had yet to sail through the China Sea, the treacherous Sunda Strait, the Indian Ocean and around Cape of Good Hope. What a time he had with roaring seas, leaking bulwarks, prowling French warships and rough English officers searching for faulty paper and unexpected prize.

From long experience Edmund Hayes and Hewitt Jackson know their ships and rigging as this study beautifully attests. Their singular partnership has resurrected much lost treasure from the past. They conclude that the tiny *Union* may be the only American sloop-rigged, fur-trading vessel ever to girdle the globe—giving us a unique voyage. And when Boit got his sailors safely home they were given three huzzas from the wharves. And a fine newspaper account appeared in the *Boston Centennial* under "Arrivals," to wit: "Sloop *Union*, Boit, Canton." Perhaps William Wordsworth said it best for those times and those youthful adventures. "Bliss was it in that time to be alive," said the poet in 1792, "but to be young was very Heaven." Such opportunities for every generation should ever obtain and we are indebted to Edmund Hayes and to his associate Hewitt Jackson for bringing them back to mind.

Thomas Vaughan
Executive Director
Oregon Historical Society

Preface

The initiation and development of the maritime fur trade with the Northwest Coast of America in the eighteenth and nineteenth centuries was largely responsible for that coast's early exploration. The recorded history of the period is derived in large part from the journals and logs of the ships that participated in this trade. One of the earliest and most important, because it covered the complete second voyage of the *Columbia Rediviva* to the Northwest Coast, was that of John Boit, Jr., its fifth officer. This Log, together with all his other logs and journals, was bequeathed to the Massachusetts Historical Society in 1919 by his grandson, Robert Apthorpe Boit, and published in the *Proceedings* of the society (Vol. 53). In December, 1921, with the permission of the Massachusetts Historical Society, the complete log was also published in the *Oregon Historical Quarterly*, of the Oregon Historical Society, with annotations by Judge F. W. Ho-

way and T. C. Elliott, two of the most respected historians of Northwest history.

Early in the 1930s, the editor read Boit's Log of the *Columbia* and, later, the classic book of Samuel Eliot Morison, *The Maritime History of Massachusetts* (1921). This kindled a desire to visit the west coast of Vancouver Island and the various anchorages of the fur-trading ships. Through correspondence with Dr. Morison relative to a number of vessels mentioned in his book, a cruise together up the Northwest Coast from Astoria to Nootka Sound was arranged and accomplished in the editor's 40-foot auxiliary ketch, the *Seaway*, during the summer of 1937. Many historic places and anchorages were visited: Friendly Cove, where Captain George Vancouver met the Spanish Governor Bodega y Quadra in 1792; Resolution Cove on Bly Island where Captain James Cook first landed in 1778; Clayoquot Sound where the *Columbia* wintered in 1791-1792; and Barkley Sound, named after the captain of the *Imperial Eagle*, who is given credit for discovering and naming the Strait of Juan de Fuca.

It was during the above cruise that such effective use was made of Boit's Log of the *Columbia*, and the suggestion was made toward arranging the publication of his "Journal and Remarks of the Sloop *Union*, 1794-1796." Many years have passed without accomplishing this end. Finally, in 1979, permission was given to the Oregon Historical Society by the Massachusetts Historical Society to publish the Log of the *Union*.

I wish to express the appreciation of the Oregon Historical Society for this permission and trust it will be a worthy companion of Boit's *Columbia* Journal.

I take complete responsibility for the editing of this important Journal and the Remarks. I wish to list and thank the following persons who have given so much of their efforts and time in its publication:

Thomas Vaughan, Executive Director of the Oregon Historical Society, for his inspiration, advice and cooperation on manuscript availability.

Hewitt R. Jackson, artist and marine researcher, for his drawings, maps and marine background.

Colleen Campbell, Richard Lowry and Tracy Robinson, for their participation in the production of this book.

Louis L. Tucker, Director, and the Officers of the Massachusetts Historical Society for their generous cooperation in this venture.

C. Jared Ingersoll, a direct descendant of John Boit, Jr., who permitted the reproduction of the original miniature of John Boit's parents and John Boit, Jr., and who also supplied a photostatic copy of the original Journal of the *Union*.

Bruce T. Hamilton, book editor and manager of the Publications Department of the Oregon Historical Society, for his technical knowledge and artistic abilities in producing this book.

Joseph A. Schiewek, Jr., whose patient and accurate transcription of John Boit's undecipherable penmanship was an achievement.

Leonard Clay, a fisherman and organizer of the West Coast Maritime Museum at Tofino, B.C., who supplied valuable information on the Indian tribes and villages of the west coast of Vancouver Island and the Queen Charlotte Islands.

Vesta Hively, my secretary, for her accurate, painstaking and speedy typing of the manuscript.

Edmund Hayes

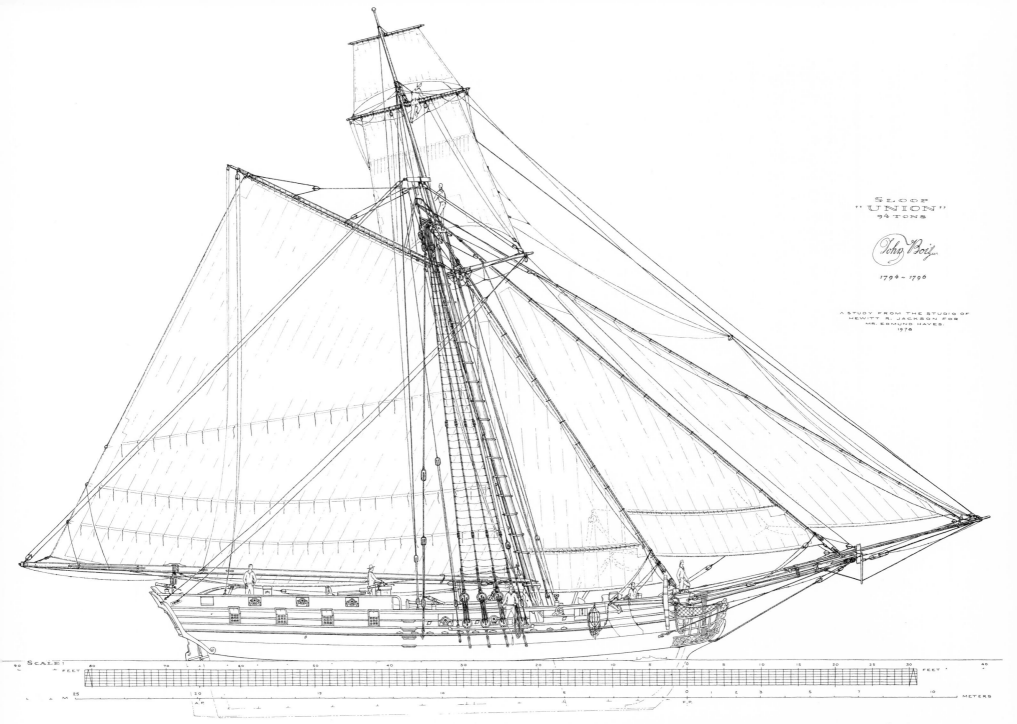

SLOOP
"UNION"
94 TONS

John Boit

1794 ~ 1796

A STUDY FROM THE STUDIO OF
HEWITT R. JACKSON FOR
MR. EDMUND HAYES.
1978

SCALE:

At the end of the two-year voyage, John Boit, Jr., wrote in his Remarks: "*I believe the* Union *was the first sloop that ever circumnavigated the globe.*"

The *Union*: Hewitt Jackson's painstaking reconstruction of John Boit's sloop reveals the rake to its mast and rigging, and how small this ocean-going ship was.

Introduction

Edmund Hayes

The Lewis and Clark Expedition (1804-1806), through its superb organization and accomplishment, gathered geographical information on the northwest quarter of the United States, which opened these lands to immigration and commercial development far sooner than otherwise would have been possible. The overland expedition was more spectacular than contemporary maritime explorations of the Pacific Coast by foreign ships of discovery and fur-trading vessels, from 1775 when the Spanish explorer Bruno Heceta lay off the mouth of the Columbia River and recorded that it must be *"the mouth of some great river, or of some passage to another sea."*[1] He was far more accurate than he knew, also he was the first European to work up the coast from California and reach the north tip of the Queen Charlotte Islands. This was 30 years before Lewis and Clark reached the Pacific Ocean.

The period between 1775 and 1806 was extremely active in maritime discovery and commercial fur trading along the coasts of present Oregon, Washington, British Columbia and Alaska. Many of the journals and logs of these ships were published at that time and no doubt encouraged President Jefferson to seek the approval of Congress to fund an expedition to explore the vast area of land between the Mississippi River and the Pacific Coast acquired in the Louisiana Purchase from France. It was even suggested that some contact be made by Lewis and Clark with one of the fur-trading vessels then on the coast and perhaps obtain passage home, thus eliminating the long trek back over the trail they had pioneered.

---

1. Quoted by Warren L. Cook in *Flood Tide of Empire: Spain and the Pacific Northwest, 1543-1819* (New Haven, 1973), p. 78.

The reference to the maritime discoveries on the Pacific Coast is not to detract from the great discoveries made by the Lewis and Clark Expedition, but to bring them into clearer focus and indicate their contribution in the development of the north Pacific Coast.

This volume contains an abridgement of the Log of the fur-trading sloop *Union*, under the command of Captain John Boit, Jr.; the *Union* made a voyage to the Northwest Coast and on around the world, between August 29, 1794, and July 8, 1796. This is interspersed with extracts from the Remarks, which Boit wrote after his return. (The Oregon Historical Society is most appreciative for the permission of the Massachusetts Historical Society to publish this abridgement of the manuscript Log and extracts from the Remarks, which were placed in their archives many years ago.)

Admiral Samuel Eliot Morison, in his classic book *The Maritime History of Massachusetts*, classifies the voyage of the *Union* as "*the most remarkable youthful exploit in this bright dawn of Pacific adventure.*"[2]

Captain John Boit was just 19 years of age and in full charge of the sloop with a crew of 22 men when she took her departure from Newport, Rhode Island, August 29th, 1794. She was 94 tons burthen, 65'5" overall length, 19'9" beam and 8'5" depth. To that time, she was the only vessel of her size and rig to circle the world. The *Lady Washington*, Captain Robert Gray, a sloop of nearly identical size, had reached the Pacific in 1788 as consort to the ship *Columbia*, but she never accomplished the encirclement of the globe. Boit's voyage took place only 16 years after the landing of Captain Cook at Nootka Sound, Vancouver Island, in 1778 and two years after the discovery and preliminary charting of Puget Sound and the Northwest Coast by Captain George Vancouver in 1792.

The sloop *Union* is of special interest to students of Northwest maritime history not only because of her exploits during the long voyage, but because she exemplified the contribution that early fur-trading vessels made to the geographical knowledge of the vast Northwest Coast and in the pioneering of its economic development.

There are many factors that give background to this voyage and afford a clearer understanding of the conditions and problems under which it was made. These factors will be outlined below.

Maritime New England

It is important to quickly trace the early maritime history of New England because of that area's preponderant involvement in the fur trade between the Northwest Coast and China following the Revolutionary War. In addition, a large percentage of the vessels, involved in the trade, and more importantly, the capable seamen to handle them came from New England. A number of points about the importance of the sea to New England have been made by Admiral Morison in his *Maritime History of Massachusetts*. The sea was the material sustenance of Massachusetts in the Colonial and Revolutionary periods. The dependence of New England on the sea for its economic existence in the seventeenth and eighteenth centuries found a satisfactory answer in its trade with the West Indies—the latter dependent on New England for salted and dried fish, timber, and other provisions, a trade which had no substitute. The high grades of fish were exported to Europe and the lower grades, mackerel, bass and alewives, supplied the West Indies.

The building of ships to transport the products of New England to foreign markets contributed greatly to its economy. Ship building by 1660 had become a leading industry in the larger and smaller ports. The colonial fleet con-

2. Samuel Eliot Morison, *The Maritime History of Massachusetts, 1783-1860* (Boston, 1921), p. 74.

sisted for the most part of small sloops and ketches, 20 to 30 tons burthen. New England built most of the ships which carried bulk cargo from Chesapeake Bay to England and southern Europe and by the end of the seventeenth century it was a thriving maritime colony consisting of a chain of prosperous trading towns and fishing villages with a merchant fleet of some 430 cargo vessels.

The eighteenth century brought an increase of activity in ship building and commerce. Even London complained their shipwrights and workmen were being drawn off to American shipyards. Peace reigned in New England from 1713 to 1776 and its maritime activities continued to multiply. The population of Boston was 7,000 in 1690 and increased to an estimated 17,000 by 1740. Immigration from many European countries added to an English Puritan base which produced a tough but restless population. The stratification of society was exemplified in dress, houses and wealth, which was not necessarily democratic. It was possible to pass from one class to another but in reality a great gulf existed between the squire and the fisherman. The rule of the sea was obedience to the master of the ship, which infused a basic discipline in the population as a whole. Merchants ruled society and politics during this period. They were a class which prospered greatly, particularly in the export trade, and lived accordingly. The backbone of maritime Massachusetts was its middle class made up largely of captains and other officers, master builders, and shipwrights.

The Revolutionary War brought a drastic change to the society and economy of New England. Many of its commercial vessels were converted into privateers by being granted letters of marque by the Continental Congress and the general courts. These grants gave the vessels permission to attack British merchant ships on the high seas and confiscate their cargoes. Needless to say, it was a risky operation for the American vessels involved, but also exceedingly rewarding to their owners and made a great

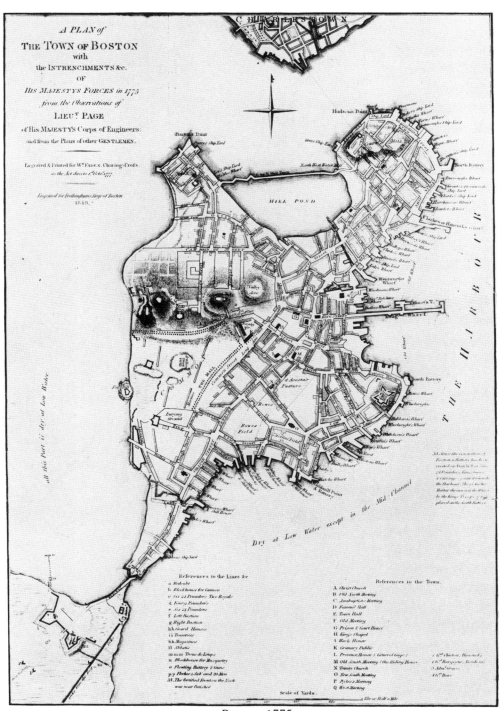

Boston, 1775.

contribution to the final success of the Colonies in winning the war. They were very effective in preying on England's commerce through intercepting their communications and supplying the Colonies with munitions, stores, clothing and the essentials of existence. Privateering fishermen and seamen learned daring seamanship and strengthened the aptitude and tradition of the Colonies. The design of sailing vessels was greatly improved to provide the necessary speed for such operations. Under these licenses to take prizes, commerce was continued with the West Indies, France and Spain throughout the war.

Although the American colonies won the war and their independence, the war's termination precipitated a severe depression. This raised havoc with the resurgence of fishing, seafaring and all maritime activity. By 1786, the exports of Massachusetts were only one-fifth of what they had been 12 years earlier. The fishing and whaling fleets had to be replaced; the codfish trade with the British West Indies, as well as the whale fisheries with England, had to be rebuilt. After four years of peace about four-fifths of the Grand Banks fleet was in commission, but by 1789 only one-third of the whaling tonnage had been restored. New England thrift was taxed to its utmost and civil disturbances were rampant. However, by 1790, a gradual growth of industry and trade took place. The population of Boston stood at 18,000, most of whom lived close to the docks and on the water. This resurgence was felt in other New England ports, including Newport, Rhode Island, from which John Boit's *Union* set sail.

The Pacific Northwest Maritime Fur Trade

Captain James Cook, R.N., that famous British navigator and explorer, made his third and last voyage to the Pacific in 1776-1780. His chief instruction and objective was to find the western entrance to a Northwest Passage between the Pacific and the Atlantic oceans. He had crossed from the Hawaiian Islands to the southern Oregon coast, and, feeling his way north, made the first landing by a European on the Northwest Coast at Resolution Cove (Ship's Cove), Nootka Sound, Vancouver Island, on the 29th of March 1778. He refitted his weather-beaten vessels, checked his lunar sights at a shore station and made numerous longboat trips around the Sound, visiting the present Friendly Cove where there was a large summer native village. More importantly, Cook observed the Indians at close range and was impressed by the large number of sea otter skins and other peltries offered him in trade. Some of these were traded to the Russians when Cook's ships called at Kamchatka, but the majority were probably taken back to England. John Ledyard, an American sailor of fortune, was a crew member and published a book about the voyage on his return to Boston, which was given quite wide circulation, particularly among the Boston merchants who already had been investigating the advantages of trade with China.

There is little doubt that the finding and reporting by Cook of the existence of large numbers of sea otters and other fur-bearing animals along the north Pacific Coast precipitated the early and rapid development of the China fur trade. The early Spanish explorers never seemed to realize the potential of this trade, nor did the early English vessels. The smaller, well-handled ships from New England, with their tough Yankee skippers, were much more effective than the English. They eventually monopolized the trade until it faded during the first quarter of the nineteenth century.

The first American vessel to initiate trade with China was the ship *Empress of China*, which arrived at Canton on August 23, 1784, after a six-month voyage from New York. Although we do not know her captain's name, we know that her supercargo was Major Samuel Shaw, a young, former army officer, who served during the Revolutionary War. He handled all the details of trading with the Chinese merchants. He completed this lucrative voyage, and returned in 1786 on the ship *Hope* out of New York to establish the first American commercial house in China, and was made honorary American Consul at Canton. He was a man of fine character and much admired by the Chinese merchants with whom he came in contact. Unfortunately, he died aboard the ship *Hope* on her return voyage to New York. Much of the material used to describe this early China trade is derived from Shaw's journals. These were compiled and published by William Crosby and H. P. Nichols of Boston, Massachusetts in 1847.

Britain was already well established in the China trade when the Americans became aware of its great potential for extending their world markets. The Chinese demanded and usually obtained goods they either needed or prized, such as Russian furs and the products of India and the Moluccas (including fabrics, opium, sharks' fins and edible birds' nests) supplied by the British merchants. Silver (specie) and credit were other requisites in short supply for the American traders. However, this group was quick to see that a large supply of sea otter and other fur pelts was readily available to them along the recently discovered Northwest Coast of America, the shoreline that extended from California to Alaska.

British fur-trading vessels were the first to visit the Northwest Coast following Cook's first landing at Nootka in 1778. They were largely out of London but some used a "flag of convenience" to avoid the burdensome restrictions of the East India Company. Unfortunately, a number of other countries participated but left no trace of their origin or a record of their voyages; it was a fertile field for illicit trade. Subsequent to 1789, and following the first voyage of the *Columbia*, the American ships rapidly took over the Northwest fur trade. Their ships were small and well adapted to navigating the treacherous coastline with its narrow channels and swift-running tides. In addition the Yankee skippers were a resourceful lot, hard traders and each ran a "tight ship."

On September 30, 1787, the fur-trading ship *Columbia* sailed from Boston for the Northwest Coast and China, to become the first American vessel to collect a full cargo of furs on the coast and dispose of them in the Canton market. During the first 10 years after Cook's landing at Nootka, 14 American vessels had traded in China with cargoes either direct from America or through exchange with India and the East Indies, but none of these had used furs in the exchange.

The first voyage of the *Columbia*, 1787-1790, was organized by Joseph Barrell, a prominent merchant from Boston, and five other men: Samuel Brown, another merchant; Charles Bulfinch, an architect; Crowell Hatch, a sea captain from Cambridge; John Derby, a wealthy shipowner from Salem and John M. Pintard, a merchant from New York; Crowell Hatch was a brother-in-law of John Boit, Jr., the future commander of the *Union*. The partners raised $50,000 to purchase and outfit two vessels, the *Columbia Rediviva* and the *Lady Washington*. John Kendrick of Wareham was commander and master of the *Columbia* and Robert Gray was captain of the *Lady Washington*. Considerable publicity was developed concerning this voyage and a medal was struck for distribution among the natives involved in the trade.

The two vessels made a very slow passage to the Falkland Islands where Commander Kendrick was disposed to winter and await better weather before rounding Cape Horn. He was dissuaded from doing so by Captain Gray, and as he expected rather stormy conditions were encountered at the Cape. After reaching the Pacific the two vessels were separated during a severe storm and, according to agreement, they made a rendez-vous at

Nootka Sound in September, 1788. They wintered at Friendly Cove until March, 1789, when the *Lady Washington* cruised north as far as Bucareli Bay, Alaska, successfully securing a good supply of sea otter skins at various villages on the Queen Charlotte Islands. Later in the summer, she returned to Nootka Sound to find the *Columbia* still at anchor without having acquired a single skin. The *Washington* made another voyage into the mouth of the Straits of Juan de Fuca with good success. Later, both vessels moved to Clayoquot Sound where all of the skins were transferred to the *Columbia*. For some unknown reason the skippers exchanged commands and the *Columbia* set sail for the Hawaiian Islands and China under the command of Captain Gray.

Captain Kendrick, in the *Washington*, made a trading cruise to the Queen Charlotte Islands and other northern waters following the departure of the *Columbia* and before the winter storms set in, then set sail for the Hawaiian Islands and China. Having practically commandeered the *Washington*, Kendrick used her for his own purposes for six years; having rerigged her as a brigantine, he made three voyages to the Northwest Coast. He carried on a desultory correspondence with her owners in Boston and always indicated an intent to eventually return the ship to them. He was accidentally killed by an unshotted cannon in the Hawaiian Islands on December 7, 1794 and the *Washington* was lost a year later near the Straits of Malacca.

Captain Gray and the *Columbia* made an uneventful voyage to China (stopping at the Hawaiian Islands for three weeks to revictual), arriving at Macao and Canton in mid-November 1789 after a passage of four weeks. His cargo consisted of 700 sea otter skins which, because of a depressed market, sold at a rather low price. This, in addition to a considerable expense to refit the *Columbia* for her return voyage to Boston and the loss of the *Lady Washington*, resulted in little profit to her merchant partners.

Captain Gray reported that on his arrival at Canton he found 14 American and 70 ships of other nations. After considerable delay in disposing of his cargo of furs and overhauling his vessel, Gray took aboard a full cargo of Bohea tea and sailed for Boston, arriving on 9 August 1790. The return voyage, down the China Sea, through the Strait of Sunda, across the Indian Ocean, around the Cape of Good Hope and up the long passage of the Atlantic Ocean.to Boston was completed "*without incident.*"

A quotation from the *Boston Columbian Centennial* of August 11, 1790 reflects the importance of the *Columbia*'s first voyage in the China fur trade.

It is with real pleasure we announce the safe arrival, in this port, on Monday last [August 9] *of the ship* Columbia, Capt. *Gray, from a voyage of adventure and trade to the Northwest Coast of America. To Messrs. Barrell, Brown, Bulfinch, Hatch, Derby and Pintard, who planned the voyage, their country is indebted, for this experiment in a branch of commerce before unessayed by Americans. And to their care in providing every necessary for the comfort and convenience of the crews—having lost but one man, by sickness since they sailed.*

The Columbia *and* Washington *are the first American vessels who have circumnavigated the Globe. We are told, that one of the natives of Owhyhee* [Hawaii] *arrived in the* Columbia.

The importance of the first voyage of the *Columbia* and the *Lady Washington*, in the Northwest fur trade, was the publicity that was given to it as the spectacular opening of an entirely new field of international trade when it was most needed by the fledgling American republic. Other constructive results were the acquisition by Captain Gray of a great deal of geographic knowledge of the Northwest Coast, together with a better understanding of trading with the natives and the marketing of furs in China.

Because of these reasons and the enthusiasm of the

ship's officers for another voyage, the partners gave their approval and immediate preparations were made to refit the *Columbia*. She took on necessary stores and trade goods and made an early departure for a summer passage around Cape Horn, leaving Boston September 28, 1790, just seven weeks after her arrival from her first voyage. Two of the original partners, Derby and Pintard, dropped out and were replaced by Captain Gray, Davenport and McClean. Captain Gray was appointed commander; Robert Haswell, first officer; John Boit, Jr., fifth officer; and John Hoskins, supercargo. The knocked-down frame of a vessel of 50 tons was loaded on the *Columbia*; this small sloop was to be completed while the *Columbia* wintered on the Northwest Coast. (It is interesting to note that John Boit, Jr. was just 16 years old when he sailed on this voyage.)

Cape Horn was rounded on March 1, 1791, with a minimum of difficulty and Clayoquot Sound, Vancouver Island was reached on June 4. The balance of the summer was spent in trading off the coasts of present Oregon, Washington, the west coast of Vancouver Island, the Queen Charlotte Islands and as far north as Dixon Entrance. Captain Haswell reported that 700 sea otter skins had been taken when the ship returned to winter on September 20, 1791, at Adventure Cove, Clayoquot Sound. Construction was immediately begun on the 50-ton sloop *Adventure*.

On the arrival of the *Columbia* at Clayoquot Sound, Captain Gray found Captain Kendrick in the *Lady Washington*. The latter completed his summer's trade for furs and was ready to sail for the Hawaiian Islands and China. No mention is made in the journals as to his use, or misuse, of the *Washington*. Kendrick departed on the 27th of September, 1791.

Except for the weather and harassment by the natives, Gray spent a satisfactory winter; the crew completed con-struction of the *Adventure* and both vessels left Clayoquot Sound on April 2, 1792, Robert Haswell acting as captain of the new ship. The *Columbia* turned south and traded from off the Straits of Juan de Fuca to Cape Blanco on the Oregon coast. Working her way north, she was spoken by his Britannic Majesty's ships *Discovery* and *Chatham* under George Vancouver and en route to the Straits of Juan de Fuca. Gray went aboard the *Discovery* and gave Captain Vancouver considerable information concerning the geography of Vancouver Island but none concerning the opening of a large river to the southward.

Gray then turned south and on the 7th of May, 1792, entered Grays Harbor and on the 10th of May entered the mouth of the Columbia River, which he named after his ship. He tarried here for 10 days, trading and observing the broad reaches of this great river. A total of 150 sea otter, 300 beaver and twice that number of other land furs was collected here, and on the 20th of May, 1792, Gray crossed out over the Columbia's bar and proceeded to Columbia's Cove just under Cape Cook (Woody Point).

At Columbia's Cove he was attacked by a considerable fleet of war canoes but repulsed them without losing any of his own men. Entering Queen Charlotte Sound, he penetrated it for a number of miles and was attacked by over 200 natives, a number of whom were killed in the encounter. Between these hostilities, he was able to collect a considerable volume of furs.

The *Adventure* had made an extensive cruise around the Queen Charlotte Islands and had collected 500 prime otter skins. Both vessels rendezvoused at Nasparti Inlet, on Vancouver Island's west coast and set sail for the Queen Charlotte Islands for further trading, however the *Columbia* struck a reef and was forced to return to Nootka Sound for repairs by friendly Spanish shipwrights. Subsequently, the two vessels made a final trip to the Queen Charlottes to top off their cargoes of skins and returned to

Friendly Cove in Nootka Sound where all the furs were transferred to the *Columbia* in preparation for her departure for Hawaii and China. To avoid the expense of sailing her back to Boston, the *Adventure* was sold to the Spanish governor for 72 prime otter skins.

The *Columbia* sailed from Port San Juan, Vancouver Island on September 3, 1792 and reached Hawaii on October 3rd, where she took on wood and water and continued on to Macao, China, arriving on December 8, 1792. Proceeding up the Pearl River to Whampoa, the furs were unloaded and sold to the Chinese merchants for $90,000, an average of $45 each. The ship was given a complete overhaul from keel to truck, which cost 7,000 Spanish dollars. A full cargo of tea, sugar and Chinese porcelain was taken aboard and the *Columbia* sailed for Boston on the 2nd of February, 1793.

The Cape of Good Hope was rounded on the 4th of May, 1793. A short stop was made at the island of St. Helena to take on wood, water and supplies. Castle William, at the entrance to Boston, was reached on the 25th of July, 1793 and the ship was given a federal salute. Thus was terminated the second voyage of an American vessel engaged in the Northwest fur trade with China.

The last entry in John Boit's Log of the *Columbia* is quite poignant:

At making Boston Light, from which place we took our departure from, we have just made 360 degrees on Longitude West, which is the Circumfrence of our Globe. . . . 'Tis impossible to express our feelings at again meeting with our friends. But the loss of an affectionate and much loved Sister during my absence, was a great obstacle to the happiness I shou'd otherways much enjoy'd.[3]

The completion of the second and last voyage of the *Columbia* was significant because of the accomplishments of both Captain Robert Gray and the vessels under his command. The first voyage initiated the development of the American fur trade with the Pacific Northwest, and also accomplished the first circumnavigation of the world by an American vessel. The last voyage was outstanding as it resulted in the discovery of the Columbia River and the acquisition of additional geographic knowledge of the Northwest Coast from present Oregon to southern Alaska.

The preceding detailed description of the two voyages of the *Columbia* are important because these voyages were quite typical of the short and intense development of the fur trade. In addition, the second voyage afforded valuable training for John Boit, Jr., and prepared him for taking command of the sloop *Union* only one year after his return to Boston.

Judge F. W. Howay, in his great study on vessels in the fur trade, states:

The maritime fur-trade on the Northwest coast was merely a series of individual efforts. It never reached the stage of unification. It was filled with opposition and secrecy. This probably accounts for the absence of any contemporary narratives after 1790, . . . Yet during all those forty years [1785-1825] the trade went on; and a large trade it was, until about 1805 when it began to dwindle. At the outset the trade was entirely British; but from 1789 onward the American traders, principally from Boston, gradually absorbed it, until by about 1800 it had become the practical monopoly of the city of Boston.[4]

3. Frederic W. Howay, ed., *Voyages of the ''Columbia'' to the Northwest Coast, 1787-1790 and 1790-1793* (Boston, 1941), p. 431.

4. Frederic W. Howay, *A List of Trading Vessels in Maritime Fur Trade, 1785-1794*, Transactions of the Royal Society of Canada, 3rd series, vol. 24, sec. II (Ottawa, 1930), pp. 111-112.

The Canton Fur Market 1785-1825

The Northwest Coast fur trade could not have taken place without the Canton fur market. Largely supplied from Russian sources in Siberia, it was greatly increased following the development, by the Russian-American Company and others, of the fur trading from the Northwest Coast, especially that coast's supplies of sea otter. While most of the traders did their business with the Chinese at the factories in Canton, they usually had their bases at Macao 50 miles down the Pearl River at its mouth.

After the long voyage westward across the Pacific the trading vessel would reach the entrance of the Pearl River, pick up a pilot off Lingting Island who might afford some protection from going ashore on one of the countless islands infested with numerous piratical craft.

The first anchorage for most fur-trading vessels was made off Macao near the south entrance. Macao was a Portuguese settlement located on a peninsula of the same name, and two islands. The fort (Monte Fort) was built in 1675 on the crown of the hill in the center of the peninsula. The settlement, along Praia (Praya) Grande, faced the old harbor and looked to the east. The whole peninsula is less than a dozen square miles.

A river pilot was picked up at Macao, and it took two days to reach Lintin Island and another day or two to anchor at the Second Bar. The following day put the vessel at Whampoa Island, the final anchorage where the cargoes were unloaded and lightered up to the factories at Canton, a distance of 12 miles.

As soon as a ship arrived at Whampoa, a fiador, or surety man, was engaged before any of the cargo was discharged. This person was one of the principal merchants through whom all transactions were channeled. The trade was handled by 13 trading companies called Co-Hang who maintained a complete monopoly. Each ship also was required to have a compradore (or middleman) who furnished provisions and other necessaries, a practice that inevitably involved devious practices and bribery. All ships had to have a bankhall, or storage shed, which was a temporary affair for the reception of water casks, spars, sails, et cetera, and apartments for many men ill after the long sea voyages of the trading ships.

A most important individual was the hoppo-man, an officer of the Chinese customs office, the Hoppo. He measured the ship for duty (government tax) before the cargo was unloaded and lightered up to Canton. He also expected a suitable gift for his wife, mother and himself; that gratuity often referred to as "cumshaw." In addition to the functionaries mentioned above, a linguist was also required to handle the transactions with the customs, and to provide sampans (boats) for the loading and unloading of cargo destined for Canton. Once at Canton, the lighters were anchored opposite the factory to which the goods were consigned.

The factories at Canton were owned by the various European nationals whose traders were doing business with the Chinese on a regular basis. The Danes, Russians, Swedes, English and Dutch traded through their own companies. The other countries used intermediaries. These factories occupied less than a quarter-mile of the Canton waterfront; they were enclosed by a fence through which stairs and gates opened from the water to each factory, and where all merchandise was received and sent away. They were actually very imposing buildings where the Chinese merchants and foreign traders met and transacted their business, and they were surrounded by extensive gardens consisting of wooded areas, artificial rocks, miniature mountains and cascades with winding paths on which the customers strolled and tried to cool off during the evening. The Europeans and Americans had a minimum of social contact with the Chinese, for they were restricted to the factories and the immediate area.

This was the fur market that made possible the large commerce carried on between the American and European trading vessels and the Chinese between 1785 and 1825. John Boit's *Union* was one of these vessels that participated in this trade at its zenith.

John Boit, Jr.

John Boit, Jr. was born at the family home, Green Lane, Boston the 15th of October, 1774.[5] Beacon Hill was only a quarter-of-a-mile to the south and Boston Common close by. Four older children were on deck when John arrived: a half brother, Henry, eleven years old; a half sister, Hannah, nine; a sister, Sarah, four; and a third sister Rebecca, two. The Boston Tea Party was ten months in the future and less than a year later, the 17th of June, 1775, the guns at Bunker Hill were heard. John Boit, Jr. was cradled in the events leading up to the Revolutionary War.

Boit was undoubtedly educated at the Boston Latin School, located on the present site of the Parker House near King's Chapel; the chapel where he was buried many years later, after his adventurous years at sea. Although he evidently left school at the age of 16 that he must have had a well-grounded education is reflected in his journals and log books (some poems are scattered through them).

Boit's father was an importer, although little is known about him, his older brother went to sea, and his brother-in-law, Crowell Hatch, was a ship broker, sea captain and

one of the partners who financed the first and second voyages of the *Columbia*.

John begged his father and brother-in-law to let him sign on as a sailor before the mast, on the second voyage of the *Columbia*, but they were reluctant to do so, probably because of his age. However, the decision was reached to make him fifth officer under Captain Gray, an appointment that seemed to work out very well and he was given assignments carrying real responsibilities. One of these was keeping a journal of the voyage, which has been used extensively by historians because of its continuity and descriptive quality. A considerable portion of the official log of the *Columbia* has been lost.

Returning to Boston on July 25, 1793, Boit was made a mate on the ship *Eliza* on a voyage to Dublin, Ireland with passengers and general cargo. This service terminated at Charleston, North Carolina, where he was discharged in April, 1794 and returned to his home.

There is little direct evidence as to how Boit became involved with the voyage of the sloop *Union* except that it is noted in the ship's log that he took charge of her at Newport, Rhode Island and spent July and early August in *"giv'g the sloop a complete overhaul for a circumnavigation voyage & in taking on board stores & provisions for three years."*

It is natural to suppose that John Boit had been convinced by his recent voyage in the *Columbia* that there were real opportunities in the Northwest fur trade, and that he talked his brother-in-law, Crowell Hatch, into forming a syndicate to underwrite the purchase of the *Union* and the cost of re-fitting her for the world voyage. That this was what happened indicates that the new owners had great confidence in this 19-year-old skipper and his crew of 22 men. The Log and Remarks covering this voyage that make up the contents of this book, show that this confidence was well founded.

The *Union* returned to Boston on the 8th of July,

---

5. Robert A. Boit, *Chronicles of the Boit Family* (private edition, 1915), Chap. 2, "Bibliography of John Boit, Jr."

John Boit, Sr.

John Boit, Jr.

Sarah Brown Boit

(Originals in the collection of C. Jared Ingersoll)

1796, and John Boit's accomplishment is well expressed by Frederic W. Howay:

The fact that he [Boit], *a mere boy in his teens, was entrusted with the command of this vessel* [Union] *to sail to the Northwest Coast, engage in the maritime trade there, proceed thence to China to exchange the sea-otter skins for Oriental goods, and finally return to Boston, speaks volumes for his complete mastery of his profession, his management of men, and his general ability. He handled his crew like an old hand, fought off an Indian attack, and ended a successful voyage by bringing the little sloop back to her home port. But the only notice taken of such a remarkable achievement was the laconic note under "Nautical Intelligence" in the* Columbian Centennial [Boston] *of July 13, 1796: Arrived since our last* [issue] . . . *sloop* Union, Boit, Canton.[6]

After only a month ashore from this arduous voyage of two years, Boit was made commander of the ship *George*, a captured English store vessel, which he delivered in a sinking condition to a purchaser on the Isle de France (Mauritius). On his return to Boston, the 26th of November, 1797, he remarked "*God send that I may never sail in the like of her again.*"[7]

On the 20th of August, 1799 he married Eleanor Jones, one of those "*pretty girls*" of Newport mentioned in his Log of the *Union*'s departure from that port for the Northwest Coast.

From the 10th of August, 1801 to the 13th of October, 1806, he made three voyages as master of the ship *Mount Hope*, 600 tons, a large ship for that period. From 1806 to 1816, he was listed as a merchant and in 1816 became a

6. Howay, *Voyages of the "Columbia,"* p. xxiii.

7. Howay, *Voyages of the "Columbia,"* p. xxiii.

partner with Joseph Bray in an importing business at 43 India Wharf. In 1822, after 16 years as a merchant ashore, he returned to the sea, his first love, and assumed command of the brig *Sally Ann* from Boston bound to Havana. In 1824, he commanded the brig *Barbara* in the same trade. The Boston directories of 1825-1826 listed him as mariner with a residence on Federal Street, Boston.

In July, 1826 John Boit was listed as captain of the ship *Mercury* bound for London. This must have been his last command for he died on the 10th of March, 1829 at the age of 55. He left seven children, Ellen M., Caroline, Henry, Mary, Harriet, Edward Dailey and Julia Overing.

Frederic W. Howay gives an excellent summation of John Boit's character:

John Boit was a man of good education, with a fine appreciation of the better things in life. He had, evidently, an acquaintance with and a love of the best in English literature. His log books are crammed with quotations from the standard authors. He even tried his hand at poetic composition, and his ten-line poem "Hoisting the Sails" is of real merit. He was a fine seaman: his rapid rise is sufficient evidence of his capacity as a navigator. In the back of the volume containing his log of Mount Hope Boit kept a commonplace book. In it he entered the following quotation as a good summary of fine character:

'I live in terms of good neighbourhood with all about me; sometimes I go to their homes, sometimes invite them to mine; my table is neat and clean, and sufficiently affluent, without extravagance.

'I slander no one, nor do I allow backbiters to come near me; my eyes pry not into the actions of other men, nor have I any impertinent curiosity to know the secret of their lives.

'I go to church ev'ry Sunday, and the poor men partakes of my substance; I make no ostentation of the good I do, that I may defend myself against the attacks of hypocrisy and vain glory, well knowing that the best fortifyed heart is hardly proof against these sly deceivers.

'As far as I have an opportunity, I am a reconciler of differences among my neighbours. And I have an entire dependance on the mercies of God our Saviour.'[8]

The "Chronicles of the Boit Family" carries this quotation, *"In the old credit books of Baring Brothers & Co. in London, stands the name of John Boit with the record, 'His word is as good as his bond.'"*

The Sloop Union

The Sloop Union was built at Somerset, Massachusetts in 1792. Her specifications were: tonnage 94 tons, length 65'6'', beam 19'9'', draft 8'5''. One deck, one mast, woman figurehead, Registered July 8, 1793. Owners William Burroughs (merchant), John Nicolas (trader), Benjamin Hicks (mariner) of Newport, master, John Finch. She was re-registered August 26, 1794. Owner Caleb Garner (merchant) Newport, Crowell Hatch and Peter Brooks (merchants) Boston, Mass., master John Boit, Jr. Surrendered July 22, 1796 at Boston, vessel sold.[9]

The selection of a suitable vessel for trade with the Northwest Coast of America and the circumnavigation of the globe was an important decision on the part of John Boit, Jr. and his syndicate of owners. Reference has already been made to the depleted condition of Colonial merchant marine at the end of the American Revolution and the losses through privateering and other natural causes. Fishing fleets and those involved in the overseas trade were particularly affected. This must have presented difficulties in finding not only a suitable secondhand ves-

---

8. Howay, *Voyages of the "Columbia,"* p. xxv.
9. "The Ship Registers and Enrollments of Providence, Rhode Island, 1773-1939," vol. 1 (Providence, Rhode Island, 1941).

SLOOP UNION'S *arrival at* BOSTON *passing* THE FORT.

John Boit's own rendering of the *Union*. The sloop sailed into Boston Harbor on 8 July 1796, almost 23 months after its departure from Newport, Rhode Island. Boit recorded: "At 4 PM A pilot took charge of the Sloop to take her to Boston, the Lighthouse bear'g WBN 3 leagues. . . . *At noon anchor'd abreast the town. Saluted the town was return'd with their welcome huzza. So ends this voyage.*"

sel but also the construction of a new one. The *Union* was almost new, only one year off the shipways when she was acquired by the syndicate, which speaks well of its credit for economic conditions were very depressed following the American Revolution.

The question arises why a sloop-rigged vessel was selected, and one of such limited size.

Sloops and shallops, usually small, one-masted boats, were used extensively along the Atlantic Coast from Maine to Florida and from the earliest Colonial times down through the nineteenth century.[10] Their earlier use was largely for tenders to larger vessels and later, transportation between coastal communities. Over the years they

10. See William A. Baker, *Sloops & Shallops* (Barre, Massachusetts, 1966).

gradually were increased in size and rigging, particularly on the Hudson River, where in 1780 they were building 60-foot vessels of 75 tons or larger, primarily for the New York to Albany trade. One of these, the *Experiment*, completed a voyage to China in 1787 and returned to New York a year and a half later.[11] The sloop *Lady Washington* was a 90-ton vessel and, as mentioned earlier, accompanied the *Columbia* to the Northwest Coast on her first voyage in 1787. She made several voyages between the Northwest Coast and Canton, finally going aground on an island in the Straits of Malacca. The *Union* was almost identical in size and rig to the *Lady Washington*.

Because of the shortage of commercial vessels in the late eighteenth and early nineteenth centuries, a crash program of shipbuilding took place along the New England coast. Many large and small shipyards sprang up in the coastal communities, especially in the harbors and estuaries whose rivers gave access to the heavy stands of pine and oak in the interior; excellent sources of high-quality shipbuilding timber. It is quite apparent from this situation that sloops of 50 to 100 tons were highly desirable and were constructed in the make-shift yards of that period. Their design and specifications were relatively simple, and were undertaken by Yankee shipwrights and journeymen available in increasing numbers along the coast. It had been proven that these small sloops were quite capable of making long, trans-oceanic voyages and had certain advantages over larger vessels in the Northwest fur trade. Their broad beams and full-bodied lines gave them great tonnage capacity for their overall length and good stability. The relatively light draft permitted entry into shoal bays and river entrances; also they had the ability of standing upright in case of running aground.

The *Union* had 22 men, as it was customary to have

11. C. G. Davis, "The Hudson River Sloops," *Yachting Magazine* (September, 1932), p. 40.

"extras" on the long voyages. A drawback to the sloop rig was its one mast, which, if lost, meant the probable destruction of the entire ship, whereas a two- or three-masted vessel could usually be jury-rigged and survive. It is evident that the *Union* turned out to be an excellent choice, not only for trading on the Northwest Coast but also for her circumnavigation of the globe.

The excellent sketches and drawings of the *Union* that illustrate this book, and the various charts showing her voyage, were created by Hewitt Jackson of Bellevue, Washington. He is a marine artist, an ex-sailor before the mast and a naval architect without papers. His principal field of research and activity covers ships of the late-eighteenth and early-nineteenth centuries. His pictures and drawings of ship models in the collections of the Oregon Historical Society in Portland, Oregon have made a valuable contribution to Northwest maritime history. Mr. Jackson has prepared a summary of his research on the sloop *Union* which is included in this publication; this will help establish the authenticity of the drawings and be of special interest to students of maritime architecture of the late eighteenth century.

The Extraordinary Voyage

John Boit took charge of the sloop *Union* on July 17, 1794 at Newport, Rhode Island, and until 29 August 1794 was extremely busy outfitting her for the long voyage to the Northwest Coast of America and thence around the world, an extremely short time for such preparations.

Newport had always been an important New England port because of her superb harbor favored by almost constant westerly winds. There was an extremely roomy roadstead in which ships of any size might come to anchor before entering the inner harbor with its shipways, rope walks, chandleries and food shops, making it an excellent outfitting port. It was one of the early stations of the budding United States Navy and used by the frigate *Constitution* and ships of her class. George Channing, a contemporary ship merchant, wrote: *"It was a grand sight—the arrival and departure of so many gallant-looking ships, among them the Constitution . . . the Congress, President and United States."*[12]

Many vessels, engaged in foreign trade, used Newport for incoming and outgoing cargoes, which were barged to and fro from the smaller ports between Boston and New York.

The crew of the *Union*, with the addition of local stevedores, was busy day and night putting aboard various types of cargo. The equipping of the *Union* must have been the same as the materials brought aboard the *Columbia* on her second voyage which were: Equipment: rope, caulking material, canvas, tar, turpentine, spare oars, iron for fastenings, medicine chests, anchors, glass and putty, nails of all sizes, pewter plates and dishes, axes, kettles, chisels, draw shaves, bricks, hammers, sledges, vices, needles, etc., etc.[13]

Food, wood and water were, of course, the most essential items. A scale of victualing for a small crew of 20 men (the *Union* had 22) for a period of one month was published in England in 1867[14] and included the following stores: salt beef and pork 700 lbs.; flour 120 lbs.; rice 80 lbs.; peas 40 lbs.; sugar 60 lbs.; tea 9 lbs.; water 420 gallons for a total weight of 4,016 lbs. In addition at least 10 cords of wood and dunnage would be required weighing at least another ton. Water could be partially replaced during the voyage by stretching tarpaulins underneath the sails to catch the rain, but wood could only be found ashore. It is difficult to understand how the *Union* could have carried enough wood to last from 24 January 1795, when she left the Falkland Islands, to 16 May 1795, when she reached Nasparti Inlet, Vancouver Island, without one stop en route.

While the crew of the *Union* was busy overhauling the ship and loading her with cargo for a three-year voyage, John Boit must have spent many hours with the skippers of the various vessels in the harbor at Newport, discussing Atlantic and Pacific routes, which were largely determined by the winds and currents prevalent in different months of the year. At that time there were few hydrographic or meteorological stations from which to obtain this information. That information could only be secured from seamen who were regularly using the world's seas. The winds and currents of the Atlantic Ocean were reasonably well known but beyond Cape Horn the south Pacific Ocean was much less familiar, except perhaps to the Spanish, and the Northwest Coast from Oregon north had only recently been discovered.

The importance of these winds and currents to the sailing ships cannot be overestimated. The energy to propel these vessels was entirely derived from the prevailing winds as well as the currents created by them.

The hydrographer of the United States Navy in the 1973 edition of *Ocean Passages of the World* (3rd ed.) makes this generalization pertaining to ocean currents and winds:

Currents flow at all depths in the oceans but in general the stronger currents occur in the upper layers. . . . The main cause of surface currents in the open ocean is the direct action of the wind on the sea surface and a close correlation accordingly exists between their direction and those of the prevailing winds. . . . Thus the northeast and southeast trade winds of the two hemispheres are the mainspring of the surface current circulation. In the Atlantic and Pacific oceans the two trade

---

12. George Channing, *Early Recollections* (Newport Historical Society, 1804), p. 133.
13. Howay, *Voyages of the "Columbia,"* p. 448.
14. See *Merchants and Ship Masters Manual* (England, 1867).

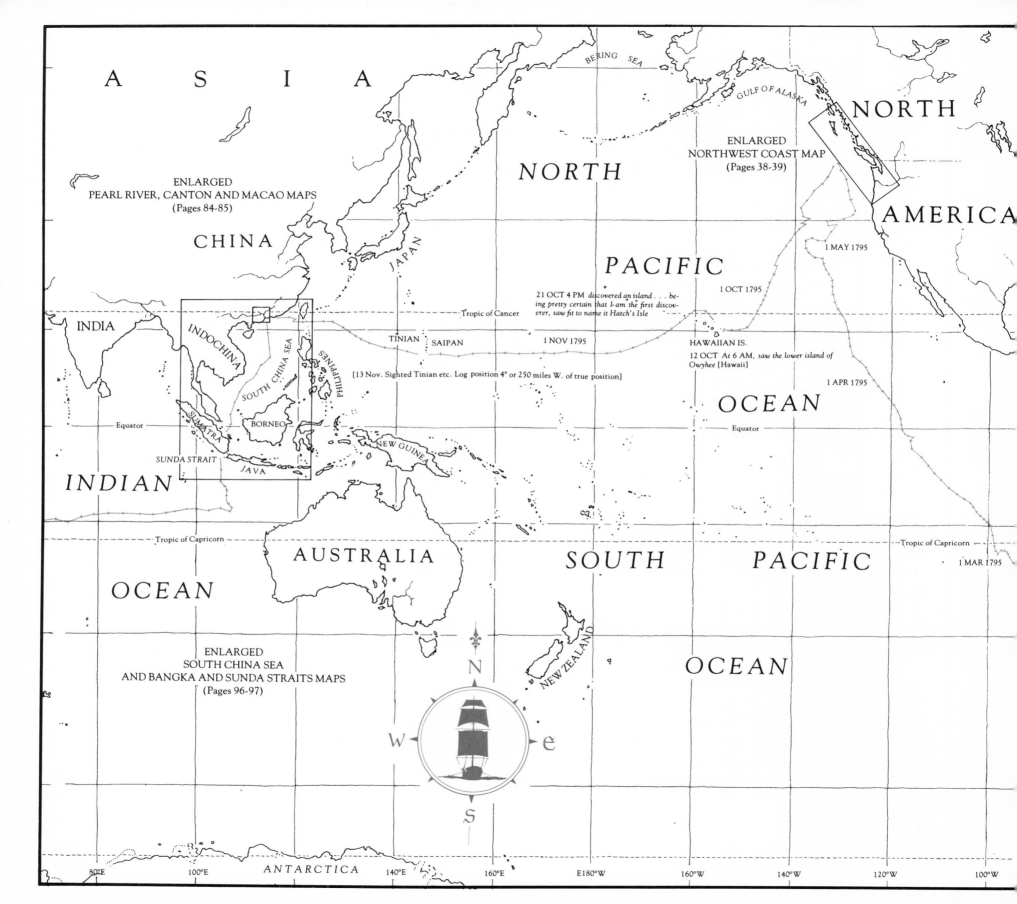

ASIA

NORTH

BERING SEA

GULF OF ALASKA

NORTH

ENLARGED
NORTHWEST COAST MAP
(Pages 38-39)

AMERICA

ENLARGED
PEARL RIVER, CANTON AND MACAO MAPS
(Pages 84-85)

CHINA

PACIFIC

1 MAY 1795

JAPAN

1 OCT 1795

21 OCT 4 PM *discovered an island . . . being pretty certain that I-am the first discoverer, saw fit to name it Hatch's Isle*

Tropic of Cancer

INDIA

INDOCHINA

TINIAN   SAIPAN   1 NOV 1795

HAWAIIAN IS.
12 OCT *At 6 AM, saw the lower island of
Owyhee* [Hawaii]

1 APR 1795

PHILIPPINES

SOUTH CHINA SEA

[13 Nov. Sighted Tinian etc. Log position 4° or 250 miles W. of true position]

OCEAN

SUMATRA   BORNEO

Equator   Equator

INDIAN

NEW GUINEA

SUNDA STRAIT

JAVA

OCEAN

AUSTRALIA   SOUTH   PACIFIC

Tropic of Capricorn   Tropic of Capricorn

1 MAR 1795

OCEAN

ENLARGED
SOUTH CHINA SEA
AND BANGKA AND SUNDA STRAITS MAPS
(Pages 96-97)

OCEAN

NEW ZEALAND

N

W   E

S

80°E   100°E   ANTARCTICA   140°E   160°E   E180°W   160°W   140°W   120°W   100°W

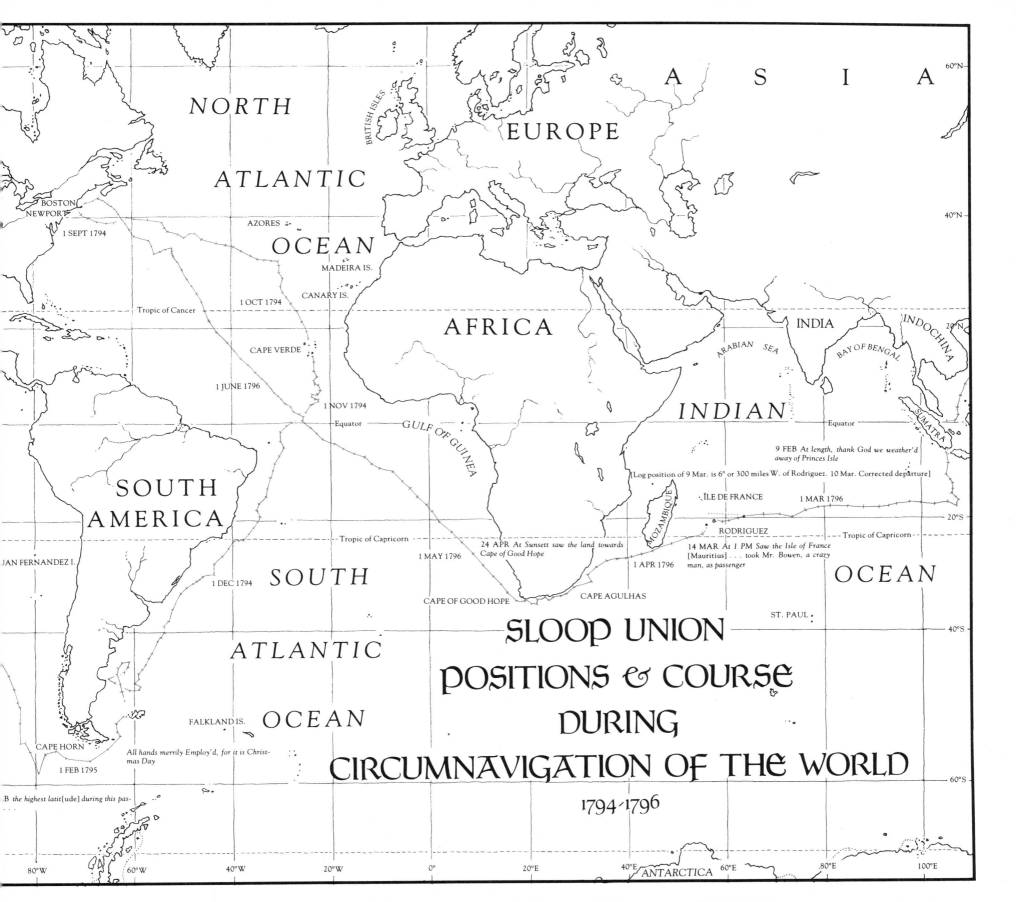

NORTH

ATLANTIC

OCEAN

EUROPE

ASIA

60°N

40°N

BRITISH ISLES

BOSTON
NEWPORT

1 SEPT 1794

AZORES

MADEIRA IS.

CANARY IS.

1 OCT 1794

Tropic of Cancer

CAPE VERDE

AFRICA

INDIA

20°N

ARABIAN   SEA

BAY OF BENGAL

INDOCHINA

1 JUNE 1796

1 NOV 1794

Equator

GULF OF GUINEA

INDIAN

Equator

SUMATRA

9 FEB At length, thank God we weather'd
away of Princes Isle

[Log position of 9 Mar. is 6° or 300 miles W. of Rodriguez. 10 Mar. Corrected departure]

ÎLE DE FRANCE

1 MAR 1796

SOUTH
AMERICA

MOZAMBIQUE

RODRIGUEZ

Tropic of Capricorn

20°S

JAN FERNANDEZ I.

Tropic of Capricorn

24 APR At Sunsett saw the land towards
Cape of Good Hope

1 MAY 1796

14 MAR At 1 PM Saw the Isle of France
[Mauritius] . . . took Mr. Bowen, a crazy
man, as passenger

OCEAN

1 DEC 1794

SOUTH

1 APR 1796

CAPE OF GOOD HOPE

CAPE AGULHAS

ST. PAUL

ATLANTIC

OCEAN

SLOOP UNION

40°S

FALKLAND IS.

POSITIONS & COURSE

CAPE HORN

1 FEB 1795

All hands merrily Employ'd, for it is Christmas Day

DURING

60°S

B the highest latit[ude] during this pas-

CIRCUMNAVIGATION OF THE WORLD

1794-1796

80°W

60°W

40°W

20°W

0°

20°E

40°E   ANTARCTICA   60°E

80°E

100°E

winds drive an immense body of water west over a width of some 50° of latitude. . . . A similar westerly surge of water occurs in the South Indian Ocean by the action of the southeast trade wind. The trade winds in both hemispheres are balanced in the higher latitudes by wide belts of various westerly winds. . . . The direction of the current circulation is clockwise in the north hemisphere and counter clockwise in the south hemisphere.

Throughout this age of sail, it was the general custom for sailing masters to "speak" and contact ships passing one another on the high seas. The usual purposes were to check calculated positions, the probable conditions of winds and currents, and also exchange the latest world news—which was probably not very "late."

It is interesting to trace the *Union*'s passage around the world and the manner in which Boit made use of world winds and ocean currents to expedite his voyage. Leaving Newport on the 1st of September, 1794, a slightly SE course was followed, aided materially by the Gulf Stream with its two- to three-knot current and the westerly winds. Upon reaching the northeast trade winds and the Canary Current along the African coast gradually this course was changed toward the south. This brought the *Union* to the Cape Verde Islands, which were passed, close aboard, on the 1st of October, 1794. A southerly course from there brought the ship through the variables and doldrums until it entered the southeast trades and the south equatorial current, when the course was changed to southwest to take advantage of the Brazil Current running along the South American coast. This course lasted until the ship was opposite the Rio de la Plata. At that point the adverse Falkland Current was met, the ship had slow going until the Falkland Islands were reached.

Leaving the Falkland Islands on the 23rd of January, 1795, on a south-westerly course, the *Union* increasingly felt the "Howling Forties" blowing with gale force around Cape Horn and the strong southern ocean currents

created by these winds. Many ships took two to three weeks to round this dreaded promontory, while a few turned east to pass around the Cape of Good Hope and run their "easting down" to reach the South Pacific. The *Union* fortunately made a quick passage of the Horn and, after entering the Pacific, turned on a northerly course to take advantage of the southeast trades and the Peru Current along the Chilean coast. After leaving the Cape and through these latitudes the weather is usually favorable and mild, a most agreeable change from the frost and ice off the Horn.

In crossing the Equator the doldrums were encountered for a short distance until the northeast trades were reached with some assistance from the North Equatorial Current. On reaching the 30th parallel north, contrary westerly winds and the southerly California Current slowed down the progress of the little ship until she reached Columbia's Cove, Vancouver Island on the 16th of May, 1795. The *Union* completed her trading on the Northwest Coast on the 12th of September, 1795, and cleared for the Hawaiian Islands from Vancouver Island. The winds offshore are rather variable at this time of year but generally westerly. The North Pacific Current flows south and southwest, both favoring a direct southwest course to the Hawaiian Islands.

The ship made a very brief stop at the Islands before sailing for Canton, China, on the 17th of October, 1795. The winds at this time of year are generally the northeast trades. The current, the south equatorial, flows from east to west, permitting a direct course to Canton, which was reached the 1st of January, 1796. The departure for Boston was made on the 13th of January, 1796.

The course from Macao down the China Sea was almost due south with variable winds and currents. Currents were influenced by the restriction of these waters between the mainland of China and the islands to the east.

The Strait of Sunda presented a number of problems to

sailing vessels of this period. The northwest monsoon winds blew strongly across the south entrance of the strait making it difficult to beat to windward in the narrow channel, which held up the *Union* for several days.

Once through this passage, a south course was laid to the 18th parallel south in the Indian Ocean whence she turned directly west to take full advantage of the southeast trades and the south equatorial current. This course was continued until the 14th of March, 1796, when she reached Isle de France (Mauritius), tarrying there until the 29th of March, 1796. A slightly southwest course was laid to pass south of the island of Madagascar and the Cape of Good Hope, taking full advantage of the southeast trades.

Once around the Cape of Good Hope, a northwest course bore the ship along with the continued aid of the southeast trades and the Benguela Current, following the west coast of Africa. This course was maintained until the northeast trades were entered, which pushed the small sloop nearly across the Atlantic where it encountered the variables in to Boston, the *Union*'s home port.

The *Union*'s Log may be roughly divided into three parallel but distinct parts; the first being the days at sea; the second, the days on the Northwest Coast trading for furs; and the third, the days at the main ports of call, including the Falkland Islands, Columbia's Cove, Vancouver Island, the Hawaiian Islands and at Canton, China.

The days at sea can be monotonous and repetitive, as no doubt they were to John Boit and his crew. They are of interest in the observations that were made relative to the birds, fish, whales and other sea life. They also reflect the changes of weather in different sea lanes. Lastly, they are an enumeration of the activities and jobs necessary to keeping a small ship at sea and relieving the crew of boredom, in other words, maintaining a "happy ship."

The second part of the Log covering the days on the Northwest Coast touches on the trade with the natives for furs and the constant vigilance necessary to avoiding attack. In addition, it describes the problems involved in handling a small vessel when following uncharted shorelines beset with fast-running tides and dense fog, together with a prolonged attempt to enter the Columbia River, where the *Union* was nearly lost.

The third part is of the most interest. Included among others are accounts of the Falkland Islands and its myriad sea and land life, and the reprovisioning there of the ship for its bout with Cape Horn and the long voyage to the Northwest Coast.

This third part reveals Boit's acumen through his long account of an offshore stop at the big island of Hawaii, with observations on the hazard of small vessels like the *Union* being overcome by the large native war canoes, and the political turmoil being created by Kamehameha I in his campaign to conquer all the Hawaiian Islands. A great deal of this information was obtained from an English beachcomber, John Young, who came aboard the *Union* while Boit was purchasing food and supplies from the native canoes alongside the *Union*. Young appeared to be a chief of staff for Kamehameha, and supplied a rather complete report on the fur-trading vessels that had touched at the Hawaiian Islands in the recent past. In addition, he gave a veiled implication that Boit would be well served not to anchor too far inshore, where his ship could be readily overcome by the large war canoes. Boit had arrived off the island of Hawaii on October 13th and for three days and nights had cruised back and forth trading for food, taking on water and wood and obtaining information that probably saved the *Union* from capture by the natives. In any event, at midnight of the 16th of October, 1795 he recorded:

After mature consideration, & summing up All the information into a point, which I got from Young, I came to a conclu-

sion that it was not safe to run down among the Islands, with my small vessel, at least without a good stiff breeze & indeed I had no sufficient inducement, to tarry any longer among them, having on board 16 large Hogs, 10 Small pigs, 2 doz. Fowls, & a large supply of Water & Musk melons, breadfruit, plantains, sweet potatoes, Yams, Taro, Sugar Cane & Cocoa Nuts, . . . At Midnight a fine breeze sp[r]ung at SE, Upon which I haul'd upn a wind to the N & E, with a determination, to pass to the N of the Island [of] Mowee, & so run down to the Northward of all the Islands.

Boit's stay at Canton to sell his furs and recondition his ship for the long voyage back to Boston, is rather cryptically and briefly noted, but reflects great ability and foresight in his responsibilities as a shipmaster.

The Log indicates the danger faced by the *Union*. In a heavy gale, off the Cape of Good Hope, Boit nearly lost his ship when it sustained heavy damage. Fortunately, this was repaired and she barely avoided being dismasted, which would have been almost fatal for a ship of her size and rig.

Hopefully, the previous background may give the reader a contemporary picture of the time and conditions under which John Boit sailed his little sloop around the world and participated in the apex of the sea otter trade on the Northwest Coast.

Editorial Principles

John Boit's Log of the *Union* and his Remarks have been treated, not as sacrosanct literary texts, but as primary resources that contain pertinent information that should be easily understood by the reader.

The texts of the Log and the Remarks (the latter set in italic type throughout) are abridgements of the original documents. Countless repetitive entries have been dropped (generally references to the weather, sail changes, and variations in the course), such as, "Noon pleasant," "Midnight squally," "tops'l down," "Single reef'd ye Mainsail," etcetera. Elipsis have not been placed in their stead in order for the texts to remain readable. Significant changes of course, wind details, major sail changes and shipboard activities have been retained. Boit's narrative descriptions of landfalls and events have been included.

Boit's idiosyncratic spelling and capitalization (common to the period) have been kept to retain the color and character of his style and to give the entries a certain rhythm that would be otherwise lost. Boit's capitalization, combined with the formal syntax, contrasts nicely with the rather casual punctuation. Boit, for example, consistently spelt *off* as *of* and *sennit* as *sinnett*; the original spelling has been retained in these cases. In these abridgements, silent emendations have been made to catch Boit's penslips, where spelling is not clear at first reading; these regularizations, while not common, are necessary to make the texts more coherent. Terminal punctuation has been added where needed. Daily distances of the voyage have been given, latitude and longitude are given every few days.

The sea day extends from noon to noon (or meridian to meridian); the procedure in port changed to the normal midnight-to-midnight rendering. Ship names have been italicized, following modern usage.

A note on the commonly mispronounced word *ye*, used by Boit throughout the texts. *Ye* is a form of *the*, and properly pronounced as *the*. The *y* does not represent the English *y*, but is an ancient runic letter (known as *thorn*) no longer in use that represents the *th* sound in English. The *Oxford English Dictionary* states: "It is still often used pseudoarchaically, jocularly, or vulgarly (pronounced as *ye*) . . . [as] in shop-signs like 'Ye Olde Book Shoppe'." *Ye* as a contracted form of *the* was still used by many correspondents and diarists as late as the nineteenth century.

Bruce T. Hamilton
Book Editor
Oregon Historical Society

The Sloop Union

JOURNAL AND REMARKS OF A VOYAGE AROUND THE WORLD

1794-1796

by

John Boit, Jr.

Color Frontis

The *Union* in Columbia's Cove, September 1795. At anchor here from 1 to 11 September 1795, the *Union* prepared for sea. On 12 September, the crew "unmoored in the morning and at 8 PM left Columbia's Cove bound for Canton in China." (Original by Hewitt Jackson in the collections of the Oregon Historical Society)

Newport, Rhode Island to the Falkland Islands

29 August 1794 to 21 January 1795

In July 1794, I took charge of the Sloop *Union*, burthen 98 Tons, she then laying at Newport, Rhode Isle, Bound for a Voyage to the N.W. Coast of America, China, Isle of France, & back to Boston. Own'd by Crowell Hatch & Caleb Gardner Esq. Employ'd during the months of July & beginning of August, giv'g the Sloop & Complete overhaul for a Circumnavigating Voyage, & in Taken on board Stores & Provisions for Three years, likewise a Cargo consisting of Sheet Copper, Bar Iron, Blue Cloth, Blankets, Trinkets of various kinds etc. etc. All which articles where suitable for traffick with the NW Indians, for firs propper for the Canton markett. The Sloop was Completely fited for the voyage, with a Crew of 22 In Number. Had good quarters, & mounted Ten Carriage Guns & Eight Swivells on the rails. On the 28th August, '94, Got under way & dropt into Coastal Harbour, & Got all in readiness for Sea.

John Boit

Adieu to the pretty girls of Newport

*August 29th, 1794**
Pleasant weather. At 5 AM Weigh'd & came to sail with the wind at NNW. At 6 Abrest the Light house. At 11 Block Island bore WBN 6 leagues dist. from which I take my departure, it lying in Lat. 40°55′N & Long. 71°35′W of Greenwich.
Dist per log 6 Knots[1]

August 30th, 1794
[Course NEBE, EBN, ENE. Wind SSE, SEBS, SE]
Fresh breezes and pleasant weather. At 1/2 past 12 PM Block Island bore NWBW 9 Lea's, in squarsail. All hands employ'd unbending cables & stowing the Anchors. In flying Jib.
Lat Obsd 40°14′N Long 69°58′W

August 31st, 1794
Moderate breezes. Employ'd making Sinnett.[2] At 5 AM saw a Ship, upon a wind to the East'd. At 6 Wm. Carr one of the Seamen fell from the square sail yard overboard. Wore round out boat & got him again, not much hurt. At 8 Made sail.
Dist pr log 83 Knots

September 1st, 1794
Pleasant breezes. At Meridian in squaresail set ye† foresail & flying Jib. At 5 AM in foresail, set the square sail. All hands employ'd breaking out for peas, making Mats etc. Noon pleasant.
Lat Obsd 38°48′N Long 66°49′W
Dist pr log 83 Knots

September 2nd, 1794
At 9 PM Jib'd[3] ship. Midnight squally. At 2 AM in mainsail. At 3 Set Do.‡ By two Distances of the sun & moons§ nearest limbs, I determin'd the Long to be 63°44′15″

West. At 7 jib'd ship.
Dist pr log 109 Knots

September 3rd, 1794
[Course E½S, EBS. Wind WBN, SW]
Light winds & Pleasant weather. At 11 AM in squarsail, set fores'l. Spoke a Sloop from Wiscasset. Mick Camell master, bound to St. Croix.
Dist pr log 79 Knots

September 4th, 1794
[Course SEBE, E½N, EBS. Wind SSW, SEBS, SWBS]
Light breezes. At 4 AM Set ye Tops'l, Jib, & Squares'l. At 6 parted ye Clue of ye mainsail. Fitted a new clue, set ye sail. Noon squally.
Dist pr log 70 Knots

September 5th, 1794
[Course ESE. Wind SSW]
Light breeze. People employ'd making sinnett etc. Midnight squally with thunder and lightning. In topsail & flying jib. Heavy rain, reef ye Mainsail. St. Anthony's [Cape Verde Is.] bears S54°E Dist 2230 miles. Noon pleasant.
Lat Obsd 39°2′N Long reduc'd by Obs 57°3′39″W
Dist pr log 93 Knots

September 6th, 1794
[Course ESE. Wind SWBS]
Fresh gales & pleasant weather. At 4 PM In topsail & flying Jib in single reef of the Mainsail. At 5 Set ye topsail.

---

*Entries run from noon to noon.
†See Editorial Principles (p. xxxix).
‡To economize on words, Boit made frequent use of 'Ditto' in this abbreviated form.
§Boit used the nautical symbols ☉ for sun and ☽ for moon throughout the Log.

4

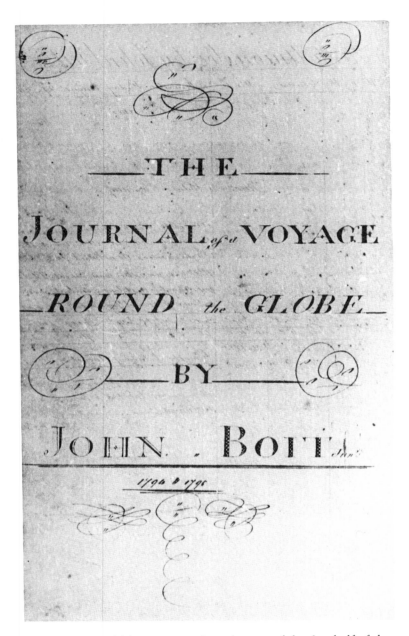

John Boit's careful lettering on the title page of the first half of the original manuscript Log of the sloop *Union*.

Midnight strong gales, with a high sea. In 2d reef of ye Mainsail. At 1 AM In Foresail. At 10 Heavy squalls, Down tops'l Yard.
Dist pr log 138 Knots

September 7th, 1794
[Course SEBE, ESE. Wind SWBS, NNW]
Fresh gales with frequent heavy squalls, accompanied with much rain. At 7 PM Jib'd ship, Down mainsail, set ye squarsail. Noon flying clouds, with a high sea.
Dist pr log 118 Knots

September 8th, 1794
[Course ESE. Wind NEBN]
Fresh Breezes & cloudy weather. People variously employ'd. All hands employ'd breaking out the hold for beef.
Dist pr log 71 Knots

September 9th, 1794
[Course ESE, SEBE. Wind calm, SW]
All hands employ'd weaving mats for the shrouds,[4] & making sinnett. A swell from ye NEBN for which I allow 24 M[iles].
Dist pr log 34 Knots

September 10th, 1794
[Course ESE. Wind SW]
Pleasant weather. At 8 Saw a Ship standing to the East'd.
Dist pr log 104 Knots

September 11th, 1794
[Course ESE, SEBE. Wind NE, calm]
Fresh breezes, with rain & a swell from the N. People employ'd in their departments. Midnight squally with heavy thunder & Ligh[tnin]g.
Dist pr log 51 Knots

5

Entries in John Boit's Log of the *Union* for 6 through 9 September 1794. Nine days and eight hundred leagues out of Newport, Rhode Island, the *Union* was well on its way, sailing under "flying clouds, with a high sea."

September 12th, 1794
[Course NEBE, NEBN. Wind ESE, East]
All hands employ'd making mats, Sinnett etc. Carpenter in his department. Two sail in sight to the West'd. Noon Pleasant. *The Sloop proves a good seaboat but is a dull sailer.* *
Dist pr log 27 Knots

September 13th, 1794
[Course EBN. Wind SEBS]
Light airs & pleasant weather. Lowerd down the Mainsail & new leather'd the Jaws of the Gaff. Two sail still in sight.
Dist pr log 44 Knots

September 14th, 1794
Light winds and pleasant weather. At 2 PM Low'd Down the Mains'l to repair. Leatherd the Collars of the Stays etc. Tailor steadily employ'd making coats for trade.
Dist pr log 40 Knots

September 15th, 1794
Fresh Breezes & pleasant weather. At 5 PM Spoke the Bark *Columbia* Jeremiah Bunker Master, from New York bound to South Georgia out 17 Days, reckoned himself in the Long of 40° West.
Lat Obsd 35°43'N Long 42°12'15''W
Dist pr log 106 Knots

September 16th, 1794
[Course SEBE. Wind SW]
Fresh breezes & pleasant weather. Midnight squally in Topsail single reef'd ye Mainsail, heavy rain.
Dist pr log 128 Knots

---

*All entries from John Boit, Jr's, later Remarks are set in italic throughout the text.

September 17th, 1794
Brisk breezes & pleasant. Employ'd breaking out ye hold for water, fill'd 3 Puncheons up with salt water. Tailor employ'd as usual.
Dist pr log 84 Knots

September 18th, 1794
[Course SEBE. Wind WSW]
Pleasant weather. Caught a Dolphin.[5] *Came to allowance of water and provisions. Crew all in good health. Every Sunday, weather permitting, have all the chests and bedding on deck & fumigate the forecastle with vinegar & gun powder, just givin' it a good washing. The regulations of the sloop is very strict as respects cleanliness & no hash is allowed to be eat by the people. Allow them tea or coffee both morning and evening for to keep the scurvey off.*
Dist pr log 67 Knots

September 19th, 1794
[Course SEBE. Wind WNW]
Fresh breezes & pleasant weather. All hands employ'd making sinnett for waiste netings etc. Isle of St. Antonia bears S29°E Dist 1080 Miles. A large swell heaving after us.
Lat Obsd 33°30'N Long 35°5'W
Dist pr log 111 Knots

September 20th, 1794
[Course SEBE. Wind NWBW, NE]
Light breezes & pleasant weather. All hands variously employ'd. Carpenter stocking a Kedge anchor.
Dist pr log 103 Knots

September 21st, 1794
[Course SEBE. Wind NW]
Light winds and warm weather. Caught two Dolphin.
Dist pr log 45 Knots

September 22nd, 1794
[Course SEBE. Wind SWBW]
Midnight lively breezes. All hands employ'd cleaning Muskets & Grafting straps for Blocks.
Dist pr log 92 Knots

September 23rd, 1794
[Course SE. Wind SW]
Steady breezes and pleasant weather. All hands employ'd as Yesterday. Isle of Sal bears S20°E 954 Miles. [6]
Dist pr log 84 Knots

September 24th, 1794
[Course SEBS, ESE. Wind SWBS, SBE]
Light winds & pleasant weather. Employ'd making sinnett.
Lat Obsd 31°13′N Long 27°56′W
Dist pr log 50 Knots

September 25th, 1794
[Course SWBS, S. Wind SEBE, SE]
Light winds & pleasant weather. Haul'd down the Mainsail & fixed a new Clue & otherways repair'd it. Caught a Dolphin & a bill fish. Midnight pleasant with a high head beat sea. Bonnetts round ye ship.
Dist pr log 48 Knots

September 26th, 1794
[Course SBW, South, SBE. Wind SE, ESE]
Moderate breezes & pleasant weather with a high head beat Sea. Employ'd making sinnett for waste nettings, [7] tailor in his department.
Dist pr log 66 Knots

September 27th, 1794
[Course SBE, SSE. Wind EBS, East]
Fresh gales & cloudy weather with a high sea. Single reef'd ye Mains'l Down squars'l Yard. At 7 AM fresh squalls, Dou[ble] reef'd ye M'Sail. At 9 Out reefs. Noon fresh gales with flying Clouds.
Dist pr log 77 Knots

September 28th, 1794
[Course SBE, South. Wind ESE, SEBE]
Fresh gales with frequent squalls. A high sea from ye SE quarter.
Dist pr log 70 Knots

September 29th, 1794
[Course South, SSE. Wind ESE, EBS]
Fresh breezes & pleasant weather. Caught a bill fish. Employ'd breaking out for beef. Sent up the Topsail Yard. St. Anthony bears S13°E 540 miles Dist. *This day took the NE trade winds.*
Dist pr log 75 Knots

September 30th, 1794
[Course SSE, SEBS. Wind EBN, ENE]
Light winds and pleasant weather. All hands employ'd making sinnet & runing Balls etc.
Dist pr log 68 Knots

October 1st, 1794
[Course SSE, SEBS. Wind ENE]
Light winds & pleasant weather. At 7 AM Spoke an English Letter of Marque ship, of twelve Guns, from London bound to Martinique, out 25 Days, reckon'd himself in the Long of 28°W.
Dist pr log 78 Knots

October 2nd, 1794
[Course SSE. Wind ENE]
Moderate breezes & pleasant weather. Got the new Mainsail on deck & fitted ye Clew. Carried away ye Topsail tie,

fitted a new one, in flying Jib. The Customary opperations was perform'd on crossing ye Tropic line. Isle of Sal bears S23°E Dist 390 Miles. Isle of St. Anthony bears S12°E Dist 330 miles.
Dist pr log 120 Knots

October 3rd, 1794
[Course SBE. Wind EBN, ENE]
Fresh breezes & cloudy weather. Many Skip Jacks round ye Sloop. Tailor constantly making coats for trade. Midnight pleasant. Many Boobies flying round. At 10 Sent Down the Topsail & Cross Jack Yard, the Topsail being rent.
Lat Obs 20°45′N Long 24°57′W
Dist pr log 136 Knots

October 4th, 1794
[Course SBE. Wind ENE]
Brisk breezes with flying clouds. Sent up ye Topsail & Squarsail yard & set ye topsail. At 5 PM Set ye flying Jib. Midnight Do. weather caught many flying fish. Sail maker employ'd mending the foresail. Some birds round. St. Anthony bears S47°W Dist 113 Miles. Sal Bears S15°E Dist 112 Miles.
Dist pr log 149 Knots

October 5th, 1794
[Course S½E, SBW. Wind NEBE, NE]
Fresh breezes & pleasant weather. At 7 PM In 1 reef of ye Mainsail in topsail & Squarsail of Bonnetts from ye Jib & foresail. At 10 Hove too under ye ballenced Mainsail & foresail. *At midnight hove too, at daylight hove off. At 7 AM saw the Isle of Sol, one of the Cape de Verde bearing SW 7 leagues. Very highland in the body of the Isle but makes down in sevrall low points especially in the SE.*
Dist pr log 121 Knots

October 6th, 1794
[Course SWBS, SWBW. Wind NEBE]
Begins lively breezes at NE. At 6 PM the SE Point of Sol bore NNW 5 leagues haul'd to the westward to go between Sol & Bonnavista & although the passage is not above 8 or 9 leagues we could not see Bonnavista as the weather was very smoaky, at midnight edg'd away to the south'd for the Isle of Mayo & St. Jago. At daylight saw them both. Very high land. At meridian we where between the islands with a fresh gale distant from Isle of May 2 leagues.
Lat Obsd 15°6′N Long 23°12′W
Dist pr log 132 Knots

October 7th, 1794
[Course SWBS, SW. Wind ENE, North]
Fresh breezes & pleasant weather. At 1 PM Abrest of Mayo Town, saw a Sloop lying at Anchor in the roads. At 6 the South end of Mayo Isle bore E. English roads bearing NEBE 5 leagues. The SE pt of St. Jago bore WBNW½N dist 3 leagues. Bore away to ye South'd & set all sail. Midnight pleasant caught a large Shark. At 7 AM The South pt of the Isle of Mayo bore NNW Dist 9 or 10 leagues. Unstock'd ye Anchors & stow'd them inboard, employ'd making Sinnett etc.
Dist pr log 59 Knots

October 8th, 1794
[Course S½E, South. Wind SWBW, NNE]
Unbent ye Old topsail to repair & bent a new one in its room, unbent ye Squaresail. At 6 PM Saw the high peak on ye Isle of Mayo. Caught 70 Dolphin this 24 hours. Hoisted out the boat & hog'd the Barnacles of the bottom. At 10 In Boat, bent & set ye squarsail. Noon exceeding warm.
Dist pr log 21 Knots

October 9th, 1794
[Course South, S½E. Wind NEBE, NEBN]
Light winds & pleasant weather, sail maker employ'd repairing the Old topsail, pass'd many strong rips & some Whale streaks. All hands employ'd breaking out the hold for fresh water, the weather being very hot I thought proper to increase there allowance to 6 pts pr Day. Tradesmen in there department.
Lat Obsd 12°42′N Long 22°56′W
Dist pr log 80 Knots

October 10th, 1794
[Course S½E. Wind NE]
Light winds & pleasant warm weather. Some porpoises came along side, the Dog immediatly sprung overboard after them but was got again with much trouble. Caught thirty Dolphin. Saw some landbirds.
Dist pr log 66 Knots

October 11th, 1794
[Course South. Wind NE]
Light winds and pleasant weather. Seamen employ'd making Sinnett and robins [robands]. Sail maker, Carpenter & tailor in there departments. Pass'd many strong rips, occasion'd by a Current, which I suppose to be setting to WSW. Got ye Cloths on deck to air.
Dist pr log 60 Knots

October 12th, 1794
[Course South. Wind NE]
Light winds and pleasant warm weather. All hands variously Employ'd. Pass'd many strong ripples.
Dist pr log 73 Knots

October 13th, 1794
[Course SBE, SSE. Wind NE, NEBE]
The NE winds still prevail; having had many strong rips for this

some time past, hove out a boat [at 1 PM] and tried the current, found it to sett to the WSW 8-1/2 miles pr hour. At 6 In boat saw Ship to ye North. Porpoises round the Sloop.
Dist pr log 68 Knots

October 14th, 1794
[Course SE, SBE. Wind SBW, SW]
This day the NE trades left us—They had been very light for some days past. Wind at SSW, caught severall dolphin saw a whale & plenty porpoises.
Lat Obsd 8°15′N Long 22°23′15″W
Dist pr log 52 Knots

October 15th, 1794
[Course SEBE, SSE. Wind SWS]
Variable unsettled weather attended with some hard squalls & heavy rain. Many Porpoises round, struck two but ye iron would not enter. At 7 Unbent ye Mains'l to repair.
Dist pr log 37 Knots

October 16th, 1794
[Course South, SSW. Wind WNW, ENE]
Calm & pleasant, all Hands variously employ'd. At 6 Heavy squalls with rain. St. Paul's rocks bears S42°W Dist 460 Miles. Ferdinando Noronah bears S46°W Dist 910 miles. Saw ye Trunk of a large tree afloat. Caught 3 Dolphin, saw a Whale.
Lat Obsd 6°39′N Long 21°25′0″W
Dist pr log 53 Knots

October 17th, 1794
[Course South, SSW, SEBS, ESE. Wind EBS, SE, SSE, South]
Light winds with frequent rain squalls. Caught three Dolphin & two Sharks. At 6 TK [tacked] Ship to ye East'd. Some rain, but a Smooth sea. Caught a Shark & a Dol-

phin. Found one of the Hogs dead, which I Suppose was owing to its eating so many fish. Heavy rain. Caught a Gang Cask of water.
Dist pr log 48 Knots

October 18th, 1794
[Course SBW½W, SE, SSW. Wind SEBE, SSW, EBS]
Flattering squally weather with frequent rain. Another Hog took his departure for the other world. Bonnetto & some birds round. Carpenter making a set of Oars for the Yawl. Seamen making fenders for Do. Sail Maker & tailor in theirs departments.
Dist pr log 36 Knots

October 19th, 1794
[Course SSW, SBE½E. Wind SE, EBN]
Light winds & variable unsteady weather. Seamen & Tradesmen diligently employ'd in there Departments. Many lands birds, & plenty of fish round.
Dist pr log 29 Knots

October 20th, 1794
[Course SBW, SSW. Wind SEBE, SE]
Squally attended with some rain & heavy thunder, and sharp light[n]ing. Caught a Dolphin. Seamen & tradesmen all employ'd in there departments.
Lat Obsd 5°37′N Long 22°13′W
Dist pr log 36 Knots

October 21st, 1794
[Course SWBS, SW. Wind SEBS, SSE]
Light airs & pleasant weather. All hands variously Employ'd. Midnight a dull time enough. Carpenter employ'd making scrubing brushes, painted ye Oars, etc.
Dist pr log 32 Knots

October 22nd, 1794
[Course SW½W, SEBS. Wind SBE, calm]
Light breezes and flattering weather. All hands employ'd. Struck a porpoise, but lost him. A strong currant setting to ye NW for which I allow 18 Miles.
Dist pr log 21 Knots

October 23rd, 1794
[Course SBE, SE, SEBS. Wind calm, SSW, SWBS]
Light airs with frequent rain squalls. Caught a Gang cask of water. Employ'd making Sinnett fenders for the Yawl, tailor as usuall. Many land swallows round, saw some Sharks & King Fish. A Current setting to ye NW. Allow'd 18 Mi.
Dist pr log 29 Knots

October 24th, 1794
[Course SW½W, WSW, SWBW, Wind SE½E, SBW, South]
Light airs & cloudy, with some rain. At 5 PM Wore ship to the Eastward. At 7 TK Ship to ye West'd. Sail maker repairing the square sail & tops'l. Noon fresh breezes, with flying clouds. St. Paul rocks bears S36°W Dist 320 Mi. Ferdinando Noronah Do. S45°W Dist 770 Mi.
Lat Obsd 5°13′N Long 23°21′W
Dist pr log 56 Knots

October 25th, 1794
[Course ESE, South. Wind South, ENE, SW]
Moderate breezes & a high sea. A Strong currant, setting to ye NW 36 Miles this 24 Hours.
Dist pr log 46 Knots

October 26th, 1794
[Course SE½E, WSW, ESE. Wind SBW½W, South, calm]
Light winds & flattering weather. A Curr't to ye North &

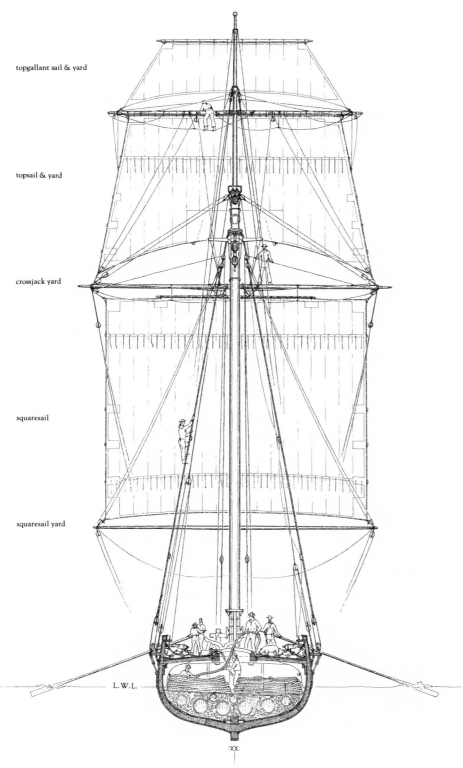

topgallant sail & yard

topsail & yard

crossjack yard

squaresail

squaresail yard

L.W.L.

West. At 9 Mistrusted a change in ye Cur't. Out Boat, & found the Current to set to ye SBE½E.
Dist pr log 29 Knots

October 27th, 1794
[Course SEBE, SBE. Wind SBW, NW[
Light winds with frequent squalls. Seamen & tradesmen in there departments. Employ'd making sinnett, tailor making up Cloth for trade.
Dist pr log 41 Knots

October 28th, 1794
[Course SE, SEBE. Wind SSW, SBW]
Light winds attended with squals of hard rain. Some Sharks round. Employ'd making Sinnet, & fitting painters for ye Boats.
Dist pr log 41 Knots

October 29th, 1794
[Course SEBE, SEBS. Wind SBW, SWBS]
Lower'd down the Mainsail & repaired it. Caught a Shark. Caught a large Porpoise, people variously employ'd.
Dist pr log 39 Knots

October 30th, 1794
[Course SE, SW, WSW. Wind SBW, SSE, South]
Moderate breezes & cloudy. All hands employ'd in there departments. St. Pauls rocks bears S59°W Dist 360 Miles. Midnight Do. weather, caught a Shark. Seamen pointing ropes. Noon flying clouds.
Lat Obsd 13°57'N
Dist pr log 53 Knots

The *Union* (left): Cross section of the *Union's* main hatch, showing midship and body stowage, mast, spar and squaresail details. "L.W.L." is low water line. (Hewitt Jackson)

October 31st, 1794
[Course WSW, ESE. Wind South, SBE]
A Large swell from ye SW'd. A Sea from ye SSW For which I allow 12'. Squally with some rain.
Dist pr log 55 Knots

November 1st, 1794
[Course ESE, SW. Wind South, SBE]
Moderate breezes with frequent rain squalls. Caught two Bonnetto. Porpoises round. St. Pauls rocks bears S53°W. Dist 250.
Dist pr log 53 Knots

November 2nd, 1794
[Course SBW, SW, SWBS. Wind ESE, SEBS, SSE]
Moderate breezes with flying clouds. Some Hard rain. Noon pleasant agreeable weather.
Dist pr log 55 Knots

November 3rd, 1794
[Course WSW, SW½W. Wind SBW, SBE]
Light winds. At 3 PM TK Ship, Caught a Dolphin. Carried away ye Clue of ye Mains'l & again repair'd it.
Lat Obsd 2°36'N Long 46°30'E
Dist pr log 63 Knots

November 4th, 1794
[Course SWBW, SWBS. Wind SBE, SEBS]
Brisk winds with flying clouds & hazy weather. Pleasant got ye Cloths on deck to air found them in good order. Seamen and tradesmen Employ'd as usuall.
Dist pr log 81 Knots

November 5th, 1794
[Course SWBS, SW, SSW½W. Wind SEBS, SSE, SE]
Fresh gales & pleasant, with flying Clouds, with a high sea from ye SE. All hands employ'd breaking out the After hold for provisions etc. Saw some Birds. A Curr't to ye NW.
Dist pr log 80 Knots

November 6th, 1794
[Course SSW. Wind SE]
Moderate breezes & pleasant weather. Carried away ye Tops'l tie, & again repair'd it. Employ'd making woulding [welding] for ye Cables.
Dist pr log 80 Knots

November 7th, 1794
[Course SWBS, SW. Wind SEBS, SSE]
Brisk breezes & pleasant weather. Seamen making Mats, robins & Sinnett, Got ye Blankets, & Sails on deck to air.
Dist pr log 75 Knots

November 8th, 1794
[Course SWBS, SW½S. Wind SEBS, SSE]
Moderate breezes & pleasant weather. Midnight do wind & weather. Vast flights of Flying fish round, together with many Jellys, which sailors call Portugueze Men of war. People employ'd knoting yarns, thruming Mats pick'g Oakum etc.
Lat Obsd 1°51'S Long 28°55'W
Dist pr log 78 Knots

November 9th, 1794
[Course SW½S, SBW½W. Wind SEBS, SEBE]
Brisk breezes & pleasant agreeable weather. All sail out.
Dist pr log 84 Knots

November 10th, 1794
[Course SSW, S½W. Wind SE, ESE]
Steady breezes with pleasant weather. People employ'd Picking Oakam, knoting Yarns etc. Tradesmen as usuall.

All hands Employ'd, fitting two pair of lower shrouds. We being obliged to take ye Old ones, to make runing riging of, our Stock being nearly exausted.
Dist pr log 86 Knots

November 11th, 1794
[Course SBW, SSW. Wind SEBE]
Steady breezes and pleasant weather. Caught a Noddy. Lower'd down ye Mainsail & repair'd a hole in it. Saw some Men of War & tropic Birds.
Dist pr log 70 Knots

November 12th, 1794
[Course SSW, SBW. Wind SEBE, SBW]
Steady breezes & pleasant weather. Saw an Albacore. Caught a Noddy, & some flying fish. All Employ'd picking Oakum & spining Spun Yarn.
Dist pr log 91 Knots

November 13th, 1794
[Course SSW, SSW½W. Wind ESE, EBS]
Light breezes with frequent squalls, seamen & tradesmen variously Employ'd. Caught a Noddy.
Lat Obsd 8°33'S Long 30°39'W
Dist pr log 81 Knots

November 14th, 1794
[Course SSW, SBW½W. Wind SEBE]
Fresh breezes & pleasant weather, people Employ'd picking Oakum etc. At 10 Parted ye, the strap of ye throat tie block, & again repair'd it.
Dist pr log 110 Knots

November 15th, 1794
[Course SBW½W, SBW. Wind ESE, SEBE]
Fresh breezes and pleasant agreeable weather. Saw some porpoises. Employ'd breaking out ye hold for fresh water, & filling up the empty Casks, with salt water.
Dist pr log 102 Knots

November 16th, 1794
[Course SBW. Wind ESE]
Fresh breezes and pleasant weather.
Dist pr log 107 Knots

November 17th, 1794
[Course SBW½W, SBW. Wind SEBE, ESE]
Moderate breezes & pleasant. At 2 PM Some hard squalls with rain. Employ'd variously.
Dist pr log 116 Knots

November 18th, 1794
[Course SBW, SBW½W. Wind EBS]
Moderate breezes & pleasant weather. Unbent the Old topsail, it being torn & brought ye New one to ye Yard. Employ'd fitting new straps to the Main sheet Blocks, Taring the riging, making Sinnett etc.
Lat Obsd 17°2'S Long 33°41'W
Dist pr log 100 Knots

November 19th, 1794
[Courses SBW, SWBS. Wind ESE, SEBE]
Moderate breezes & pleasant weather. Caught a Dolphin. Employ'd pointing the ends of the Towline, picking Oakum etc. Carpenter making a Deep Sea reel.
Dist pr log 87 Knots

November 20th, 1794
[Course SWBS. Wind ESE, ENE]
Moderate breezes & pleasant weather. Variously employ'd. Sat up the riging, Saw a Brig in the SE quarter. A smooth sea.
Dist pr log 76 Knots

November 21st, 1794
[Course SSW. Wind ESE]
Light breezes & pleasant weather, Seamen & Tradesmen as usual Employ'd. Caught two sharks. Employ'd Crowning the spare Cables. The Brig still in sight to the SE.
Dist pr log 65 Knots

November 22nd, 1794
[Course SWBS. Wind NEBE]
A smooth Sea. Got part of the Cloaths on Deck to air. Employ'd knoting Yarns etc.
Dist pr log 99 Knots

November 23rd, 1794
[Course SW½S, WSW. Wind NNE, NW, South]
Lively breezes & pleasant weather. All sail out. At 9 AM, Squally hard rain.
Dist pr log 132 Knots

November 24th, 1794
[Course WSW, SWBW. Wind South, SBE]
Squally with some rain. Carried away the after leach rope of the Mainsail & repair'd it again. All hands employ'd knoting Yarns & spining spunyarn, & various other nessescary Jobs. St. Catharine Isle bears S68°W Dist 570 Mi.
Dist pr log 63 Knots

November 25th, 1794
[Course WSW, ESE, SWBW. Wind South, SSW, SBE]
Fresh breezes & Cloudy with frequent squalls & a high sea from the S & E. All hands employ'd knoting Yarns & Spining Spun Yarn. NW heave of ye Sea.
Lat Obsd 23°22'S Long 39°46'W Correct for 3 Days.
Dist pr log 62 Knots

November 26th, 1794
[Course WBS, SSW. Wind SBW, NNE]
Light winds & less weather, saw a Shark. At 8 PM lower'd the Main sail. Midnight flattering. At 1 AM Set the Squarsail & Mains'l. At 6 Low'd the M'sail & repair'd & set it again.
Dist pr log 31 Knots

November 27th, 1794
[Course SWBS, SBW. Wind NEBN, NE]
Moderate breezes & pleasant. At 7 PM Jib'd Ship. Carried away the throat rope of the Mains'l & again repair'd it.
Dist per log 129 Knots

November 28th, 1794
[Course SSW½W. Wind NBE½E]
Fresh breezes & pleasant weather.
Lat Obsd 27°12'S Long 42°8'W
Dist pr log 159 Knots

November 29th, 1794
[Course SWBS. Wind NEBN]
Moderate breezes & pleasant weather. Carpenter, & Caulker employ'd caulking & paying the Long boat, Tailor Constantly making up Cloth for traffic.
Dist pr log 101 Knots

November 30th, 1794
[Course SWBS, SSW, SBW. Wind NE, NW, WBN]
Fresh breezes & hazy weather. By the Mean of three Dist's of the sun & moon, I determin'd the Long. to be 42°2'0''W'd of Greenwich Obs'ry.
Dist pr log 169 Knots

December 1st, 1794
[Course SE, ESE, WSW. Wind SSW, South, SBW]
Light winds & variable with frequent rain squalls. At 3

PM TK Ship to the West'd. At 4 Wore Ship to the Eastward. At 5 fresh gales. Double reef'd the Mainsail. Parted the Jib sheets Blocks, & Split the sail. Parted the Head of ye Mainsail, haul'd down the sail and repair'd it, A large sea runing. At 11 Set all sail.
Lat Obsd 30°46'S Long 44°18'W
Dist pr log 68 Knots

December 2nd, 1794
[Course SWBW, SSW. Wind SBE, WNW]
Employ'd stowing & lashing the Boats etc. Got ye Spare-sails & Blankets on deck to air, Employ'd scraping the Long boat.
Dist pr log 50 Knots

December 3rd, 1794
[Course SBN½W, SE, SBE. Wind West, SSW, SW]
Light winds & pleasant, pay'd the bottom of the Long-boat. Midnight pleasant saw a turtle. Lower'd down ye Mainsail to rapair, sail maker employ'd repairing of it.
Lat Obsd 31°38'S Long 46°20'W
Dist pr log 39 Knots

December 4th, 1794
[Course SWBS. Wind WNW]
Calm & pleasant weather. Saw a number of Turtle, Caught one with grains. Saw some Albatrosses flying round. All hands employ'd cleaning Muskets, Cutlashes etc. All sail out.
Dist pr log 104 Knots

December 5th, 1794
[Course SSW, SWBS. Wind NW, NE, ESE]
Light winds & pleasant. Lower'd down the Mainsail & repair'd it. Saw many turtle. Heavy gales & high sea, down square sail Yard.
Dist pr log 73 Knots

December 6th, 1794
[Course SSW½W, SBW. Wind EBS, NE]
Fresh breezes & cloudy. At 2 PM Single reef'd the Main-sail. A high sea runing. Midnight lovely gales. At 4 AM Observ'd ye Water to be colour'd.
Dist pr log 168 Knots

December 7th, 1794
[Course South, SSW. Wind NEBN, NBE]
Fresh gales & hazy, the water much colour'd. At 7 PM rounded too & sound'd but got no bottom with 85 fm of line. Midnight pleasant, sounded, no bottom with 100 fm. A great number of birds flying round. Cape Blanco bears S44°W Dist 760 Mi.
Dist pr log 188 Knots

December 8th, 1794
[Course SSW, SBW, ESE. Wind NBW, NNW, South]
Fresh gales & flying clouds with a high sea. In topsail, & 2d reef of Mainsail. Set the Jib, & took the Bonnett from the squarsail. At 2 AM The wind chang'd in a squall, split the Jib, unbent it, & brought another too. Heavy gales. At ½ past 11 Hove too under a trysail—the sail maker & others repair'g the Mainsail.
Dist pr log 121 Knots

December 9th, 1794
[Course SEBS, SSW. Wind SBW, SWBS, WNW]
Stiff gales with a high sea, Laying too under a trysail. Sound'd no bottom with 70 fm.
Lat Obsd 40°45'S Long 53°15'W
Dist pr log 66 Knots

December 10th, 1794
[Course SSW, South, SSE. Wind WBN, West, SW]
Heavy gales with a high sea. Vast many birds round. Ballenc'd reef'd the Mainsail. At 2 In Mainsail, set ye trysail.

Midnight Hard squalls, with rain & sleet, ship'd many seas.
Dist pr log 69 Knots

December 11th, 1794
[Course SEBS, SSE, SWBS. Wind SWBS, SW, NW]
Fresh gales with a high sea. At Meridian Down trysail, set the Mainsail Jib & fores'l. At 5 PM Out reefs, Sent up the topsail & squarsail Yards. At 2 AM Hard gales, Double reef'd the Mainsail. The water exceedingly colored, sounded no bottom with 100 fm of line.
Dist pr log 108 Knots

December 12th, 1794
[Course SWBS, South, SBE. Wind WNW, WSW, SW]
Fresh breezes & pleasant weather, saw a Whale, & a seal, also much Kelp. *Shot two albertross, porpoises around, water discolour'd.* All hands employ'd breaking out for Beaf, scraping the Masts. Caulker, caulking ye forecastle, tailor in his department.
Lat Obsd 44°30′S Long 55°41′W
Dist pr log 66 Knots

December 13th, 1794
[Course SWBW, South, SSE. Wind WNW, WBN, SW]
Light winds & cloudy, saw a number of Whales, Shot 2 Albatrosses, & got one of them which weigh'd 150 lbs. & measured from tip to tip 13 feet.
Dist pr log 88 Knots

December 14th, 1794
[Course W½SBE of SEBS, SWBW. Wind SW, NWBW]
Heavy gales, laying too. At 7 AM Out all reefs, Set ye flying Jib. Vast many birds flying round—& ye water much colour'd.
Dist pr log 37 Knots

December 15th, 1794
[Course SWBW, SSW, SW. Wind NW, West, WBN]
Heavy gales & Cloudy. At 2 AM Sounded, no bottom with a long pole.
Dist pr log 78 Knots

December 16th, 1794
[Course SEBS, SSE. Wind SWBS, SW]
Heavy gales with a mountanious sea accompanied with hail & Sleet. Hove too under the trysail. Noon do. weather, (worse can't be).
Dist pr log 40 Knots

December 17th, 1794
[Course SW, WSW, SSE. Wind WNW, NNW, SW]
Heavy gales, saw some Kelp & seals, shot an Albatross. Got the Jib boom in upon deck. Hard squalls with hail and sleet. A high cross sea running. Ship'd many seas. Cape Blanco N84°W Dist 380 Mi.
Lat Obsd 48°0′S Long 55°25′W
Dist pr log 70 Knots

December 18th, 1794
[Course SSE, SBE. Wind SW]
Moderate breezes & tolerable pleasant. All hands nessescarily employ'd. Midnight a heavy gale of wind, hove too under a reef'd trysail. Ship'd many seas. Squally with snow & sleet, saw much Kelp etc. Noon heavy gales, & exceeding Cold.
Dist pr log 22 Knots

December 19th, 1794
[Course SBE, NWBW, South. Wind SW, SWBW]
Heavy gales with a mountanious sea. Saw porpoises Kelp, & many birds. Parted ye After leach rope of Mainsail & Split it, unbent the sail, & bent a new one. All hands Employ'd braking out the hold for water, and for the better

arrangement of it. Sail maker on ye Sparesails.
Dist pr log 28 Knots

December 20th, 1794
[Course SWBW, WSW, West. Wind NWBW, NNW, SE]
Light winds & pleasant weather. Shot an Albatross, finished stowing the Hold. Ship'd many seas. Noon heavy gales & a high sea.
Dist pr log 109 Knots

December 21st, 1794
[Course West, WBN. Wind South, SSW]
Strong gales with frequent hail squalls & a high sea. Got no bottom with 70 fm of line.
Lat Obsd 47°43′S Long 59°39′W
Dist pr log 122 Knots

December 22nd, 1794
[Course WNW, WBN. Wind SWBS, SW]
Strong breezes & hazy weather. At 7 PM Colour'd the water again. Shot an Albatross. Out all reefs. Sound'd, no bottom.
Dist pr log 81 Knots

December 23rd, 1794
[Course SWBW, SSE, SW. Wind NWBW, SW, WNW]
Moderate breezes & pleasant with a smooth sea. Seamen employ'd on the repairs of the riging. Sail maker on the Old Mainsail, Scrap'd the Mast etc. Sounded no bottom with a long pole. Saw a Water Witch, Whales etc. At 10 TK Ship to the South'd & West'd.
Dist pr log 55 Knots

December 24th, 1794
[Course SSW, NWBW, WNW. Wind West, SWBW]
Fresh breezes with flying clouds. Sailmaker employ'd on ye

Old Mainsail. Saw a penguin. Seamen making Nettles, Cable bends etc. All hands employ'd as usuall. Saw a Whale, Seal, Kelp etc.
Dist pr log 85 Knots

December 25th, 1794
[Course NWBW, WBS. Wind SWBW, SWBS]
Strong gales with frequent heavy hail squalls. At 10 AM Out all reefs, On Bonnetts. Smooth sea. All hands merrily Employ'd, for it is Cristmas Day, happiness to all friends & well wishes to ye Sloop *Union* & her Crew.
Dist pr log 80 Knots

December 26th, 1794
[Course WSW, SSW. Wind SBW, West]
Steady breezes & pleasant weather. Saw two seals, & Many Birds. Noon pleasant, sound'd, & got bottom with 56 fm of line, fine Black & white sand, with Yellow specks.
Lat Obsd 45°24′S Long 58°52′W
Dist pr log 62 Knots

December 27th, 1794
[Course South, SSW, WNW, WBN. Wind WSW, SW, SSW]
Light winds with a smooth sea. Many Whales playing round the Sloop. Employ'd upon ye riging & sails.
Dist pr log 42 Knots

December 28th, 1794
[Course SWBW. Wind calm, NW]
Pleasant & a remarkable smooth sea. Many Whales round. Birds, kelp etc. as usuall.
Dist pr log 34 Knots

December 29th, 1794
[Course WSW, SWBW. Wind NNW, calm]

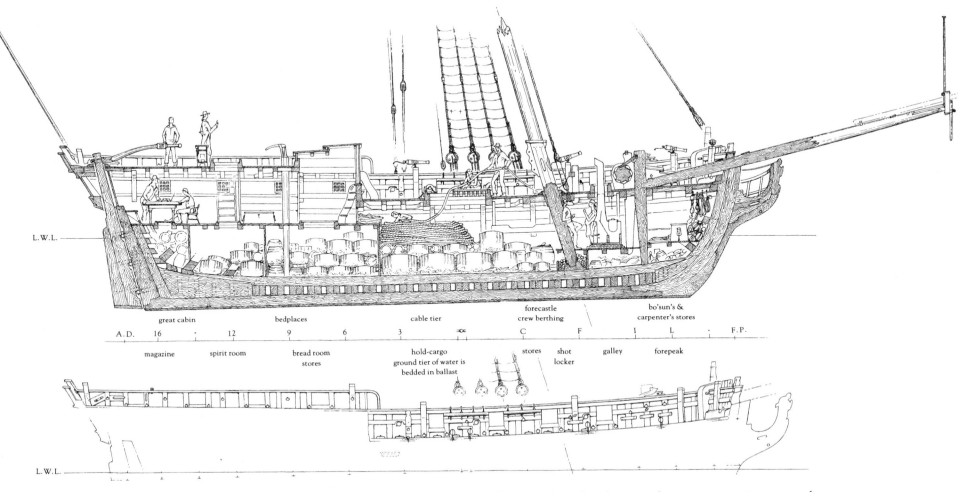

The *Union*: Inboard profile (upper) shows the structure of the ship, berthing and stowage. Lower profile shows the quarter board and bulwark details. (Hewitt Jackson)

[Note: Letters and numbers between the two cross sections are used as a reference for the cross sections and profiles that follow, and for the cross section on p. 12]

Lively breezes & pleasant with a smooth sea. Shot an albatross & got him. Stock'd the Anchors & Got them on the bows. Sound'd & got bottom in 52 fm, Grey sand & broken Shells.
Dist pr log 56 Knots

December 30th, 1794
[Course SSW, SBW, SWBS. Wind NEBE, EBN, NE]
Fresh breezes & pleasant weather, saw Vast many Whales,

Birds, Kelp, etc. At 4 PM Sound'd 52 fm, Mud & fine sand.
Dist pr log 137 Knots

December 31st, 1794
[Course WSW, SEBS, SSE. Wind NNE, SW, SSW]
Fresh breezes with flying clouds. Shot 3 Albatross's & two Sea hens & got them. At 7 PM Saw Cape Blanco bear'g west 10 or 12 leag. Dist. At 8 The South'st extreme of the

19

land in sight. Soundings 55 fm, fine sand & small stones. At 2 AM sound'd 45 fm Do. bottom. At 5 Set all sail, the water colour'd with shoals of a small redfish.
Dist pr log 85 Knots

January 1st, 1795
[Course SE, SEBE, SBW. Wind SSW, SBW, NBW]
Fresh breezes & pleasant with a head beat sea. Got Soundings in 62 fm. All hands employ'd picking Oakum & repair'g riging & Sails.
Lat Obsd 48°47'S Long 62°22'W
Dist pr log 47 Knots

January 2nd, 1795
[Course SBE½E, SE, East. Wind NNW, NNE]
Pleasant weather. Shot a Penguin. Bent the Cables, Sail Maker on the Spare Mainsail, saw Penguins Seals, Sea Lions, Albatross etc.
Dist pr log 145 Knots

January 3rd, 1795
[Course East, ESE, EBS. Wind NNW, NBW, NW]
Fresh breezes with a thick fog. No bottom with 100 fm of line. At 6 Hove too, a thick fog. At 7 AM saw the Jasons Isles[8] bear'g ENE 8 or 9 leagues Dist. Noon pleasant the Jasons Isle 3 leagues.
Dist pr log 67 Knots

January 4th, 1795
[Course EBN½N, SSE, SEBS. Wind NNW, NW, SW]
Moderate breezes & flattering weather. At 3 PM The wind heading for Port Egmont, Bore away for the New Island harbour. At 5 More clear, bore away for ye New Isles. At 6 Saw ye West[ernmost] bear'g SEBE 3 leagues. At Meridian the West'd bore WBS, Ball Isle ESE 3 leagues Dist, Lat Obsd 51°43'S. Loop Head bear'g EBS 3 or 4 leagues. Out Yawl & sent her, in a head to sound. At 7 PM Came too,

in New Isle harbour, in 8 fm Water, Mud & sand. Moor'd with ½ a Cable each way, ye Watering place a ¼ Mile Dist. Clear'd the Decks.
Dist pr log 64 Knots
N.B This Day's work contains 36 H[ours]

January 5th, 1795
[Wind SW]
Moderate breezes & pleasant, all hands employ'd, breaking out the hold. Erected a tent on Shore, land'd ye Empty water Casks, & Spare Sails, with ye Cooper & Sail maker to repair them. Brought of 2 long boat loads of Stone ballace [ballast]. Shot many Game.

January 6th, 1795
[Wind NNW]
Light winds & pleasant. Took of three load more of Ballace, making in all 12 tons, a party filling water at the tent, others aranging the hold. I went in ye Yawl to hunt after game. Shot 3 or 4 Doz. of Geese & ducks & my Dog run down three Wild Hogs, weig'd 140 [pounds] each, which I got. Latter part fresh gales. Employ'd salt'g down Pork.

January 7th, 1795
[Wind NE]
Pleasant agreeable weather. Got of fourteen Hh'ds [hogsheads] of Water, & stow'd them away. The Yawl up ye Sound after Geese & Ducks, of which we kill as many & serves all hands constantly. The Dog run us Down 2 More Hogs. At 8 The Yawl retur'd loaded with Geese.

January 8th, 1795
[Wind WNW]
First part thick hazy weather, with some rain. Cooper, setting up Bread Hh'ds, shakes for water Hh'ds & repair'g the empty Beef barrels, to hold water. Unbent ye Jib & foresail, & sent them on shore to repair. The Brig *Sally* of

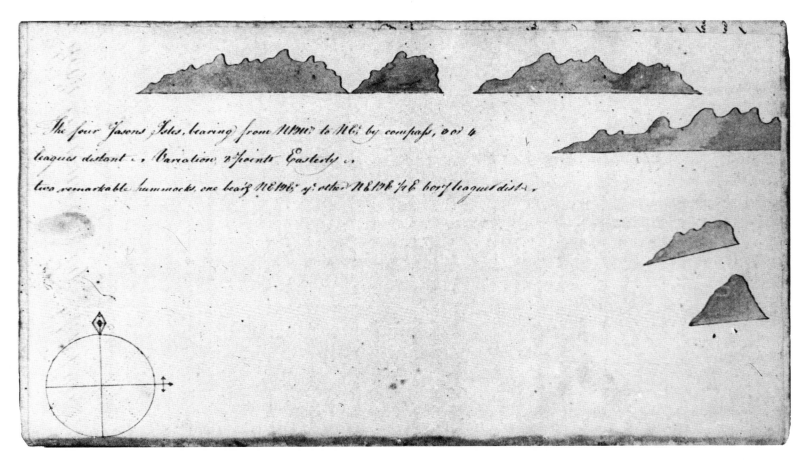

The four Jasons Isles, bearing from NNW to NE by compass, 3 or 4 leagues distant. Variation 2 points Easterly. two remarkable hummocks, one bearg NE½E, ye other NE½E ½E bore 5 leagues dist.

In January 1795, John Boit drew these profiles of Jasons Isles and "two remarkable hummocks," located west of the Falkland Islands. With poor weather hampering navigation at the time, Boit's ability to recognize the Jasons Isles helped the *Union* to approach the Falklands.

London, Capt. Nicol arriv'd in ye harbour, out 4 Months from Falmouth, on a Whaling Voyage but had not got any Oil. So ends.

January 9th, 1795
[Wind SW]
Light winds & cloudy weather. Got all ye riging on deck to repair. A party on shore hunting after Hogs of which the Dog caught one. Shot many Geese & Ducks. Capt. Nicol gave me a harpoon. Got the y[ar]d riging over head [aloft] again, kept down 2 pair of Shrouds, & replaced them with new ones.

January 10th, 1795
[Wind NW]
Small breezes & pleasant. Seamen turning in Dead eyes, & taring & rattling down ye riging. Carpenter repair'g the Channels, which he found very defective. Borrow'd the Snows Cooper to assist ours. Shot many Geese & ducks. Salt'd down 2 barr'l of Pork.

January 11th, 1795
First part light winds & pleasant. Give ye people the use of ye day to themselves to go on shore & recreate themselves, among the Grass. The Dog caught three large

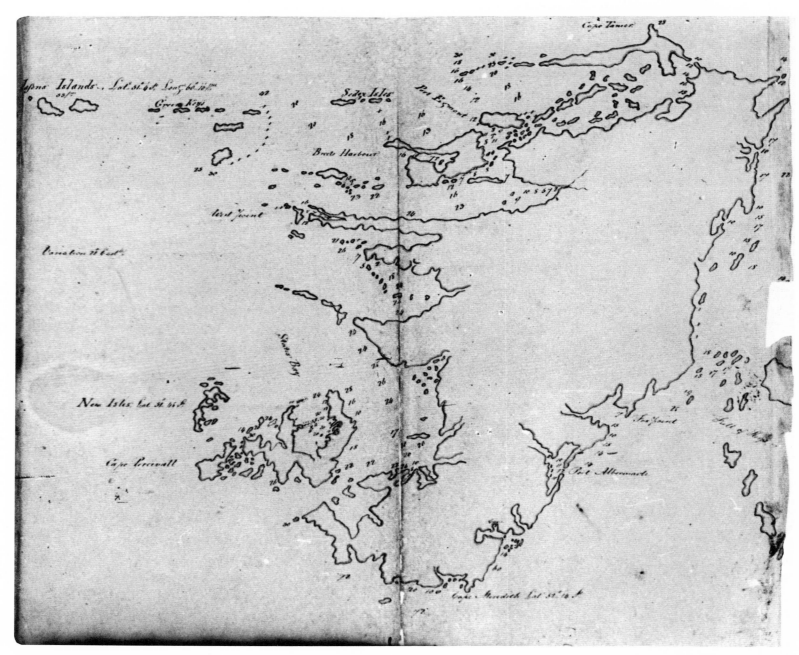

West Falkland Island, as drawn by John Boit, Jr., in January 1795. The *Union* reached the Falkland Islands early in the month, and remained in the area for almost three weeks. During that time Boit completed several maps and illustrations for the Log. The accuracy of Boit's map of the islands seems to indicate that he may have had access to charts made by other navigators.

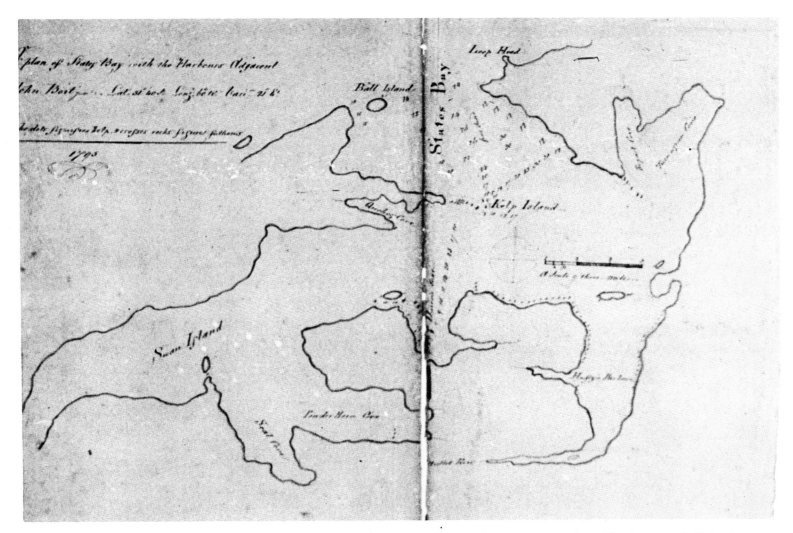

One of John Boit's maps of the Falkland Islands area. Boit described it in the Log as: "A Plan of States [Queen Charlotte] Bay with the Harbours Adjacent," noting that "The dots signify Kelp, & crosses rock, figures fathoms."

Hogs, one of which I gave to Capt. Nicol, but he insisted it should be an Indian gift, & so gave in return as much Elephant blubber, as made 15 Gall. of Oil, together with a spare double Block, & some sheaves & laniard stuf, all which articles, I stood much in need of. Latter part fresh gales, the people fetch'd on board, above 60 Geese & Ducks.

January 12th, 1795
[Wind NW]
Fresh breezes & tolerable pleasant. I exchang'd 1 pair of Swivels[9] [small cannon], with Capt. Nicol, for a pair of two pounders, with carrages & utensils. He complimented me with the Ods. Seamen & tradesmen constantly employ'd in there departments.

January 13th, 1795
[Wind NW]
Fresh gales & pleasant, sail maker constantly employ'd on shore upon ye sails. Carpenter in his department. Seamen upon ye riging—so ends this day.

January 14th, 1795
[Wind NNW]
Moderate breezes & pleasant weather. Hog'd[10] both sides, & cleared the bottom, pay'd the bends & sides, sat up the riging, brought off the spare sails from the Shore. The boat went after Celery & found plenty. The Snow *Sally*, Capt. Nickell, sail'd for West point in pursuit of Elephant.

January 15th, 1795
[Wind NW]
Strong gales & hazy weather, ye Snow *Sally* arriv'd again in the harbour she not being able to reach Westpt. the wind being contrary. A party on shore hunting shot many Geese & Ducks, the Dog caught two fine hogs.

January 16th, 1795
[Wind WNW]
Pleasant agreeable weather, a party on shore washing, another hunting, ye Dog caught us five Hogs, salt'd down two bbl. of fresh pork. Got ye remainder of our water on board, & stow'd it away. Present'd Capt. Nickell with two Hogs, he not being able to catch any for want of a Dog.

January 17th, 1795
[Wind SW]
Small breezes & pleasant weather. The Snow *Sally*, Capt.

Nickell, sail'd again for West pt., with a fair tide, both boats away in pursuit of game. At night ye boats return'd with, five Hogs, & six seals, & above 60 Geese & Ducks besides much drift wood & wild Celery.

January 18th, 1795
[Wind WNW]
Light winds & pleasant weather, all ready for sea. Wind bound, both boats away after stock. At eve they return'd with abundance of fowl, & one Seal.

January 19th, 1795
[Wind NW]
First part light airs, of tent & every thing else of Consequence from ye shore, began to unmoor. Middle part a heavy gale of wind, moor'd ship again, it blow'g too hard to get under way.

January 20th, 1795
[Wind WSW]
Fresh gales with flying clouds, a party went after Geese & Ducks, & Got plenty. Carpenter caulking in ye quarter lights. Latter, more moderate, got ye small bowes anchor on the bow.

January 21st, 1795
[Wind WSW]
Strong gales with heavy gusts from the mountains, lying wind bound, a party on shore after game. Shot 20 Geese, & ye Dog caught two Hogs. Latter part strong gales with Hail & rain.

The Falkland Islands to Columbia's Cove, Vancouver Island

22 January to 16 May 1795

January 22nd, 1795
[Wind WNW]
Moderate breezes & fair weather. At 10 PM Hove up the Anchor, & beat down under Kelp Isle & came to anchor, with the best bowes, in 8 fm water, mud & sand. Loop Head bear'g NBW. Green Isle SSW, States Harbour SE, & ye East'st pt. of Kelp Isle NBW½W 1 Mile Dist. Sent the Longboat along shore after drift wood, & ye yawl after game, both well man'd. At eve they return'd, the Longboat loaded with wood & ye Yawl with plenty of Geese & Ducks. Hoist'd in ye Longboat, & let go ye small bowes, under foot.

January 23rd, 1795
[Wind WSW]
Pleasant breezes and fair weather. At 4 PM Hove up ye Anchors, & came to sail standing upon a wind to ye N &

W. At 6 Abrest of Ball Isle, in Yawl & stow'd ye boats, Stow'd ye Anchors & quoil'd ye Cables below. At Meridian the NW extreem of the New Isles bore SBW½W 9 leagues. Gibralter rock NNE½E, the Entrance of West point harbour NEBN 4 leagues.
Lat Obsd 51°39'S

January 24th, 1795
[Wind SWS, SWBW]
Light winds & pleasant weather, with a large swell heaving into the bay. Cape Percivall bear'g SBW. Midnight pleasant with light winds, many Seals round. Noon pleasant, Cape Percivall bear'g SEBS 10 or 12 leagues Dist.

January 25th, 1795
[Wind SW, SBW]
Midnight squally. Took in & set sail occasionally, saw a

large fire on ye New Isles. At Meridian ye NE part of ye New Isles bore NEBN ye Eastermost part of Swan Isle in sight. Cape Percivall bear'g EBN, 5 or 6 leagues Dist. from which I take a departure it lying in Lat 51°54′S & Long 60°10′W of Greenwich.

January 26th, 1795
[Course SBE, South, SW. Wind SWBW, WSW, WNW]
Fresh breezes with a high sea. Seamen & Tradesmen employ'd in their depart's. Unbent ye Cables & quoil'd them below.
Dist pr log 95 Knots

January 27th, 1795
[Course SWBW, South, SBW. Wind WBN, West, WSW]
Moderate breezes & pleasant weather, all sail out, observ'd many strong tide rips, saw Kelp & many birds. At 7 AM Light winds & thick weather. Noon hazy.
Lat Obsd 53°34′S Long 63°9′W
Dist pr log 75 Knots

January 28th, 1795
[Course SE½S. Wind ENE]
Moderate breezes. Pass'd many Currant rips. Saw Blackfish.
Dist pr log 50 Knots

January 29th, 1795
[Course SSW, EBS. Wind calm, West, North]
At 4 AM Saw States Isle bear'g from SE to SBE, 12 leagues dist. Jib'd Sloop & took in the Squarsail. Strong tides, but smooth sea. Cape St. Juan bore S¾W 10 leagues Dist.
Dist pr log 77 Knots

January 30th, 1795
[Course SSE, South. Wind NNE, NBE]

Fresh gales. At 2 PM Cape St. Juan [Eastern end of States Island] bore SW½W 8 or 9 leagues dist. A high following sea. Noon steady breezes, with an exceeding thick fog.
Dist pr log 147 Knots

January 31st, 1795
[Course SSW, SWBW. Wind ENE, ESE]
Fresh breezes. Foggy disagreeable weather. In 2d reef of the Mainsail a high sea runing. Cape Noir bears N35°30′W Dist 240 Miles. Cape Horn Do. N22°E Dist 120 Miles. [Position nearly directly south of Cape Horn.]
Dist pr log 156 Knots

February 1st, 1795
[Course SWBW, WSW. Wind SE, ENE]
Fresh breezes & thick dirty weather with frequent rain squalls. Got the Anchors on deck & lash'd them etc.
Lat Obsd 57°10′S Long 72°11′W
Dist pr log 150 Knots

February 2nd, 1795
[Course WNW, NWBW, WBN. Wind NNE, NBE, NBW]
Moderate breezes & cloudy, with a following swell. Double reef'd the Mains'l, of Bonnetts. At 10 On Bonnett to the foresail.
Dist pr log 102 Knots

February 3rd, 1795
[Course SW, SWBW. Wind WNW, NWBW]
Fresh breezes & pleasant weather with a mountanious sea, from ye West'd. At 5 AM Squally. Noon Stif gales, with Sleet.
Dist pr log 86 Knots

February 4th, 1795
[Course SW, SWBW, WBS. Wind WNW, WBN]

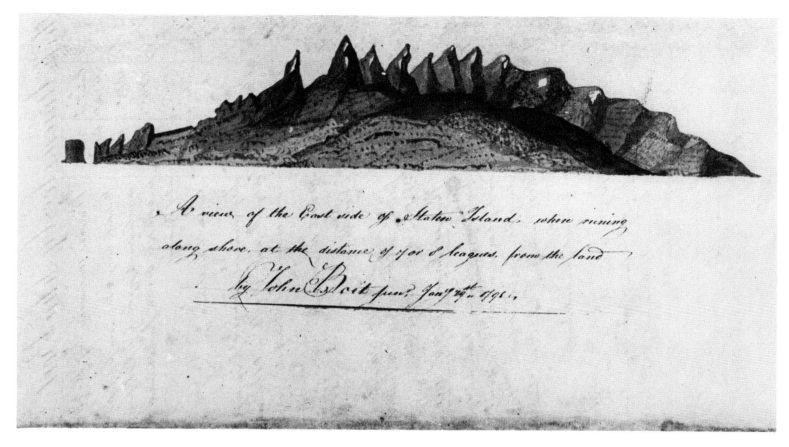

East side of Staten Island (Isla de los Estados, off Tierra del Fuego), drawn by John Boit, 29 January 1795. The *Union* passed it one day before rounding Cape Horn. Boit sketched this view "when runing along shore, at the distance of 7 or 8 leagues from the land."

This day's Latit is the highest latit during this passage, having generally experienced fresh gales from the east with high seas. Had albatross & land birds round. At 3 Down Jib & hove too, under a ballenc'd Mainsail.
Lat Obsd 57°42′S Long 78°15′W
Dist pr log 47 Knots

[The *Union* is now around Cape Horn after a relatively easy passage.]

February 5th, 1795
[Course WBN, WNW, NWBW. Wind NBW, North, NBE]
Moderate breezes & tolerable pleasant. Midnight squally with sleet. At 11 Out all reef's, on bonnetts.
Dist pr log 108 Knots

February 6th, 1795
[Course NWBW, WNW. Wind NBE, NBW]

Moderate breezes with rain & a high sea. At 1 PM Parted ye clew of ye Mains'l. Unbent ye sail, & brought another too.
Dist pr log 65 Knots

February 7th, 1795
[Course NBW, NBE, WBS. Wind WBN, NW, calm]
Fresh breezes with flying clouds. Midnight calm, & a high sea which caus'd the Sloop to labour exceedingly. Many Albatross flying round. Cape Disseada bears S85°W Dist 290 Mi.
Lat Obsd 54°39′S Long 81°1′W
Dist pr log 76 Knots

February 8th, 1795
[Course NNW, North, NW. Wind West, WNW, SWBW]
Brisk gales & tolerable pleasant weather.
Dist pr log 99 Knots

February 9th, 1795
[Course NWBN, NW, NNW. Wind SWBW, WBS, West]
Fresh breezes with pleasant weather. Sail maker repair'g ye foresail. Struck a porpoise but ye Iron brak'g, lost him. Some Land birds, & Albertross round.
Dist pr log 129 Knots

February 10th, 1795
[Course NWBW, NNW, NW. Wind WSW, West, NE]
Fresh breezes with a high sea. Ship'd many seas. A disagreeable head beat sea.
Dist pr log 98 Knots

February 11th, 1795
[Course NNW½W, NW, West. Wind WBS, SW, West]
Flattering breezes & cloudy. Kill'd a Hog. Calm, with a

rolling sea. People employ'd on ye repairs of ye riging.
Dist pr log 72 Knots

February 12th, 1795
[Course WSW, NBW, NW. Wind NW, WBN, SWBW]
Fresh breezes with tough squalls. Double reef'd ye Mainsail, a high sea. Massasuero bears N11°E, Dist 820 Miles.
Lat Obsd 47°11′S Long 83°12′W
Dist pr log 136 Knots

February 13th, 1795
[Course NWBW, NW½N. Wind SSW, SWBS, SW]
Fresh gales with frequent hard Squalls. Ship'd many seas. Some Albertrosses, & Sandpipers round.
Dist pr log 163 Knots

February 14th, 1795
[Course NW½N, NWBN. Wind SW, WSW]
Steady breezes with flying clouds. Out reefs, on bonnets.
Dist pr log 122 Knots

February 15th, 1795
[Course NNW, NNW½W. Wind West, WBS]
Moderate breezes. Employ'd getting ye people Chests & beding on deck to air, & smoking the Forecastle with Gun powder. Massasuero bears N29°E 540 Mi Dist.
Dist pr log 92 Knots

February 16th, 1795
[Course NWBN, NW. Wind WBS, SW]
Steady breezes & pleasant weather, with a smooth sea, all sail out. All hands employ'd.
Dist pr log 147 Knots

February 17th, 1795
[Course NW, NWBN. Wind SSW, SW]
People employ'd overhauling the topm't riging, knoting

yarns, Carpenter fitting gun for to make rope with.
Dist pr log 100 Knots

February 18th, 1795
[Course NW. Wind SSW, EBS]
Light winds and pleasant weather. Employ'd knoting Yarns, Got the topmast an end & the Jib boom out, Sat up the riging & other small jobs. Saw Some Skip jacks, a Albertross etc. Massasuero bears N67°E Distant 440 Miles. The Line [equator] in Long 120°W bears N37°57'W Dist. 2,789 M.
Dist pr log 99 Knots

February 19th, 1795
[Course NW. Wind EBS, variable]
Light winds & pleasant. Employ'd drawing & knoting Yarns, Set up the topmast Shrouds, Bent ye Flying jib. A 8 AM Sent up the Topsailmast Yard & Set the Sail. Got part of the Cloths on deck to air.
Lat Obsd 35°45'S Long 88°51'W
Dist pr log 78 Knots

February 20th, 1795
[Course NW, NWBN. Wind EBS, ESE]
Got ye Cable below. Employ'd knoting Yarns and making Nettles. Carpenter fitting a new Waste for the sloop.[11] Tailor making great Coats for trade. Seamen making rope, & reef plats [ties].
Dist pr log 64 Knots

February 21st, 1795
[Course NWBN. Wind SEBS, East]
Brisk winds and pleasant weather. All hands Steadily employ'd.
Dist pr log 159 Knots

February 22nd, 1795
[Course NWBN. Wind EBN]
Lively breezes with flying clouds, with a smooth sea. Saw flying fish. Cape St. James bears N22°27'W dist 5,350 Mi.
Dist pr log 139 Knots

February 23rd, 1795
[Course NWBN. Wind SEBE, variable]
Pleasant weather with a smooth sea. Seamen employ'd making rope & spining Yarns. Carpenters on the waste tailor in his department.
Dist pr log 120 Knots

February 24th, 1795
[Course NW. Wind East, SE]
Moderate agreeable weather. Midnight very pleasant. Tradesmen in there departments—kill'd a Hog.
Dist pr log 96 Knots

February 25th, 1795
[Course NW. Wind SEBE]
Pleasant breezes with a smooth sea. Saw Tropic Birds. Seamen knoting Yarns, Carpenters Caulker & Tailor in there departments.
Lat Obsd 26°32'S
Dist pr log 89 Knots

February 26th, 1795
[Course NW. Wind EBS]
Light airs & very pleasant weather. At 2H10'40'' Ap time, By the Mean of three sights of ye sun & moon nearest limbs I determined the Long to be 91°0'56''W. Tradesmen employ'd in there departments, Seamen making rope.
Dist pr log 45 Knots

February 27th, 1795
[Course NW. Wind SEBS, SE]
Fresh gales with a still calm accompanied with a high Sea but smoth water. Caught an Albacore, but lost him. Saw the shadow of a Shark. Seamen & Tradesmen diligently employ'd doing nothing by mischeif.
Dist by guess work 12 Knots

February 28th, 1795
[Course NW, WBN. Wind calm, ENE, NBW]
Very pleasant, Laying too in a calm. Seamen employ'd pointing the ends of the Cables for Splicing.
Dist pr log 19 Knots

March 1st, 1795
[Course WBS, West, WBN. Wind NWBN, NNW, NBW]
Light winds and pleasant weather. Employ'd cleaning out ye Forecastle.
Lat Obsd 25°47'S Long 92°57'W
Dist pr log 62 Knots

March 2nd, 1795
[Course NW½W, NW, NNW. Wind NNE, NEBN]
People employ'd making points & pointing ropes. Carpenter on the Waste. Snider making Great Coats.
Dist pr log 47 knots

March 3rd, 1795
[Course NNW, NBW. Wind NE, East, SE]
Light winds with a long south'y swell. Sat up the riging & various other nessescary jobs.
Dist pr log 61 Knots

March 4th, 1795
[Course NBW, NNW. Wind SE, SEBS]
Fresh breezes with a tumbling swell. At 8 PM Saw a Brig to ye NE & soon after spoke her, but could get nothing from them but No Understand etc. She was standing upon a Wind to the SW, & did not shorten Sail for me. They appear'd to be somewhat frighted. I suppose she was a Spanierd, from Acapulco, bound to Boldivia or Chile.
Dist pr log 113 Knots

March 5th, 1795
[Course NNW. Wind SEBS]
Brisk breezes & pleasant. Seamen employ'd making Mats & picking Oak'm. Carpenter upon ye Waste, Tailor making great Coats etc. Sail maker making Yawl's sails.
Lat Obsd 20°39' Long 94°50'W
Dist pr log 124 Knots

March 6th, 1795
[Course NW½W. Wind SSE, SBE]
Lively breezes and pleasant. At noon jib'd Sloop. Seamen and Tradesmen Variously employ'd. Steady breezes, with a southly swell.
Dist pr log 107 Knots

March 7th, 1795
[Course NW½W. Wind SSE, SSW]
Light winds & pleasant weather. Seamen grafting the rings of ye Spare Anchors, & picking Oakum. Some Skip Jacks round, but very coy. Seamen Employ'd making board'g Nettings etc.
Dist pr log 67 Knots

March 8th, 1795
[Course NW½W. Wind SW, calm]
Midnight inclining to a Calm. Employ'd getting the people Chests & beding on deck to air, & smoking the forecastle with Gunpowder & Vinegar.
Dist pr log 43 Knots

March 9th, 1795
[Course NBW, NNW. Wind calm, WBN, West[
Warm pleasant weather. Seamen to work on Boarding nettings Carpenter on the Waste tailor as Usual. A large swell constantly heaving from the SSE. Saw a Man of War bird.
Dist pr log 21 Knots

March 10th, 1795
[Course NW½W. Wind variable, SE]
Light airs & pleasant warm weather. Saw many Water Jellies, a Water Snake etc. Employ'd as Yesterday. Plenty of Cats paws, but no steady breeze.
Lat Obsd 17°3'S Long 97°49'W
Dist pr log 30 Knots

March 11th, 1795
[Course NW½W. Wind SEBE, NEBN]
Light winds & pleasant weather. Saw flying fish & some drift feathers. By two sights of ye sun & moon Near't Limbs I determined the Long. Ye moon was too low to put much Confidence in ye Obs'n.
Dist pr log 81 Knots

March 12th, 1795
[Course NW½W. Wind NE, ENE]
Light winds, Caught a Bonetto saw a Man of War bird, & a small land bird etc. Employ'd setting up ye Bowsprit Gammond.
Dist pr log 97 Knots

March 13th, 1795
[Course NW½W. Wind ENE, NE, ESE]
Steady breezes and pleasant weather. Sat up the Stays, Carpenter mak'g parts of Guns, Tailor as Usuall.
Dist pr log 110 Knots

March 14th, 1795
[Course NW½W. Wind EBN, ESE]
Steady breezes & pleasant, seamen & tradesmen Various-ly Employ'd. Many tropic birds & flying fish round. Mid-night pleasant, all sail out. Porpoises round.
Dist pr log 110 Knots

March 15th, 1795
[Course NW½W. Wind ESE, SEBE]
Brisk breezes & pleasant weather. Finish'd ye boarding Nettings, many Tropic Birds & flying fish round.
Lat Obsd 11°10'S Long 108°28'W
Dist pr log 134 Knots

March 16, 1795
[Course NW. Wind EBN, ESE]
Light breezes with frequent rain squalls. Carpenter mak-ing Parts for Guns. Caulkers Caulking ye Yawl.
Dist pr log 130 Knots

March 17th, 1795
[Course NW. Wind SEBE]
Moderate breezes & pleasant weather. Employ'd painting the New Waste. Caulking the Long Boat etc.
Dist pr log 127 Knots

March 18th, 1795
[Course NW. Wind SE]
Lively breezes & pleasant weather with a following swell. Some Tropic birds & many flying fish round. Carpenter fitting Hawse pieces Aft. Cape St. James bears N15°W. Dist 3620 Mi. Owyhee Do. N58°W. Dist. 2910 Miles. rocca Partida Do. 33°W Dist 1600 Miles. Isle Galego Do. N71°E Dist 770 Miles.
Dist pr log 146 Knots

March 19th, 1795
[Course NWBN. Wind SE]
Fresh breezes & flying clouds. All sail out. Caulker caulking ye quarter deck. Painted the Bowsprit, etc.
Dist pr log 141 Knots

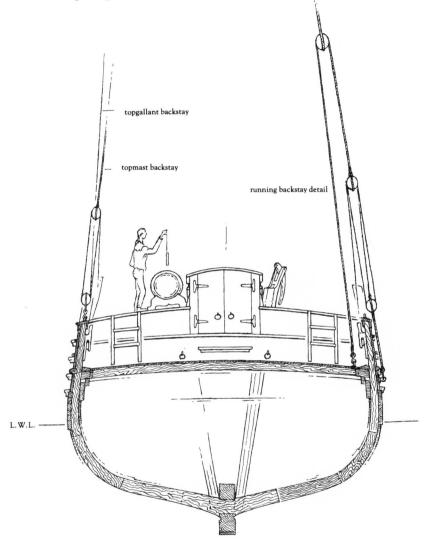

topgallant backstay

topmast backstay

running backstay detail

L.W.L.

The *Union*: Cross section at 3 (see profile on p. 19) showing the quarterdeck, bulkhead, pumps, hold and backstay details. The crew member is drawing water from the cask with a water thief. (Hewitt Jackson)

March 20th, 1795
[Course NWBN. Wind SE, ESE]
Moderate winds & fair weather, seamen and tradesmen Employ'd in there Various departments. Saw a land bird. Squally with much rain, Employ'd catching Water.
Lat Obsd 2°45'S Long 114°54'W
Dist pr log 90 Knots

March 21st, 1795
[Course NWBN, West, WNW. Wind EBN, NE, North]
Light winds & squally. Caught a Bonnetto, Saw many turtle. Unbent ye tops'l it being Split & brought ano'r too. Low'd down the Mainsail & repair'd a hole in it, Struck a porpoise & lost ye harpoon.
Dist pr log 53 Knots

March 22nd, 1795
[Course NWBN. Wind calm, SE, ESE]
Warm weather, Caught two turtle with the grainz. Some Bonnetto round. Employ'd washing out the forecastle, & smoking it with Gunpowd.
Dist pr log 56 Knots

March 23rd, 1795
[Course NNW. Wind EBS, SE]
Light winds & very pleasant weather. Caught two Bonnettoes. Carpenters, fitting Yawls masts, Caulker upon the decks, Tailor making coats. Seamen squaring ye rattlings.
Dist pr log 45 Knots

March 24th, 1795
[Course NNW. Wind SE]
Light winds with a smooth sea, tare'd down the riging. All hands nessecar'ly employ'd. Fish round.
Dist pr log 61 Knots

March 25th, 1795
[Course NNW. Wind ESE]
Moderate winds & pleasant with a smoth sea. Caught a porpoise, Saw Bonnetto. Carpenter employ'd fitting swivell stocks for the Yawl. Saw some large Albacore & turtle.
Lat Obsd 0°32′N Long 116°48′W
Dist pr log 74 Knots

March 26, 1795
[Course NNW½W, NNW. Wind EBN, East]
Steady breezes & pleasant. Caught a turtle, & four Bonnetto. Caught a Blackfish that weigh'd 450 lbs & a large porpoise, saw many large Scooles of Small fish. *This day took the NE trade winds.*
Dist pr log 86 Knots

March 27th, 1795
[Course NNW, NWBN. Wind EBN, ENE, NE]
Steady breezes, painted the Main boom, Carpenters making lockers for the Yawl, Seamen trying out Blubber, tailor as Usuall. Many Porpoises & Albacore round.
Dist pr log 93 Knots

March 28th, 1795
[Course NWBN, NW, NW½W. Wind NE, NEBN]
Steady breezes & pleasant weather. A Strong Current Setting to ye WNW. Squally with hard rain.
Dist pr log 113 Knots

March 29th, 1795
[Course NW, NW½N, NNW. Wind NEBE, ENE, NE]
Fresh breezes & flying clouds. People Variously employ'd. Caught a large porpoise. Employ'd getting the people chests & bedding on deck to air & sprinkling the fore Castle with Vinegar. A Strong Currant to ye West'd.
Dist pr log 97 Knots

March 30th, 1795
[Course NWBN, NW. Wind NE, NNE]
Fresh breezes with a pitching sea with flying clouds. Many birds on the Wing. All hands employ'd cleaning Small arms.
Lat Obsd 7°33′N Long 124°5′W
Dist pr log 105 Knots

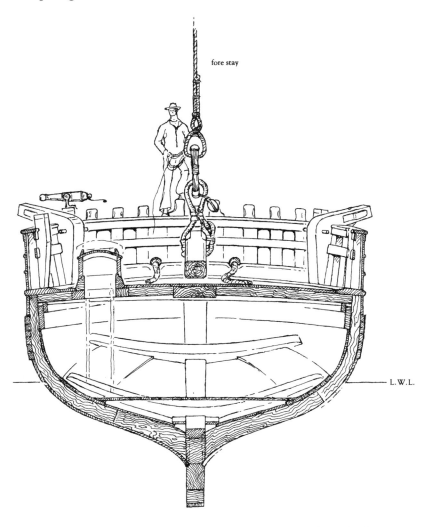

The *Union*: Cross section at L (see profile on p. 19) through the forepeak structure, with howse and cathead details and fore stay. (Hewitt Jackson)

March 31st, 1795
[Course NWBN, NW. Wind NE, NNE, NEBN]
Fresh breezes with a confus'd Sea which makes the Sloop labour exceedingly. All hands employ'd breaking out the Hold for the better arrangement of it. Parted ye Topsail tie, fitted & rove a new one, furl'd ye tops'l & down Squ're S'l Yard. Hoist'd ye Cannon on deck. Employ'd scraping them. Noon a pitching time.
Lat Obsd 8°54'N Long 125°1'W
Dist pr log 93 Knots

April 1st, 1795
[Course NW, NWBN. Wind NNE, NEBN]
Fresh breezes with flying clouds & hazy weather, & a tumbling sea. Carpenter making Swivell stocks.
Dist pr log 91 Knots

April 2nd, 1795
[Course NWBN, NNW. Wind NE, ENE, NE]
Moderate breezes & flying clouds with a cross Sea. Bend the flying jib. Many birds & flying fish round. A labouring sea. Down topsail Yard. Carpenter making Cartridge Chests. Some Black fish round.
Dist pr log 93 Knots

April 3rd, 1795
[Course NWBN, NW. Wind NE, NNE]
Fresh breezes with rain squalls & dark weather. Accompanied with a heavy sea from the NE. Many birds on the Wing. Mounted two Six pounders on the Main deck, Seamen fitting Gun tackles & scraping Cannon.
Dist pr log 90 Knots

April 4th, 1795
[Course NW, NWBN. Wind NNE, NEBN, NE]
Fresh breezes & pleasant, with a head beat Sea. Mounted 8 Swivels on the Waste & 6 three pounders on the quarter deck. Employ'd fitting breechings & tackles.
Dist pr log 84 Knots

April 5th, 1795
[Course NWBW, NW. Wind NBE, NE]
Fresh breezes & pleasant with a tumbling Sea. Lower'd down the Mainsail & repair'd a hole in it.
Lat Obsd 14°33'N Long 129°16'W
Dist pr log 92 Knots

April 6th, 1795
[Course NNW, NBW½W. Wind NEBE]
Fresh breezes with flying clouds. Few birds, & no fish in Sight. Carpenter making beds & Coins for the Cannon etc.
Dist pr log 114 Knots

April 7th, 1795
[Course NBW½W. Wind ENE]
Fresh gales with low'ry weather. Single reef'd the Mains'l. Of Bonnett from the foresail. A heavy Sea from ye North'd. Carpenters Casting lead Aprons for the Guns. Cape St. James bears N2°W Dist 202 Miles.
Dist pr log 123 Knots

April 8th, 1795
[Course NBW½W, NNW. Wind ENE, NE]
Brisk breezes with a swell from the North'd. Carpenters Making tomkin for the Guns, & fitting ladels & Spunges for Do. Employ'd runing bullets & repairing the rigging.
Dist pr log 100 Knots

April 9th, 1795
[Course NW. Wind NE, ENE]
Gentle breezes & pleasant weather. At 3 PM Sent up the Topsail & Cross Jack Yard & Set ye topsail. Carpenter making Cartridge chests. Seamen blacking the Mast

head, tailor & Sail Maker in there Departments. Scaled ye cannon.
Dist pr log 97 Knots

April 10th, 1795
[Course NW, NNW. Wind NNE, NE]
Seamen runing bullets, run a Spare Set of Sounding leads. Many tropic birds on the Wing. Tar'd the Bowsprit riging.
Lat Obsd 22°24'N Long 132°2'W
Dist pr log 82 Knots

April 11th, 1795
[Course NW, NWBN. Wind NNE, NEBN]
Moderate breezes & pleasant. Painted the Sloops Mouldens & Channels, Scaled the Main deck Guns. Carpenters Making formers for the Guns. Tailor making Coats, Seamen fixing laniards for the Swivels, & Scraping the Yawl. Painted the Sloops Stern.
Dist pr log 67 Knots

April 12th, 1795
[Course NW½N, NNW. Wind NEBE, NE, ENE]
Brisk breezes & pleasant weather. Employ'd getting the people Chests on deck & Smoking the Forecastle with Vinegar.
Dist pr log 108 Knots

April 13th, 1795
[Course NNW, NWBN. Wind NNE, NEBN]
Squally disagreeable weather, with a head beat Sea. Down tops'l & Squars'l Yards, the topsail being Split. Carpenters repair'g Muskets, Seamen making Wads, Scaled the Swivels.
Dist pr log 89 Knots

April 14th, 1795
[Course NNW½W, NBW. Wind NE, ENE]

Brisk breezes with frequent squ'll. Seamen making Wads. Carpenters making loop holes in the companion way.
Dist pr log 105 Knots

April 15th, 1795
[Course NBW½W. Wind NEBE, EBN]
Moderate breezes & pleasant weather. Saw two large Birds, resembling the black Albertross.
Lat Obsd 29°20'N Long 134°23'W
Dist pr log 90 Knots

April 16th, 1795
[Course NBW½W, NW. Wind ENE, NE, NNE]
Moderate breezes & pleasant weather. Seamen and tradesmen Variously Employ'd. Cape St. James Dist 1200 Mi.
Dist pr log 71 Knots

April 17th, 1795
[Course NW, NWBN. Wind NNE, NE]
Fresh gales with a head beat Sea which makes the Sloop pitch very bad.
Dist pr log 82 Knots

April 18th, 1795
[Course NWBN, NBW½W. Wind NEBN, NNE]
Fresh breezes with dark cloudy weather. All hands getting the Cables on desk, for the handier Stowing them below again. Carpenter fitting Anchor stocks.
Dist pr log 72 Knots

April 19th, 1795
[Course NW, NWBN. Wind NNE, NEBN]
Light winds & cloudy weather. Sat up the riging. Painted ye head rails. Saw some Whales & a few birds.
Dist pr log 51 Knots

April 20th, 1795
[Course West, WBN. Wind NNW, NBW]
Light breezes and cloudy with a smooth Sea. Carpenter fitting Anchor Stocks, tailor making Coats, Seamen Scraping the Longboat, painted the Yawl.
Lab Obsd 33°14′N Long 138°11′W
Dist pr log 73 Knots

April 21st, 1795
[Course WBN, WNW, NWBN. Wind NBW, North, NBE]
Fresh breezes accompanied with thick disagreeable weather, fitted New Boom tackel pendents. Carpenter fitting New Stantions Aft for boarding Nettings.
Dist pr log 85 Knots

April 22nd, 1795
[Course NWBW, NNW. Wind NBE, NE]
Brisk breezes with thick rainy weather. At 2 PM In flying jib. At 8 In Topsail, Down Squars'l Yard. Employ'd parcelling the Spare Cables painting Anchor Stocks, picking Oakum, & making Cable bends. Painted the Oars.
Dist pr log 88 Knots

April 23rd, 1795
[Course NNW, NBW, North. Wind NE, NEBE, ENE]
Brisk breezes & cloudy weather. Saw a flock of Wild foul on the wing. At 11 Stiff gales, Down Squars'l in tops'l, Double reef'd ye Mains'l.
Dist pr log 80 Knots

April 24th, 1795
[Course NBE½E, NNE. Wind NW, NNW]
Heavy gales with a high Sea. Carried away the strap of the Peak tie block. Split the Foresail. Midnight hard gales with Sleet. At 6 AM Down Foresail, & hove too, under a

ballenced Mainsail, bent a New Jib. Noon an exceeding heavy Gale.
Dist pr log 63 Knots

April 25th, 1795
[Course [Hove Too]. Wind NNW]
Heavy gales with Stiff Sleet Squalls. Down Mainsail & Set ye Trysail. Unbent ye Mainsail & brought a new one too. Tailor constantly making coats. Carpenter in his department. Seamen making robins & Nettles.
Lat Obsd 36°14′N Long 137°39′W

April 26th, 1795
[Course ENE, NE, NNE. Wind North, NNW, NW]
Strong gales with a Mountanious Sea, a Vast many Portugueze Jellies round. Sail maker repairing the Old Mainsail. A few birds round & vast Shoals of Jellies.
Dist pr log 25 Knots

April 27th, 1795
[Course NNE, NBE, NBW. Wind NW, NWBW, WBN]
Fresh breezes with flying clouds. Get ye wet sails on deck to air. Carpenter fitt'g Swivel Stocks to the Longboat. Sail maker on ye Old Mainsail.
Dist pr log 87 Knots

April 28th, 1795
[Course NNE, North, NBE. Wind NW, WNW, West]
Fresh gales & disagreeable lowr'g weather. Unbent ye Old flying jib & bent a New one. Saw a Number flocks of Sand birds. Still vast quantities of Jelly's round.
Dist pr log 100 Knots

April 29th, 1795
[Course NBE½E, NNE. Wind NW, NWBN, NBW]
Fresh breezes & cloudy weather. Seamen & tradesman

Variously employ'd, Vast Shoals of Jelly's round. Sail maker repairing the Old jib, Carpenter on the Longboat, tailor as Usuall. Saw a Diver.
Dist pr log 79 Knots

April 30th, 1795
[Course WBS, West, ENE. Wind North, NBW, NNE]
Light winds & cloudy weather. Smooth sea. Unrig'd ye Jib boom to repair ye riging.
Dist pr log 48 Knots

May 1st, 1795
[Course NBE, NNE, WNW. Wind NWBW, NW, North]
Light winds & foggy weather. Saw two Sea Gulls & a land bird. Vast many Jelly's round. Saw a Whale.
Lat Obsd 39°22′N Long 138°50′W
Dist pr log 43 Knots

May 2nd, 1795
[Course NBE, North. Wind NW, WNW, NWBW]
Light winds with calms Alternatively. Sent up the Tops'l & Cross Jack Yards & set the Tops'l. Seamen & tradesmen Employ'd in there Various departments.
Dist pr log 63 Knots

May 3rd, 1795
[Course NNE, NE½N, NE. Wind NW, NNW, NBW]
Fresh breezes with rain squalls. At 6 Sent down the Cross jack Yard. Saw a Shag and Severall Divers, Got the Old Mainsail up to air. Jellies Still round.
Dist pr log 79 Knots

May 4th, 1795
[Course NNE, North, NNW. Wind NW, WNW, WSW]
Light winds & pleasant weather. Employ'd cleaning out

the Forecastle & Smoaking it with Vineger. *Divers whales. Crew all healthy.*
Dist pr log 50 Knots

May 5th, 1795
[Course NNW, NNW½W. Wind SW, SSW]
Moderate breezes & Cloudy weather. Sail Maker, making Blunderbuss Coats. No Jellies round. Saw two Shags, & a number of Guls. Got ye bower Anchors on the bows, Sail maker making reef cloths.
Lat Obsd 42°58′N Long 137°10′W
Dist pr log 120 Knots

May 6th, 1795
[Course NNW½W, NBW½W. Wind SBW]
Light winds with a rolling swell. Saw Porpoises, Whales & Sea parrots. Carpenter grinding Axes. Made some Mast hoops.
Dist pr log 96 Knots

May 7th, 1795
[Course NBW½W, NNW. Wind SE, ESE, EBN]
Light winds & cloudy. Saw a number of Sea parrots, & many scales of Slime. Saw some feathers. Saw a large flock of Wild Geese flying to the N & W'd.
Dist pr log 109 Knots

May 8th, 1795
[Course NWBN, NW½N, NW. Wind NE, NNE, NBE]
Brisk breezes & hazy. At 4 AM rainy in topsail. Saw blackfish, Sea parrots, Gulls etc. Carpenter burnishing Muskets.
Dist pr log 109 Knots

May 9th, 1795
[Course NW, NWBN, ENE. Wind NNE, NEBN, North]
Light breezes & pleasant weather. *A large flock of wild geese*

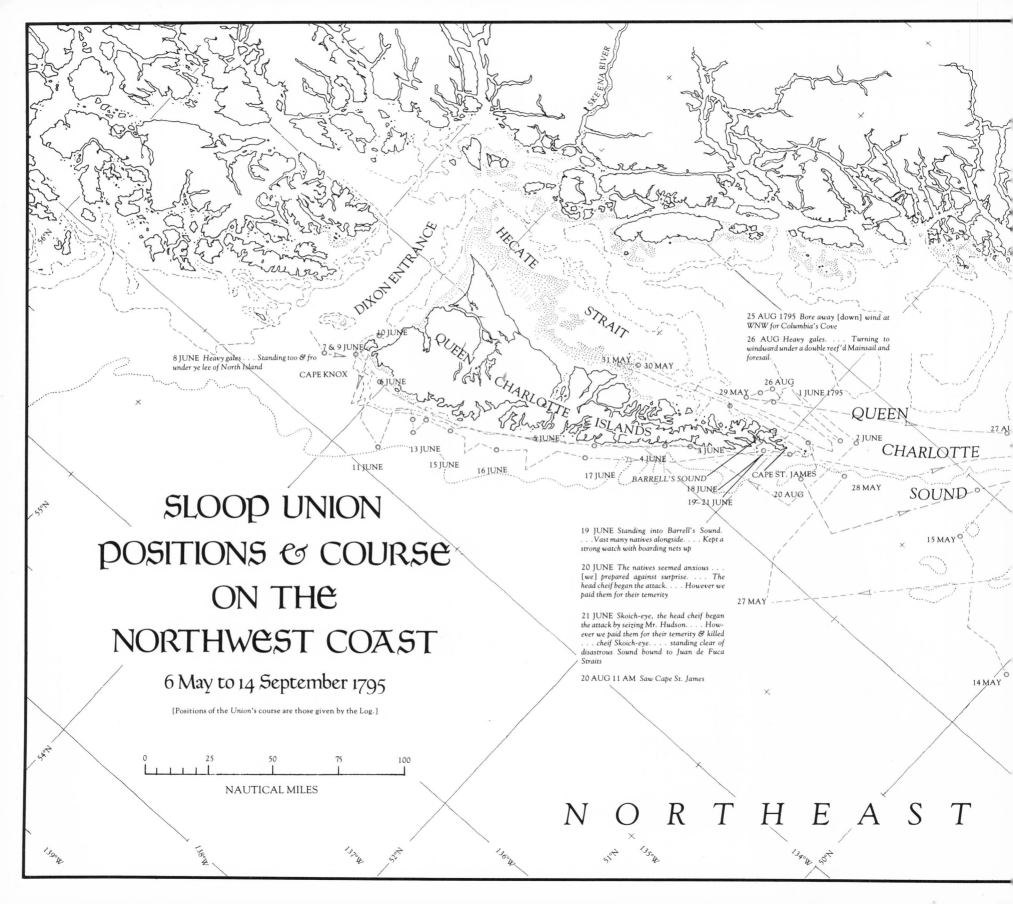

SKEENA RIVER

DIXON ENTRANCE

HECATE

STRAIT

QUEEN

CHARLOTTE

ISLANDS

25 AUG 1795 *Bore away [down] wind at WNW for Columbia's Cove*

26 AUG *Heavy gales. . . . Turning to windward under a double reef'd Mainsail and foresail*

10 JUNE

8 JUNE *Heavy gales . . . Standing too & fro under ye lee of North Island*

7 & 9 JUNE

CAPE KNOX

6 JUNE

31 MAY   30 MAY

26 AUG

29 MAY   1 JUNE 1795

QUEEN

5 JUNE

3 JUNE

2 JUNE   CHARLOTTE

27 A

13 JUNE

4 JUNE

11 JUNE

15 JUNE

16 JUNE

17 JUNE

BARRELL'S SOUND

CAPE ST. JAMES

28 MAY   SOUND

18 JUNE

20 AUG

19–21 JUNE

15 MAY

SLOOP UNION
POSITIONS & COURSE
ON THE
NORTHWEST COAST

6 May to 14 September 1795

[Positions of the *Union's* course are those given by the Log.]

19 JUNE *Standing into Barrell's Sound. . . . Vast many natives alongside. . . . Kept a strong watch with boarding nets up*

20 JUNE *The natives seemed anxious . . . [we] prepared against surprise. . . . The head cheif began the attack. . . . However we paid them for their temerity*

21 JUNE *Skoich-eye, the head cheif began the attack by seizing Mr. Hudson. . . . However we paid them for their temerity & killed . . . cheif Skoich-eye. . . . standing clear of disastrous Sound bound to Juan de Fuca Straits*

20 AUG 11 AM *Saw Cape St. James*

27 MAY

0   25   50   75   100

NAUTICAL MILES

56°N

55°N

54°N

139°W   138°W   137°W   52°N   136°W   51°N   135°W   134°W   50°N

14 MAY

N O R T H E A S T

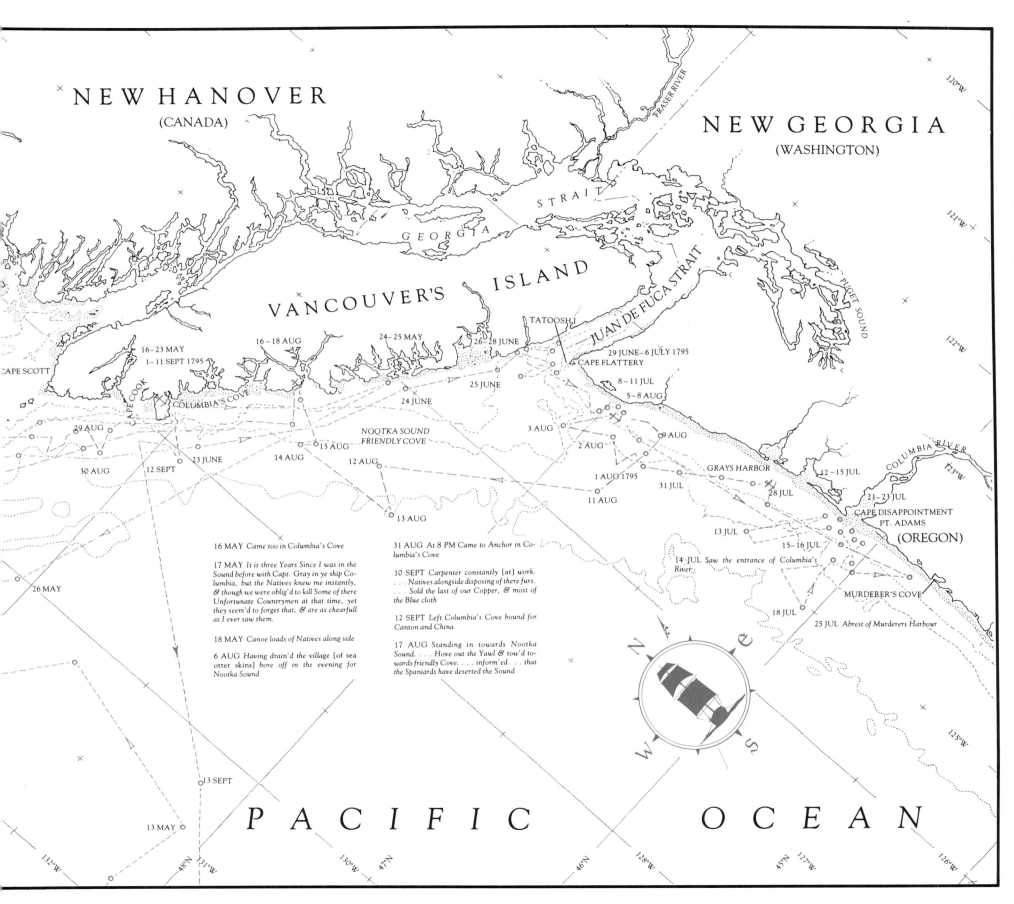

NEW HANOVER
(CANADA)

NEW GEORGIA
(WASHINGTON)

FRASER RIVER

GEORGIA STRAIT

VANCOUVER'S ISLAND

PUGET SOUND

TATOOSH I.

JUAN DE FUCA STRAIT

CAPE SCOTT

16–23 MAY
1–11 SEPT 1795

16–18 AUG

24–25 MAY

26–28 JUNE

29 JUNE–6 JULY 1795
CAPE FLATTERY

CAPE COOK

25 JUNE

8–11 JUL
5–8 AUG

COLUMBIA'S COVE

24 JUNE

29 AUG

3 AUG

9 AUG

NOOTKA SOUND
FRIENDLY COVE

2 AUG

COLUMBIA RIVER

15 AUG

30 AUG

12 SEPT

23 JUNE

14 AUG

12 AUG

GRAYS HARBOR

1 AUG 1795

31 JUL

12–15 JUL

11 AUG

13 AUG

13 JUL

14 JUL Saw the entrance of Columbia's
River.

15–16 JUL

21–23 JUL
CAPE DISAPPOINTMENT
PT. ADAMS

(OREGON)

26 MAY

16 MAY Came too in Columbia's Cove

17 MAY It is three Years Since I was in the
Sound before with Capt. Gray in ye ship Columbia, but the Natives knew me instantly,
& though we were oblig'd to kill Some of there
Unfortunate Countrymen at that time, yet
they seem'd to forget that, & are as chearfull
as I ever saw them.

18 MAY Canoe loads of Natives along side

6 AUG Having drain'd the village [of sea
otter skins] bore off in the evening for
Nootka Sound

31 AUG At 8 PM Came to Anchor in Columbia's Cove

10 SEPT Carpenter constantly [at] work.
. . . Natives alongside disposing of there furs.
. . . Sold the last of our Copper, & most of
the Blue cloth

12 SEPT Left Columbia's Cove bound for
Canton and China

17 AUG Standing in towards Nootka
Sound. . . . Hove out the Yawl & tow'd towards friendly Cove. . . . inform'd . . . that
the Spaniards have deserted the Sound

MURDERER'S COVE

18 JUL

25 JUL Abrest of Murderers Harbour

N E W S

13 SEPT

13 MAY

PACIFIC

OCEAN

120°W

121°W

122°W

123°W

125°W

132°W 131°W

130°W

48°N

47°N

46°N

128°W

45°N 127°W

126°W

*passes us. Porpoises & albatross round. Fastened swivell stocks
to the boats.* Employ'd making Mats.
Dist pr log 67 Knots

May 10th, 1795
[Course NEBE½E, EBN, NW. Wind North, NBE, NNE]
Fresh breezes & pleasant weather. Employ'd making Mats
& cleaning Small Arms.
Lat Obsd 48°8′N Long 139°45′W
Dist pr log 82 Knots

May 11th, 1795
[Course NW, ENE, NEBE. Wind NNE, North, NBW]
Moderate breezes & pleasant weather. Employ'd cleaning
out the Fore Castle & Smoaking it with Vinegar & Gun-
powder.
Dist pr log 46 Knots

May 12th, 1795
[Course NE, NBE, NBW. Wind NNW, NWBW, West]
Light breezes & flattering weather. Seamen Employ'd
thruming Mats. Stock'd the Sheet & Kedge Anchors.
Dist pr log 82 Knots

May 13th, 1795
[Course North, NNE, NE. Wind WNW, NW, NNW]
Fresh gales with foggy disagreeable weather. Saw a flock of
Ducks.
Dist pr log 64 Knots

May 14th, 1795
[Course N½E, North, NBW. Wind NWBW, WNW,
WBS]
Light breezes & flattering weather. Seamen & Tradesmen
Variously employ'd. Bent the Bower [anchor] Cables &
fitted New Shank painters.
Dist pr log 79 Knots

May 15th, 1795
[Course WBN½N, ENE, North. Wind NBW, North,
WNW]
Fresh breezes & cloudy. At Meridian TK to the West. At
1 PM TK to the East, a Strong current Setting to the
South. *Crew saw this severall days many whales & porpoises,
blocks of ducks, & geese, driftwood. All signs of the vicinity of
land.*
Lat Obsd 50°47′N Long 133°45′W
Dist pr log 124 Knots

May 16th, 1795
[Course EBN½N. Wind NWBW]
Fresh breezes & hazy. At 10 PM In Topsail & Squarsail; at
11 Double reef'd the Mainsail & run under short Sail. At
Midnight hove too & sounded but got no bottom. At 7
Saw the land ranging from NNE to East, 12 leag. dist, We
being 260 Days from Newport & all well & hearty, no
signs of ye Scurvey. At 3 PM Hauled into Bulfinches
sound & at 6 Came too in Columbia's Cove.[12] Many of
the Natives along Side, & appear to be very friendly.
Lat Obsd 50°21′N
Dist pr log (36 hours) 135 Knots

Trading
on the
Northwest Coast

17 May to 11 September 1795

May 17th, 1795
[Wind SW]

Light airs & pleasant. Early in the morning, Moor'd Head & Stern. A Vast many Indians along Side, of whom I purchased Many valuable furs, a number of Deer, & vast quantities of fish & Greens. A party well arm'd on Shore after Wood & Water, others restowing the Hold, took off ten H(ogs) h(ea)ds of water from ye Shore. It is three Years Since I was in this Sound before, with Capt. Gray in ye Ship *Columbia*, but the Natives knew me instantly & though we where oblidg'd to kill Some of there Unfortunat Contrymen at that time, Yet they seem'd to forget that, & are as chearfull as I ever saw them.

May 18th, 1795
[Wind SE]

Fresh gales with constant heavy rain. A Vast many Canoe loads of Natives along side, of which I purchas'd many prime Skins, a Deer, & many fish for Blankets & blue Cloth, for Copper they don t set much Store by, & Chizz'l they won't take as presents. Took of Eight Hhds of Water & Stow'd it away, & two load of Wood.[13] Latter part more pleasant.

May 19th, 1795
[Wind south]

Light winds & Cloudy weather. Canoes along Side as Yesterday, with many valuable furs which I purchas'd, brought of four Hhds of Water & Stow'd it away & two load of wood, loos'd Sails to Dry. Latter part Do. weather.

May 20th, 1795
[Wind SE]

Light with rain, took of two load of wood from the Shore.

Many Natives along Side, Still trading away there Skins, & plenty of fish, deer, ducks etc. Hog'd both Sides, & Scraped the bends & waste. The Natives seem to be vey anxious for me to tarry among them along time. So ends.

May 21st, 1795
[Wind SSE]
Heavy gales with constant Showers of rain. No Canoes in sight this day. Got of two long boat loads of Wood from the Shore, & fill'd ye remainder of our water Casks, & Got it on board, together with some broom Stuff.

May 22nd, 1795
[Wind SSE]
Fresh gales & Cloudy. Scrap'd & Slush'd[14] down the Mast, New leather'd the jaws of the boom & Gaft. Got a quantity of broom Stuff & spruce bows[15] from the Shore, many Natives alongside of whom I purchas'd a few Skins. Ends with rain.

May 23rd, 1795
[Wind WNW]
Light breezes & pleasant weather, pay'd[16] our Sides & bends. Carpenter making boarding Netting Stantions. Many Canoes along side of whom I purchas'd a good lot of Skins, which I believe to be the cheif that they had, but they was very desirous of my Visiting them in a few months again. At 1 Unmoor'd, & at 1/2 past Weig'd & came to sail, hoisted in ye boats & Stow'd the Anchors. At 3 being clear of the Sound bore away along Shore to the South'd. At 8 Nootka Sound bore East 7 leagues. So ends with stiff breezes & pleasant weather (36 Hour).

May 24th, 1795
[Wind WNW]
Fresh breezes with a high Sea, a runing along Shore to the South & East. At 10 Saw the Entrance of Ahhouset[17]

bearing East 5 or 6 leagues dist. At 10 We where abrest the Outer break. Out Yawl, & sent her ahead to look out for a harbour. At 1 PM the Yawl had out a Signall for no Safe harbour, but there being many Canoes round her, & a fine bay to leeward, occasion'd me to bear down upon her. At meridian anchored in the bay at Ahhousett in 19 fm sandy bottom. The boat came alongside and the officer reported that he had been into a snug harbour but the buttum was rocky. Our present situation is not but a few miles from Claoquat where the Columbia wintered. Capt Hannah Hatswrah principle chief of the place came alongside, followed by a vast many canoes full of indians. They all appear'd happy to see me again & inquired insistently after the Columbia [and] purchas'd many valuable furs & plenty of fish.

May 25th, 1795
[Wind ESE]
Light winds, sent the yawl to leeward under charge of Mr. Hudson, 2nd officer, in search of a better harbor. Plenty of natives [came] off trading. They informed me that Nootka Sound was entirely deserted, both by the Spaniards & English & the Spanish village destroy'd. The yawl return'd and informed there was no snug harbour in the bay. In the evening got under way bound to Queen Charlotte Isles.

May 26th, 1795
[Course West, WBN. Wind ESE, SSE, SSW]
Fresh gales with rain. At Meridian the Entrance of Nootka Sound bore NBW½W, 10 leagues. All sail out. Midnight foggy, with stiff breezes & a pitching swell. Many large Whales, playing round.
Dist pr log 137 Knots

May 27th, 1795
[Course WBN, NNW. Wind SBW, West]
Fresh gales with a tumbling swell. At 2 PM Set the topsail. At 3 In do., parted another Iron strap of one of ye larboard

dead eyes & fitt'd a rope one, this being the second on the same side which has part'd owing to the badness of ye Sloops Iron work. Down topsail & squaresail Yards. Midnight foggy. At 8 AM Saw Cape St. James[18] bear'g North Dist 15 leagues. All hands employ'd upon the riging.
Lat Obsd 51°28'N
Dist pr log 123 Knots

May 28th, 1795
[Course NBW, NNW. Wind WBN, West]
Fresh breezes with a high sea & a strong currant setting to the South'd, on bonnetts, many large whales round. At 8 PM Cape St. James bore NBW½W, 8 leagues dist. At 9 AM Abrest Cape St. James, made all sail & stood into De Fonte Straits.[19] At 10 Out Yawl & sent her along ahead. At Noon Ukers[20] Village bore NW 4 leagues dist.
Dist pr log 78 Knots

May 29th, 1795
[Wind WSW]
Light winds & pleasant [evidently hove to]. At 4 PM abreast of Ukers Village, fir'd two Cannon to rouse the Natives. At 5 A small Canoe came along side, out of which we purchased some Halibut. Ye Natives inform'd me that Uker wou'd be of on the Morrow. Midnight pleas[ant], laying of & on. At 9 AM the Cheif came of attended by a number of canoes & a fine lot of Sea Otter furs was purchased for blue cloth, for Iron they wont take as presents & Copper is not much better. Noon Calm & pleasant with a smooth sea. 75 fathom Water.

May 30th, 1795
[Wind NW, North]
Light winds & plesant weather. At 5 PM The Natives left us. Sent ye Yawl, well man'd to leeward in search of a harbour, found ye forestay parted, & got a preventer up. At 7 The Yawl return'd & the Officer reported that he went into a deep sound, but found no safe harbour. Bore away, for Cunaswaks Village.[21]

May 31st, 1795
[Wind WNW]
Light winds. At 3 PM Bore away for Ukers Village. At 6 abrest it, a vast many canoes came along side, full of ye Natives, of whom I purchas'd a fine lot of Skins. At 7 The Indians left us, bore away for ye SE entrance of Coyears harbour.[22] At 7 Many Canoes came along side from Coyars. At 8 the Cheif came of himself of whom I purchas'd a fine lot of Skins. These natives fetch'd us Beads, pewter spoons & Iron for sale. At 11 The Natives left us. So Ends with strong tides.

June 1st, 1795
[Course SBE½E, NNW. Wind SW, West, WBS]
Fresh winds with very strong tides. Standing towards Cape St. James. At 6 Saw St. James bear'g NW. At 10 past it, & stood again into Defonte Straits having been set 4 leagues to leeward by the Currant. At noon Ukers Village bore NWBW 6 leagues.
Lat Obsd 52°9'N
Dist pr log 42 Knots

June 2nd, 1795
[Course SW½S, SWBW, NNW. Wind WBN, WNW, SW]
Moderate breezes & hazy, people busily employ'd. At 6 PM TK to the South. At 7 St. James bore NWBN 6 leagues Dist. An exceeding strong current setting to the South'd & East'd. At 9 AM TK ship to the Northward. All hands employ'd, getting the Cables on deck to air, & stowing them down again.
Lat Obsd 51°34'N
Dist pr log 44 Knots

"Sloop *Union*'s Log, by John Boit Jr—Coasting Queen Charlotte Isles." From May to September 1795, the *Union* was engaged in trade for furs along the Northwest Coast of America. Boit conducted business with Indians from many villages, generally stopping for a day or two in harbors where trade seemed promising. On 31 May 1795, Boit entered in the Log: "At 3 PM Bore away from Ukers Village. At 6 abrest it, a vast many canoes came along side, full of ye Natives, of whom I purchas'd a fine lot of Skins."

June 3rd, 1795
[Course NNW, West, WNW. Wind West, SE, ENE]
Fresh breezes with a heavy swell from the SW, accompanied with rainy thick weather. At 4 AM Saw Cape St. James bear'g NE½N 9 leagues distant. All hands employ'd, lacing the boarding Nettings to the rails. At Noon The land in sight extended from NWBW to EBS ye nearer 6 leagues dist.
Dist pr log 65 Knots

June 4th, 1795
[Wind WNW]
Light winds & pleasant weather, turning [course] up to the North'd & West'd. At 4 AM Out Yawl, & I sent an Officer & crew to look into an inlet then in sight in search of a harbour. At 10 She return'd, & the Officer reported there was a deep sound but appear'd to be rocky.
Lat Obsd 52°29′N

June 5th, 1795
Took a fair breeze at SE, made all sail for the NW part of Queen Charlotte Isles. Keep generally an offing of 2 or 3 leagues. Have not seen the sight of an indian since leaving Cape Haswell [St. James]) & am of the opinion that few natives are settled on this part of the isles toward the sea. At 1 PM Dispatch'd the Yawl, well man'd in Shore in search of Anchorage. At 9 She return'd, & found none.
Lat Obsd 52°47′N
Dist pr log 41 Knots

June 6th, 1795
[Course WNW, WBN, NW. Wind SE, SBW, SEBE]
Lively breezes and cloudy weather. At 9 The Northermost land in sight bore NWBW. *Runing along the Isles, bore in, but saw neither smoke or inhabitants. Many large whales & sharks round.*
Dist pr log 91 Knots

June 7th, 1795
[Wind SSE, ENE]
Light winds & cloudy weather. At 8 PM The NW Extreem of North Isle bore NBE 4 leagues distant. The SE part of Charlotte Isles in sight ESE. The Entrance of Tadent's[23] NE. At 9 AM *abreast Tadent's village. The cheif came off with a great number of his people & several valuable furs was purchased. These natives inform'd me that a Portugueze Brig had been here & carried away two of the kings daughters to Macoa in China by consent, that he was to return them in 6 moons. We soon came on to blow a gale of wind, the canoes left us & we struck off. At noon picked up a canoe full of indians [among them] 2 chiefs almost found dead.*

June 8th, 1795
Heavy gales with rain. A Standing too & fro under ye lee of North Island. At 2 PM A large canoe come of but brought no Skins. At 3 She left us leaving ye Chief on board, ye Natives told us they had plenty of Skins. But they was saving them for Vianna a Portugueze who had carried two of there Woman to Macoa.
Lat Obsd 54°31′N

June 9th, 1795
[Wind ENE]
Moderate breezes & hazy weather. A 4 PM A Canoe boarded us, in which was Cunniah's Wife, Who made a present of two Skins for which I made a Suitable return. The Canoe had many skins on board her, but She would not sell them. At 6 The Natives all left us, except one cheif, whom I detained for fear they wou'd not come of again. At 8 AM A large Canoe come of from the Village Neden, & a fine lot of prime skins was purchased out of her, Some Small Canoes from Cunniah's with fish. *Iron & cloth most in demand but furs are at least 100 P cent dearer than when the Columbia was to the coast.*

June 10th, 1795

Moderate breezes & pleasant, Standing in towards ye Village. At 3 Was close in with it. Fir'd a gun, & hoisted the ensign, down Mainsail. At 4 A large canoe came of & brought a few Skins. Cunniah's wife was in ye Canoe, So I took her on board & let ye Cheif go, & Sent the Canoe to inform them of it at ye Village. At 8 Two Canoes came along side from Cunniah Out of which I purchased a Capitall lot of prime furs, & paid them well for them. So I

THE *UNION* OFF THE WEST COAST OF VANCOUVER ISLAND NEAR NOOTKA SOUND, SUMMER 1795 (opposite).

In the early 1790s Nootka Sound was one of the most famous locations in the world, much discussed by the European powers vying for supremacy in the North Pacific, and filled with ships as part of that diplomatic and naval confrontation.

When the *Union* arrived at Nootka Sound 17 August 1795, her crew found the area devoid of Europeans. Boit entered in the Log: "At 9 A Canoe came alongside, with a few skins, they [the Indians] inform'd us that the Spaniards had deserted the sound entirely." The only traces of the Europeans, apparently, were goods the Indians brought to the ship the next day for trade: "Green peas & Beans, Cabbges etc. which they collected from ye remains of the Spanish gardens."

Trading along the Northwest Coast commenced with a two-day stop in Bulfinch Sound (Nasparti Inlet), where the *Union* anchored in Columbia's Cove on 17 May 1795. Upon arrival, Boit noted: "It is three Years Since I was in this Sound before, with Capt. Gray in ye Ship *Columbia*, but the Natives knew me instantly."

This representation of the *Union* in the Sound includes a Nootkan Indian canoe. The Northwest Indians had an abundant supply of timber suitable for canoe construction, and they were skilled at the art. Different models accommodated a wide range of uses, which included hunting, fishing, and other utilitarian purposes. These craft were built for trade as well as for local use, and Nootkan great canoes were a familiar (and often feared) sight along the entire length of the Northwest Coast. They appear to have remained relatively constant in form throughout the canoe-building era, although the introduction in the early 1800s of iron and steel for tools allowed increased decoration. The canoe depicted here is typical of those encountered by John Boit in 1795.

made ye Old woman a present & let her go, besides making many presents to all her people. At 9 PM Made Sail for Barrells sound.[24] Noon rainy.

Lat Obsd 54°12′N

June 11th, 1795

[Course SW, SSW, SSE. Wind SSE, SE, EBS]

Fresh gales & hazy. At 8 The extreem point of ye land in sight. Extended from NE to SE. At 7 Strong gales with a high sea. Hove too under a ballenced Mains'l. At 10 out 1 reef, Set ye fores'l Jib.

Lat Obsd 53°46′N

Dist pr log 58 Knots

June 12th, 1795

[Course East, EBN, ENE. Wind SSE, SEBS, SE]

Fresh breezes with thick weather. The land in sight extending from NBW to SE, ye nearest 1 league distant. Double reef ye Mainsail. At 4 Heavy gales with a high sea, hove too under a ballen'd Mainsail, with her head to the South.

Dist pr log 48 Knots

June 13th, 1795

[Course SBW, EBS, SW. Wind SSE, South]

Heavy gales with a mountanious sea. At 7 PM Wore in Shore, set ye Foresail. At 2 AM More moderate, Set the Jib, out two reefs of ye Mainsail.

Dist pr log 22 Knots

June 14th, 1795

[Course ESE, SEBS, SWBS. Wind South, SSW, SSE]

All hands employ'd breaking out ye Hold for provision & Liquor, & various other nessescary Jobs. Ye land about 8 leagues dist.

Dist pr log 60 Knots

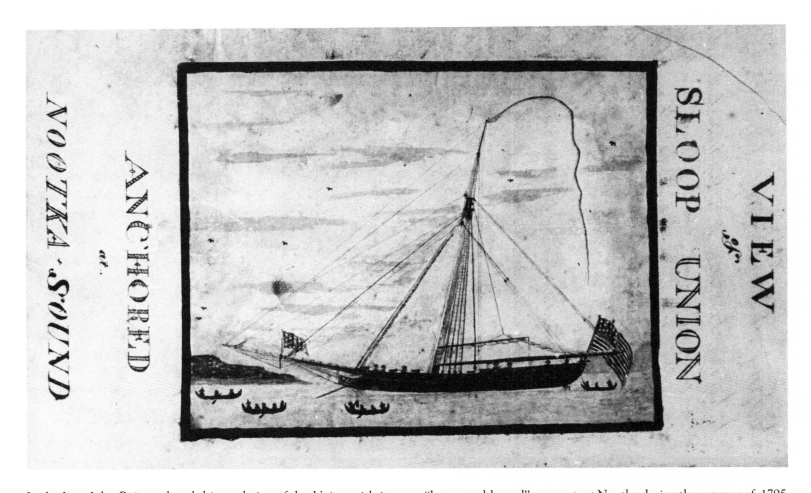

In the Log, John Boit produced this rendering of the *Union*, with its "homeward-bound" pennant, at Nootka during the summer of 1795.

June 15th, 1795
[Course South, S½W, ESE. Wind ESE, SEBE, SSW]
Fresh breezes, of bonnets from ye Jib & foresail & double reef'd the Mainsail. People employ'd steadily on ye repairs of ye riging.
Lat Obsd 53°31'N
Dist pr log 39 Knots

June 16th, 1795
[Course ESE, EBS, WBS. Wind SSW, SBE, SBW]
Light breezes with a high sea. Main boom very steady. At 9 PM Wore of Shore, Down flying Jib, in Topsail. At 2 AM Tack'd to the Eastward & Set all sail.
Dist pr log 82 Knots

June 17th, 1795
[Wind SW, NW]
Moderate breezes with a long Westerly Swell. Bore away along Shore for Barrell's sound. At 9 The land in sight from NW to ESE—in light Sails & haul'd of shore. At 4 saw Barrels Sound bearing EBN, 2 leagues. Out Yawl & I sent an Officer and Crew to examine ye entrance. At 12

48

The boat return'd & the Officer gave an unfavourable account of the sound.

June 18th, 1795

Lively breezes, bore away along shore for Coyars harbour, & Set all sail. At 9 Saw Cape St. James bear'g EBS, 8 lea. dist. Port Mangomery[25] bear'g ENE. At 8 A Canoe load of Natives boarded us, of whom we purchas'd some fish. At 10 The entrance of Coyars Sound bore NNE 4 Miles dist. Light winds.

June 19th, 1795

[Wind WBN]

Moderate breezes with fine pleas. weather. A stretching into Coyars sound. At 6 PM Came to an Anchor behind an Island[26] on ye East side of the Sound, 9 fath. Water, sand & Shells in an Excellent harbor. Moor'd with 1/2 a Cable each way. *Much better than the place where we anchored with the Columbia. Vast many natives alongside but seem to have few skins. Coyar the cheif did not come of. Pleasant weather through the night. Kept a strong watch with boarding net up as that is the identical spot where the indians try'd to cut off Capt. Kendrick in the brig Lady Washington.[27] Many natives off in the morning & brought a few skins which we purchased at a dear rate. Those following brought us ships chain bolts & other iron work, such made me mistrust that they had either cut off some vessell or else some ship had been lost [on] the coast.* People steadily Employ'd on the repair of ye riging.

June 20th, 1795

Fine pleasant weather. At 1 PM A Canoe came of from the Village and inform'd ye Natives along side, that two of there Women was drown'd by a Canoes oversettig. *Purchased this day but few skins as chief by name of Skoich Eye appear'd to be head man of the Sound & Coyar the 2d. At midnight 2 large canoes pass'd under our stern, the indians was*

crying & hooping. Therefor let them pass in peace as I suppos'd they was about burying the drown'd women. At daylight many canoes came off & appear'd to be arm'd better then common. They brought a great many otter skins alongside but would not sell them without bringing them on deck which they preferr'd. This was of course refused. The natives seemed anxious for me to wood & water & offer'd to assist. Their whole conduct appear'd to me mysterious therefor [we] kept a good look out after them & prepared against surprise.

June 21st, 1795

Calm & pleasant, above 40 canoes came into the cove full of indians (at least 30 men [in] each). I immediately suspected by their numbers that they meant to attack the Union. Called all hands to quarters; eight cheifs were on board at this time who began to be very saucy & the war canoes kept pressing alongside & the indians getting upon the nettings. Skoich-eye, the head cheif began the attack by seizing Mr. Hudson the second officer [and] at the same time the indians alongside attempted to board with the Most hideous yells. However we paid them for their temerity & killed their first cheif Skoich-eye in the 2nd mate's arms while they was struggling together. I dispatched him with a bayonet. The rest of the cheif on deck was knock'd down & wounded & we kill'd from the nettings & in the canoes alongside above 40 more when they retreated, at which time I could have kill'd 100 more with grape shot but I let humanity prevail & ceas'd firing. At 6 PM a small canoe came off from the village with 2 indians in her, holding green bows [emblems of peace]. I allow'd the cheifs on board, who was strongly iron'd, to hold convers with them [and] at dark they left us. [We] kept a strong watch. All hands to quarters through the night.

At daylight took up the anchor and came to sail, stretching toward the village on the west part of the Sound. At 9 AM severall large canoes put off full of indians waving their bows. They came alongside with fear & trembling bringing plenty of furs to ransom their cheifs with. Order'd the irons off them &

got the poor devils up and not with standing the treatment I paid full price for the skins; believe I got every piece of fur they had in the village [and] took notice that the village was deserted. [I] suppose they thought it was our intention to destroy it. At 11 AM the canoes left us the indians crying and praying for our success. Indeed the treatment they received from me was quite different from what they expected. [I] suppose in the fracas we kill'd & wound'd about 50 but the indians said we kill'd 70. None of us was hurt but their attack was very impolitic—for had they instead of being so intent to board, stood off and fir'd their arrows, no doubt they would have kill'd and wounded several of us. However I was too wellguarded against surprise for them to have been victorious. Noon pleasant gales, standing clear of disastrous Sound bound to Juan de Fuca Straits.

June 22nd, 1795
[Course ESE, EBS. Wind WBN, WNW]
Lively breezes, stretching to the South'd to clear Cape St. James. At 7 PM The Cape bore NW½W 9 or 10 leagues. All sail out. Seamen employ'd spining Spun Yarn & various other nessescary jobs.
Lat Obsd 50°39′N
Dist pr log 93 Knots

June 23rd, 1795
[Course EBS, ESE, East. Wind NW, WNW]
Brisk breezes & pleasant agreeable weather. Standing along shore, to ye South'd & Eastward. At 8 PM Split rock bore NNW½W, 8 leagues dist. Midnight pleasant gales. All sail out, with a following sea. At 1/2 past 11 AM The entrance of Clioqu[ot] bore NNW½W Distant 3 leagues, & Company's bay EBN 7 or 8 leagues distant—a Canoe in sight coming towards us.
Dist pr log 156 Knots

June 24th, 1795
Moderate breezes & pleasant weather. Hove too for ye

Canoe to come up. At 1 PM She got along side, & she was man'd with Tutuchkasettle & Yethlure two Cheifs of Clioqot & 12 Common people, they press'd me, exceedingly to go in. Purchas'd of them a few Skins. At 4 PM Two more Canoes come of with a few skins which I purchas'd. At 8 The Canoes left us. Observatory Isle bears NWBN 2 miles.[28]

June 25th, 1795
[Wind ESE]
Light winds with strong tides, vast many Whales round. At 2 TK to ye North'd. At 8 Cape Flattery bore EBS, & Clioquot Mountains NNW. Poverty Cove[29] E½N ye

---

THE *UNION*'S BATTLE WITH INDIANS AT BARRELL'S SOUND, 21 JUNE 1795
(opposite)

The *Union* entered Barrell's Sound on the southwest coast of Vancouver Island on 19 June 1795. Planning to trade with the coastal Indians at that location, Boit and his men were conscious of "mysterious" behavior by the Indians. On the morning of the 21st of June, the Indians attacked the ship. Fortunately, the sloop's crew had "kept a good look out after them and prepared against surprise." Boit recorded in the Remarks: *Skoich-eye, the head cheif began the attack by seizing Mr. Hudson the second officer [and] at the same time the indians alongside attempted to board with the Most hideous yells. However we paid them for their temerity.*

In preparing against surprise, the *Union*'s crew had put up the nets that prevented boarding. In the foreground are the head canoes used by tribes of northern Vancouver Island and the Queen Charlotte Islands. The hull form of these boats was somewhat fuller than that of the Nootkan canoes further to the south (see illustration p. 46); their distinguishing feature was a thin, plank-like "head" that extended for a considerable distance forward of the hull proper and a similar fin that extended beyond the stern of the vessel. These end pieces, carved out of the same log, and an integral part of the canoe's structure, maintained their thin section until abruptly joining the body of the canoe. Hewn from a very thin cross section of cedar, these canoes were easily damaged by grounding or rough handling. At the time of Boit's journey, they were decorated simply, with painted designs and round, carved holes.

nearest land two leagues, ye Entrance of Company Bay NBW. Nittenat ENE 8 leag. About 40 Fishing Canoes in sight at daylight, but none would venture along side, but kept at Musket shot distant.
Lat Obsd 48°47′N

June 26th, 1795
[Wind calm, WNW, NW]
Drifting to & fro with lines out & very strong tides. Sounding from 50 to 60 fm. In the evening stood toward Nettinat vil-lage.[30] *Casear, the cheif came alongside followed by many canoes & a good lot of furs was purchased. These natives appear'd very shy which made me suspect they have cut off some vessels hereabouts or else some one has been robbing them. Sea otter skins very scarce. Bore off for Cape Flattery & La Booth's Isle on the SW entrance of the Strait, they both in sight from our present situation.*

June 27th, 1795
[Wind WSW, calm]
Lively breezes & pleasant weather. At 2 PM Many Canoes with Natives came of. But not a Cheif as yet has made an appearance, which makes me suspect that they have cut of some Vessell or boat or Else somebody has play'd a trick upon them; for ye Natives seem much agitated. At 10 The fog clear'd & ye Wind came from ye West'd. Saw ye Land & bore away for ye Village.
Lat Obsd 48°48′N

June 28th, 1795
[Wind NW, calm, WSW]
Fresh breezes & pleasant weather. At 3 PM a few Canoes came of & ye Natives brought 4 or 5 Skins which I pur-chased. I ask'd why Cascar ye Cheif, did not come of but they gave me evasive answers. At 9 The Canoes left us, & I bore away for Tatooch's Isle. [31] People Employ'd clean'g out ye fore Castle. Many Salmon round.

June 29th, 1795
[Wind WSW, SE]
Light winds & pleasant. At 3 Saw Tatooch's Isle bear'g EBS 5 leagues. At 4 PM Many canoes with Natives came of & brought us a great plenty of Fish, & invited us strongly to stand in for the Village for they had great plen-ty of Skins. At 7 Clarclacko ye Cheif came of & seem'd to be very glad to see me, he came on board, & sent his Canoe & people to ye Village to tell his people to fetch of ye furs. At 11 Above 20 Canoes came of & I purchased a handsome lot of Otter Skins.

June 30th, 1795
[Course, WBS. Wind SSE, SE]
Light winds with a large swell, many Canoes with Indians along side trading away their furs. At 6 Squally with rain, ye Natives left ye Sloop, haul'd by ye wind to ye South'd. At 8 PM Tatooch's Isle bore E½N 2 leagues dist. Pover-ty Cove NE. Midnight calm with a high sea which made ye Sloop labour exceedin'ly. At 10 Saw Tatooch's Isle bear'g ESE 5 or 6 leagues dist. Calm with much rain & a high sea.

July 1st, 1795
[Wind SE, calm, SW]
Light winds & flattering weather. Standing upon a wind to ye south'd. At 11 PM Hove too, for daylight. Midnight a rolling time. Caught a Hallibut. At 6 AM A small breeze. Set sail & stood towards Tatooch's Island. Vast many Canoes with Natives fishing after Halibut.

July 2nd, 1795
[Wind SE]
Light winds & thick foggy weather. Standing too & fro, in the Straits of Juan defuca, with exceeding strong tides. No canoes to be seen.

July 3rd, 1795
[Wind SE, NE]
Fresh breezes & hazy weather. At 6 The Isle [Tatooch] hove in sight, about two leagues distant. Many Canoes came along side, with a small lot of Furs & plenty of fish, which I purchas'd. At 8 the Natives left us. At 4 PM Made sail towards the Island. At 8 Many Natives came of. At 9 The Cheif himself came of with a large quantity of War garments which I purchas'd, together with a few furs & plenty of fresh fish.

July 4th, 1795
[Wind SE, WNW]
Light winds & rainy, many of the Natives of with fish. At 4 All ye Canoes left us, Except ye Cheifs. At 6 a heavy squall, which was soon succeeded by a gale of wind, with a thick fog. Hoisted ye Cheifs canoe in. Stood upon a wind to ye Southward. At 7 Saw 4 fishing Canoes, with indians laying too one of which we saw upset but it was out of my power to lend them any assistance. Noon Set Sail & Stood for ye Isle.

July 5th, 1795
[Wind SW]
Light winds & pleasant, all sail out. At 5 PM Being within 5 Miles of Tatooch's Isle, Hove out ye Cheif Canoe & sent him, on shore. At 7 He came of again & brought a small lot of skins, which I purchased. At 8 AM A few Canoes came of with a few furs which I purchas'd together with many war garmant & plenty of fresh fish. Inclining to a Calm.

July 6th, 1795
[Wind WSW, NW]
At 2 PM Clarclacko came of with a small lot of Furs, which I purchased. The Cheif told me that I had purchas'd all ye Skins they had, & that he had lost 10 of his people in ye late gale.[32] At 9 The Natives left us, & I Stood towards Nittenat Village. At 7 AM Some of the Natives came of, with a few skins which I purchas'd. Laying too of Nittinat village.

July 7th, 1795
[Wind NW]
A great many of the Natives alongside but brought no Skins. At 4 PM Set all sail & bore away for ye Village Golintah.[33] At 8 Tatooch's Isle bore EBN½N 4 Miles dist. At 1 AM In tops'l & flying Jib & haul'd of to ye SW. At 4 Set sail & haul'd in Shore. At 8 A Canoe came of with four natives & brought a few furs. At 9 Being in 20 fm water I bore away to ye S & E.
Lat Obsd 48°7'N

July 8th, 1795
[Wind NW, SE]
At 1 PM Saw ye Island of Golintah bear'g SE½E 3 leagues. At 4 Abrest of ye Village, a number of canoes full of ye Natives came of but brought a few skins, but said there was plenty at ye Vil[lage]. At 9 AM 1 Canoe came along side with a few Skins which I purchas'd, they said ye weather was too bad, for them to come of.

July 9th, 1795
[Wind SE]
Fresh breezes attended with frequent rain squalls. At 7 PM The Island of Golintah bore NE 3 leagues dist. Double reef'd the Mainsail. Of Bonnets. At 10 Sent ye Yards aloft & set ye Topsail & stood towards Golintah it bearing NBE, 5 or 6 leagues dist.

July 10th, 1795
[Wind WSW, West]
Moderate breezes & pleasant, stand'g in for ye Village. At 6 PM We was about 4 Miles of, but no canoes came of. At

8 Hauld of to ye South & W. At 6 AM TK & stood in for the Village. At 9 two Canoes with natives came of & brought a few Skins, they told me there was plenty more at the Vill'g but I beleive they told false, for the Skins these brought was quite green.

July 11th, 1795
[Wind WBS, NW]
Laying of on ye Village Golintah. At 2 PM A few Natives came of but brought nothing, for I beleive they had no furs to bring. At 3 Set all sail & bore away for Columbia's river. All hands employ'd gett'g the Muskets in good order.
Lat Obsd 46°39′N

July 12th, 1795
[Wind NNW]
Fresh gales & hazy, a runing in for ye land. At 4 PM Saw Cape Hancock,[34] ye North entrance of Columbia river bear'g EBS 4 or 5 leagues dist. Stood in towards ye weather bar, into 14 fm but it blew so exceeding hard that it was impossible to tell ye passage in for ye sand was so great upon ye bars that it appear'd to break quite hard. I therefore thought it prudent to haul of & wait for a better time.

July 13th, 1795
[Wind NNW]
Fresh gales & hazy weather. Standing in for ye land. At 6 PM In fores'l, a strong currant setting to ye South'd. All hands nessescarily employ'd. At 4 AM TK in shore, out 1 reefd of ye Mains'l.

July 14th, 1795
[Wind NNW]
Moderate breezes & foggy, 20 fm water. At sunsett [it] clear'd. Saw the entrance of Columbia's River but we was too leeward of the bars with a strong breeze & currant against us.

July 15th, 1795
[Wind NNW]
Bearing up towards Cape Hancock but made slow progress. Sent in the yawl with the 2nd officer, well man'd & arm'd to find a passage to the south of the bars on the southern shore. At dark the boat return'd & Mr. Hudson reported that there was no passage in that direction & that there was an immense swell upon the bars, it breaking quite across from one shore to the other. Haul'd off upon a wind. Pt. Adams bear'g east. Strong currents setting to the southward.
Lat Obsd 46°4′N

July 16th, 1795
[Wind NW]
Stand in shore but could not fetch the river, indeed, if I had, should have been afraid to venture over the bars as the sea was frightful. Kept beating off, and on, this place till the 29th instant endeavauring to get into Columbia's River, but the attempt was vain as the elements appear'd to have conspir'd against us. Therefore was oblig'd as the season was advancing for to give it up. But much against my inclination, being well assur'd, had I been fortunate enough to have accomplished it many capitall sea otter skins would have been procured. Came very near losing the sloop several times on the bars, but thank God, we came off without damage.[35]

THE *UNION* ARRIVING OFF THE MOUTH OF THE COLUMBIA RIVER, 12 JULY 1795
(opposite)

Recalling Captain Gray and the *Columbia*'s extremely profitable trade here in 1792, Boit and the *Union* (during well over a week) tried nearly thirty times to cross the treacherous bar at the mouth of the Columbia River. On 16 July 1795, in the Remarks, the young captain wrote that, *the attempt was vain as the elements appear'd to have conspir'd against us. Therefore was oblig'd as the season was advancing for to give it up. . . . Came very near losing the sloop several times on the bars, but thank God, we came off without damage.*

The prominent headland of Cape Disappointment lies astern of the *Union*.

July 17th, 1795
[Wind NW]
Moderate breeze & more clear. At 1 PM TK of Shore. Adams Pt. bear'g NNE 5 leagues. Carried away the Wiff of the peak tie block & fitted a rope one—& got it aloft. Latter part as before, all sail out with strong tides.

July 18th, 1795
[Wind NNW]
Fresh breezes, standing in for ye land, Soundings in 55 fm. At 3 AM TK in shore. At 4 Saw Cape Hancock bear'g NE'd.

July 19th, 1795
[Wind NWBN]
Light flattering weather. At 4 PM Cape Hancock bore NEBN 8 leagues & Old Mans Bluff EBS½S 6 leagues dist. All sail out. Sail maker reparing the Mainsail, others making pudings etc.

July 20th, 1795
[Wind WNW]
Light airs & pleasant. Heading towards the Cape, but going at ye rate of two Knots to ye S & W. Latter part as before, little or no wind. Sixty fm water.
Lat Obsd 46°9'N

July 21st, 1795
[Wind NW]
Light breezes & pleasant weather. At 4 Cape Han'k bore NBE½E 6 or 7 leagues. TK of Shore. At 10 TK in Shore, a strong currant setting to ye South'd which seems to make it impossible to get to windward. At 2 TK of Shore. At 6 TK in Shore. At 9 TK of Shore. At 11 TK in Shore. A fine turning breeze.

July 22nd, 1795
[Wind NW]
Fresh breezes & cloudy. Standing towards Cape Hancock. We being still two leagues to leeward. At 3 PM TK to ye West'd. People nessescarily employ'd on the repairs of ye riging.

July 23rd, 1795
[Wind NNW]
Fresh gales & Coudy. At 4 TK in shore. At 6 TK of Shore, reef'd the Mains'l. At 8 PM Down foresail. Of bonnett from the Jib.

July 24th, 1795
[Wind NW]
Moderate breezes, standing in for ye land having gain'd none to Windward. At 9 PM TK of Shore. At 1 AM TK In shore. At 9 Bore away for Murderers Harbour to the South'd. Sent up the Yards & set ye top sail. Cape Hancock bear'g NBE 7 leagues.

July 25th, 1795
[Wind NNW, SE]
Fresh breezes. At 4 PM We where abrest of Murderer's Harbour.[36] Stood close but Saw no signs of inhabitants, TK of Shore. Midnight a breeze from ye South'd. Stood to ye North'd.

July 26th, 1795
[Wind SSW]
Light winds & foggy. Midnight Do., do. Noon start calm & a thick fog.

July 27th, 1795
[Wind WSW, SW]
Light winds & foggy disagreeable weather. At 6 More

clear, saw ye land ranging from NE to East. Set ye Squarsail. Midnight a thick fog. Latter part calm, people employ'd on the repairs of the riging.
Lat Obsd 45°40'N

July 28th, 1795
Light airs with frequent calms & foggy weather, a Current sett'g in shore. At 8 Heaving but 33 fm was brought up with ye Kedge [anchor]. Midnight still foggy & calm. At 3 AM A breeze sprang from the South'd, hove up ye Kedge made sail & stood of Shore.

July 29th, 1795
[Wind WSW]
Moderate breezes & foggy, standing upon a wind to ye North'd. At 6 PM Had 35 fm water. TK to the S & W.
Lat Obsd 46°48'N

July 30th, 1795
[Wind NW]
Fresh breezes, standing of Shore. At 8 PM TK in Shore, in one reef of ye Mainsail. Of Bonnets, down Yards. Midnight steady breezes. At 7 More moderate. Out reef on Bonnets. At 9 Set ye flying Jib.
Lat Obsd 47°0'N

July 31st, 1795
[Wind NW, SSW]
Light breezes, standing in for the land. At 2 PM Saw it bear'g EBN 7 leagues. At 8 TK Of Shore. Midnight light airs. At 4 AM A breeze sprang from the South'd. Sent up the Yards & Set ye Squars'l & topsail. Standing to ye N & W.

August 1st, 1795
Light breezes & hazy disagreeable weather. At 9 TK of Shore. Latter part fresh breezes. Sent the Yards down from aloft. A high sea.

August 2nd, 1795
[Wind NW]
Brisk breezes stand'g to ye North'd. At 3 PM Single reef'd the Mains'l. A swell from ye NW. Midnight Wore of Shore. At 6 AM Out Reef TK to ye North'd. Set the Foresail. A large swell from the N & W.

August 3rd, 1795
[Wind NW]
Light winds & a smooth sea. At 8 TK to the West'd. Still a strong haze over ye land. At 1 AM TK to ye North'd. At 10 Saw ye land bear'g ENE.

August 4th, 1795
[Wind NW, calm]
Light flattering weather with a strong current setting to ye South'd. At 7 PM The Islands of Asewatt bore N. 3 leagues. At 6 AM a breeze from the NW. Stood towards the Island of Golintah Which bore NE 3 leagues.
Lat Obsd 47°58'N

August 5th, 1795
[Wind WNW]
Standing towards Golintah Isle. *Pleasant weather, many canoes alongside from the village & the indians brought us a good lot of sea otter skins which we purchas'd. Having drain'd the village bore off in the evening for Nootka Sound.*

August 6th, 1795
[Wind NW]
Light winds & flattering weather. Standing to the Northward upon a wind. Seamen & tradesmen Variously employ'd.
Lat Obsd 47°54'N

"Sloop *Union*s Log, by J. Boit Jr—Bound to Nootka Sound"
Log entries for 5-8 August 1795. In early August, continuing its trade on the Northwest Coast, the *Union* was headed north and "standing towards Golintah Isle." The ship would spend another month cruising in the area before beginning the next leg of the voyage, crossing the Pacific Ocean to China.

August 7th, 1795
[Wind calm]
Calm this 24 Hours, drifting too & fro with strong tides. At 6 PM The Isle of Golintah bore NE 5 to 6 leagues dist.
Lat Obsd 47°50′N

August 8th, 1795
[Wind NW]
Light breezes. At 1 PM Hove up ye kedge & made sail. The Island of Golintah bear'g NE 6 leagues dist. At 4 Saw a Brig standing in shore.
Lat Obsd 47°50′N

August 9th, 1795
[Wind NW]
Light breezes & pleasant weather. At 1 PM TK of shore. Foggy weather, a strong steady currant setting to ye South'd.
Lat Obsd 47°31′N

August 10th, 1795
[Wind NW]
Moderate breezes. Standing of Shore by the wind. At 9 PM took the bonnett from the Foresail. At 2 In Topsail & flying jib. Noon a disagreeable fog.

August 11th, 1795
[Wind WNW, WSW]
Light winds, Standing to the Northward. At 6 PM Set the Topsail & flying jib. At 2 AM In Topsail & flying jib. At 6 Set Do., do.
Lat Obsd 47°34′N

August 12th, 1795
[Wind SW]
Light breezes, standing to ye North'd. At 2 PM Set the topsail & flying jib. At 11 In Do., do. Midnight Calm &

pleasant. People cleaning Small Arms.
Lat Obsd 48°46′N

August 13th, 1795
[Wind SE]
Light winds, Standing to the Northward. At 1 PM Saw Clioquot Mountains bearing NNE. Calm, Seamen cleaning Muskets.

August 14th, 1795
[Wind SW]
Light winds & a smooth Sea. A number of large Whales round. At 2 AM Strong breezes. In topsail, single reef'd the Mainsail, of Bonnets.
Lat Obsd 49°15′N

August 15th, 1795
[Wind SW, calm]
Steady breezes, standing in for the land. At 1 PM Haul'd to the N & W. Caught a large Shark that Weighed 300 lb.
Lat Obsd 49°15′N

August 16th, 1795
[Wind calm]
A currant Setting to ye N. Scal'd the Cannon, & reloaded them. At 6 AM Saw the entrance of Nootka sound[37] bear'g NBE, many Canoes in sight a fishing but not one came along side.

August 17th, 1795
[Wind SW]
Light breezes, a standing in towards Nootka Sound. At 2 Calm. Hove out the Yawl & tow'd towards Freindly Cove. At 8 PM brought up with the Kedge in 30 fm water, Sandy bottom. Midnight, a breeze from the North'd. Got under way, & stood too & fro. At 9 A Canoe came alongside, with a few skins, they inform'd us that the Spaniards had

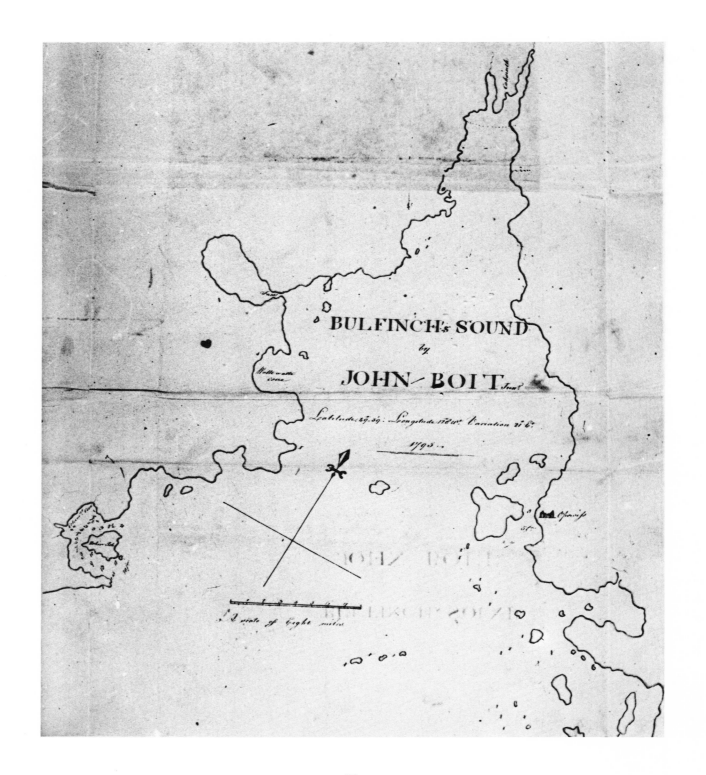

BULFINCH's SOUND
by
JOHN BOIT Junr.

1795

deserted the sound entirely & that Capt. Moore, in a brig from Bengall, had left there but five Days [before]. At Meridian came to in freindly Cove. *Vast many canoes full of the natives alongside. Among the rest Maquinna, chief of the Sound. He knew me instantly & informed [me] that the Spaniards had deserted the Sound about 4 moons, since having presented him with the houses in the Cove. These were however completely erased & an indian village erected in its place. This serves to show how preposs'd these natives are with their ancient customs, preferring their own wigwams to the fine houses the Spaniards left them. Capt. More [on] an English Brig had left the Cove but a few days previous to my arrivall but still the natives had a good collection of furs which I purchased on good terms of the natives. Many potatoes, beans, cabbages—being the remains of the beautiful Spanish gardens.*

August 18th, 1795
[Wind variable]
Moderate breezes & pleasant. Merquinna[38] the Cheif of the sound came on board & brought a fine lot of Furs which I purchas'd, the Cheif was very sick. A Vast many Canoes, with Green peas & Beans, Cabbges etc. which they collected from ye remains of the Spanish gardens. At dark the Cheif left us having parted with all his furs. At 10 PM Got underway, with a land breeze & stood out to Sea. At 5 AM Nootka bore NNE 7 or 8 leagues dist. *I got underway this day bound to the Straits of Admiral Deford.*[39] *Bore away with a fair breeze at SE to the northward.*

August 19th, 1795
[Wind EBS]
Fresh breezes, standing along shore to the N & W'd with a rolling sea. At 11 PM Down Mains'l. Set ye Squars'l &

tops'l. Midnight squally. Rainy weather. At 9 AM Jib'd Sloop & took in the Topsail.
Lat Obsd 50°17'N

August 20th, 1795
[Wind ESE]
Light breezes & pleasant agreeable weather. Seamen variously employ'd. Midnight Do., do. At 4 AM Jib'd Sloop. At 11 AM Saw Cape St. James the SE Cape of the Charlotte Isles bear'g North 8 leagues dist.
Lat Obsd 51°42'N

August 21st, 1795
[Wind SE]
Fresh breezes. Saw the Cape bear'g NBW 5 leagues. *Standing off and on abreast Ukar's & Carniswah village alternativly & purchas'd many sea otter skins.*

August 22nd, 1795
[Wind East, North]
Light airs, still standing towards the Cape. At 2 TK to the Eastward. At 7 The cape bore NBW, & the Westwardmost land in sight NW.
Lat Obsd 51°40'N

August 23rd, 1795
[Wind NBW]
Moderate breezes, standing into the straits of Admiral Defont. At 11 TK to the Southward. At 1 AM TK to the North'd. At 4 Abrest of Cape St. James. Variously Emp'd.
Lat 52°12'N

August 24th, 1795
[Wind NW]
Light airs attended with frequent calms. At 2 PM Hove out the Boats & tow'd from the Shore. At 2 A Canoe, with two indians came with a few Skins which I purchas'd.

John Boit's map (opposite) of Bulfinch Sound (Nasparti Inlet) on the west coast of Vancouver Island.

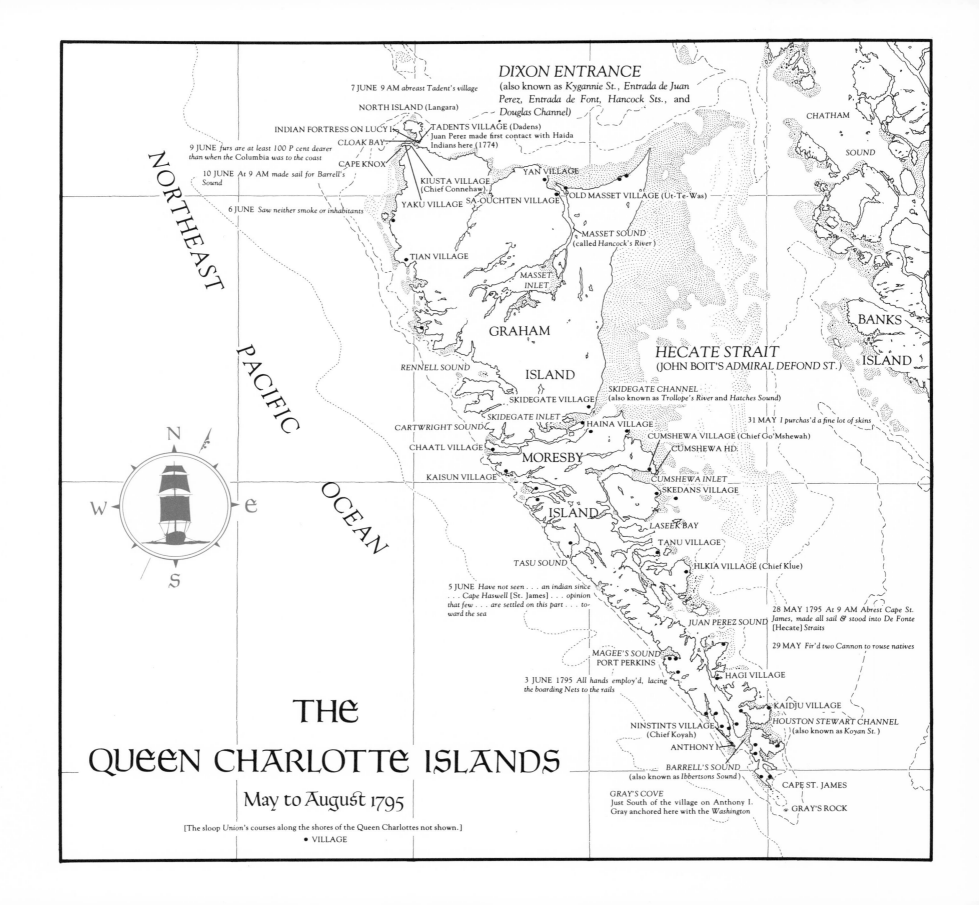

DIXON ENTRANCE
(also known as *Kygannie St.*, *Entrada de Juan Perez*, *Entrada de Font*, *Hancock Sts.*, and *Douglas Channel*)

7 JUNE 9 AM abreast Tadent's village

NORTH ISLAND (Langara)

CHATHAM
SOUND

INDIAN FORTRESS ON LUCY I.

TADENTS VILLAGE (Dadens)
Juan Perez made first contact with Haida Indians here (1774)

CLOAK BAY

9 JUNE furs are at least 100 P cent dearer than when the Columbia was to the coast

CAPE KNOX

10 JUNE At 9 AM made sail for Barrell's Sound

YAN VILLAGE

KIUSTA VILLAGE
(Chief Connehaw)

OLD MASSET VILLAGE (Ut-Te-Was)

YAKU VILLAGE   SA-OUCHTEN VILLAGE

6 JUNE Saw neither smoke or inhabitants

MASSET SOUND
(called *Hancock's River*)

TIAN VILLAGE

MASSET
INLET

BANKS

GRAHAM

HECATE STRAIT
(JOHN BOIT'S *ADMIRAL DEFOND ST.*)

ISLAND

RENNELL SOUND

ISLAND

SKIDEGATE CHANNEL
(also known as *Trollope's River* and *Hatches Sound*)

SKIDEGATE VILLAGE

SKIDEGATE INLET

31 MAY I purchas'd a fine lot of skins

CARTWRIGHT SOUND

HAINA VILLAGE

CHAATL VILLAGE

CUMSHEWA VILLAGE (Chief Go'Mshewah)

CUMSHEWA HD.

MORESBY

KAISUN VILLAGE

CUMSHEWA INLET

SKEDANS VILLAGE

ISLAND

LASEEK BAY

TANU VILLAGE

TASU SOUND

HLKIA VILLAGE (Chief Klue)

5 JUNE Have not seen . . . an indian since . . . Cape Haswell [St. James] . . . opinion that few . . . are settled on this part . . . toward the sea

28 MAY 1795 At 9 AM Abrest Cape St. James, made all sail & stood into De Fonte [Hecate] Straits

JUAN PEREZ SOUND

29 MAY Fir'd two Cannon to rouse natives

MAGEE'S SOUND
PORT PERKINS

3 JUNE 1795 All hands employ'd, lacing the boarding Nets to the rails

HAGI VILLAGE

KAIDJU VILLAGE

HOUSTON STEWART CHANNEL
(also known as *Koyan St.*)

NINSTINTS VILLAGE
(Chief Koyah)

ANTHONY I.

BARRELL'S SOUND
(also known as *Ibbertsons Sound*)

CAPE ST. JAMES

GRAY'S COVE
Just South of the village on Anthony I.
Gray anchored here with the *Washington*

GRAY'S ROCK

NORTHEAST

PACIFIC

OCEAN

N
W   E
S

THE
QUEEN CHARLOTTE ISLANDS

May to August 1795

[The sloop *Union's* courses along the shores of the Queen Charlottes not shown.]
• VILLAGE

At 7 Sprang a breeze from the NW. Hoisted in the boats & made sail. The outer rock of Cape St. James bear'g SBE the Northermost land in sight NWBW, Ukers Village W½S. Coyers Sound SW½W. At daylight stood towards Coyars Sound. Some Canoes of with a few Skins which I purchas'd also plenty of Halibutt.

August 25th, 1795
[Wind SW]
Light breezes & pleasant. Standing towards Ukers Village. *Off Uker's village. Queen Charlotte Isles. Many indians trading. At dark, it falling calm & there being no anchorage, out boats & tow'd off shore, as the surf let us in fast. The canoes left us & I believe we had got all the skins from the village. Bore away [down] wind at WNW for Columbia's Cove. At daylight Cape Haswell bore SSE.*

August 26th, 1795
[Wind SW, SE]
Heavy gales with a mountanious Sea. Turning to windward under a double reef'd Mainsail & foresail. At 9 PM Wore to the Southward. Midnight more moderate. Heavy gales, Wore Ship occasionally. More clear with a smoother Sea.
Lat Obsd 52°11′N

August 27th, 1795
[Wind WSW]
Light breezes, standing to the South'd by the wind. At 9 Bore away for Columbia's Cove, fresh breezes. Saw ye Caswell's Isles,[40] bear'g EBN½N 8 or 9 leagues.

August 28th, 1795
[Wind SW]
Light winds. At 7 The West'd of Caswells Isles bore NBE

five leagues dist'. At 8 TK to ye South'd. At 1 AM TK to the Eastward, in foresail & set the Squarsail.
Lat Obsd 50°30′N

August 29th, 1795
[Wind SSW]
Light winds & foggy weather. At 9 PM TK to the South'd.
Lat Obsd 50°20′N

August 30th, 1795
[Wind NW]
Light breezes, standing in for the land. At 7 TK of Shore. All hands Variously employ'd. Laying of and on in a thick fog.

August 31st, 1795
[Wind SW, WNW]
Moderate breezes, standing in for the land. At 8 TK Off, still foggy. At Midnight the fog clear'd. At 5 Saw Wooddy point [Cape Cook],[41] At 9 Abrest of Split rock & haul'd into Bulfinch's Sound.[42] At 11 Out Yawl. At Meridian we where within four miles of the harbour.
NB This days work contains 36 hours to commence the harbour log. At 8 PM Came to an Anchor in Columbia's Cove, & was visited by a few of the Natives. Strong gusts from ye Mount's.

September 1st, 1795
[Wind SW]
We laid in this cove till the 11th preparing the sloop for her pasage to Canton during which time we purchas'd many valuable skins from the natives who behav'd towards us with the greatest hospitality, never offering to go near our wooding & watered parties that were constantly employ'd and indeed tis doing these indians justice to say that they are by far more civilized & less savage than any I've ever met with in the NW coast of America. Pleasant agreeable weather. Sent a party

well arm'd on shore after water, got on board, & stow'd away 19 Hogsheads, & one boat load of Wood. Moor'd as Usuall head & Stern. A Number of the Natives alongsid, trading away there furs, purchas'd a handsome lot. I find these Natives full as Chearfull & Oblidging as ever & they appear'd to be very fond of this second Visit.

September 2nd, 1795
[Wind NW]
Heavy gales from the SE. Drag'd our Stern Anchor, let go the small bower under foot. Latter part more moderate, got on board the remainder of our Water. Hog'd both sides & got on board two load of wood.

September 3rd, 1795
[Wind WNW]
Fine pleasant weather. A party on shore cutting wood. Got of a quantity, pay'd the bends & various other nessescary jobs. Bought a fine lot of Skins of the Natives. So Ends.

September 4th, 1795
[Wind NW]
Still fine pleasant weather. A party on shore cutting Wood & getting it of, lifted the riging to repair, purchas'd a fine lot of furs.

September 5th, 1795
[Wind NW]
Clear pleasant weather, Seamen cuting & boating of Wood, Setting up ye riging etc. Sev'rall Canoes with the Natives trading away there Furs. Purchas'd a Large Deer of ye indians.

September 6th, 1795
[Wind West]
Pleasant agreeable weather. Employ'd cuting and getting on board wood, rattling down the riging, etc. Some of the Natives along but fetch'd no Skins. So Ends.

September 7th, 1795
[Wind North]
Pleasant weather with a fresh breeze. A party on shore cutting wood, the Carpenter with a gang After Spars. Employ'd on board Drawing and knoting Yarns, Spining Spun Yarn and making Mats. Scrap'd & slush'd the Mast's, new leather'd the Jaws of the boom and Gaft (gaff) & repair'd ye bowsprit Gammon. A few of the Natives along side, but brought but 4 or 5 Skins but plenty of Oil & Boards which I purchas'd. This day as the people where overhauling the run aft, a powder keg was found, which I caus'd to be open'd & found contain'd three large Sea Otter Skins & five Large tails, worth at Canton one hun'd and ten Dollars which is worth two hun'd & twenty at the Port of Boston. The Furs must have been Embezzel'd out of the Ships Cargo. So Ends.

September 8th, 1795
[Wind NBW]
Still pleasant weather. Carpenter ruffing out Spare Spars. Took up our Anchors & moor'd in a better birth. A party after More Spars. The Cheif of the Sound came on board & brought a fine Deer, but no Skins. Other Natives [brought] of Oil & peices of Otter fur etc.

September 9th, 1795
[Wind NBW]
Fine pleasant weather. Got ye remainder of our Spars of, Carpenter to work making them. Seamen spin'g Yarns. Others Cuting wood, & broom Stuf. Natives along side with Skins, Boards & Oil which I purchased. Latter part as before.

September 10th, 1795
[Wind NNW]
Pleasant agreeable weather. Carpenter constantly to work making a New set of small Spars for the Sloop. Got of the last of our Wood on board. A number of the Natives along side disposing of there furs. Purchas'd a quantity of Oil. Sold the last of our Copper, & most of the Blue cloth, & small Articles.

September 11th, 1795
[Wind NNW]
Exceeding pleasant weather. At 7 Unmoor'd. A party after Logs, Spruce bows & Water. A few Natives of with a few Skins, which I purchas'd, And I believe they had not many more. At 9 the party's that where on shore, got safe on board. At 10 Hove up the Anchor & tow'd out of the Cove. Light winds. So Ends.

Columbia's Cove
to the
Hawaiian Islands

12 September to 17 October 1795

September 12th, 1795
[Course SBE, SBW. Wind EBS, NE, NW]

Light airs from the Mountains. *Unmoor'd in the morning and at 8 PM left Columbia's Cover bound for Canton in China. Although at this time I was so sich as to make it very doubtful wether I should reach our destin'd port. My feelings at leaving this savage coast was the most susceptible I ever experienc'd & hope! With all & every dear anticipation was call'd on to make me happy. Although my poor frame was quite emaciated by a flux, great fever. But in God I put my trust and through his great goodness I was restored in health to the affectionate embrace of an every honor'd Father & other relatives. At sunrise took a dep[arture] from Woody Point.*

Lat Obsd 49°40′N Long 128°10′W
Dist pr log 34 Knots

September 13th, 1795
[Course SSW. Wind WNW]
Gentle breezes & cloudy. Carpenter making Scids for the Sides. At 2 PM In Squarsail, Set the Fores'l. At 5 In Tops'l & flying jib, of Bonnets. Struck a porpoise.
Dist pr log 121 Knots

September 14th, 1795
[Course SWBS. Wind NWBW]
Fresh breezes & cloudy weather. All hands Employ'd Draw'g & knoting Yarns.
Lat Obsd 46°49′N Long 132°18′W
Dist pr log 102 Knots

September 15th, 1795
[Course SWBS. Wind WNW, NW]
Brisk breezes & cloudy weather. Seamen and Tradesmen

employ'd in their Various depart's. At 7 AM Sent up the Yards & Set ye tops'l. Seamen employ'd drawing & knot'g Yarns, Carpenter making boats masts.
Lat Obsd 45°42'N Long 133°54'W
Dist pr log 93 Knots

September 16th, 1795
[Course SSW. Wind NWBN, NNE, NEBN]
Moderate breezes & cloudy disagreeable weather. Condemn'd & cut up the Old Small Bower cable for Junk, it being exceedingly worn. Set the Squaresail. A smooth sea.
Dist pr log 88 Knots

September 17th, 1795
[Course SSW. Wind NEBN]
Lively breezes with a smooth sea. Carpenter making Spare spars, Seamen drawing & knoting Yarns, & making Spun Yarn etc. Midnight cloudy, all Sail out. Owhyhee[43] bears S33°W, Dist 1640 Miles.
Dist pr log 133 Knots

September 18th, 1795
[Course SBW. Wind NEBN, EBN]
Steady breezes & cloudy weather. All sail out. Carpenter making a topsail yard. Seamen Drawing and knoting Yarns. Leather'd the Straps of the Main sheet blocks. Carpenter making a trys'l Gaf.
Dist pr log 94 Knots

September 19th, 1795
[Course SBW, SBE, South. Wind ENE, SW, WSW]
Light breezes inclining to a calm. All hands employ'd as Yesterday.
Dist pr log 45 Knots

September 20th, 1795
[Course SSE, SEBE, SE. Wind SWBS, SBW]
Moderate brezes & pleasant weather with a smooth Sea. Light winds with showers of rain.
Dist pr log 62 Knots

September 21st, 1795
[Course SE, SEBS. Wind SBW, SSW, SW]
Light breezes & cloudy weather with frequent Showers of rain. At 8 AM Set ye Topsail & flying Jib.
Dist pr log 44 Knots

September 22, 1795
[Course SBW, SSW. Wind ENE, calm, SEBE]
Light winds & thick misty weather. Seamen Variously employ'd. Caught a large Shark.
Lat Obsd 39°46'N Long 137°40'W
Dist pr log 25 Knots

September 23rd, 1795
[Course SWBW, SW. Wind SBE, SSE]
Fresh breezes with a head beat sea. Seamen & tradesmen a usuall employ'd. At 6 PM In Topsail & flying jib. At 10 Sent down ye Yards.
Dist pr log 70 Knots

September 24th, 1795
[Course SEBE, SEBS, SSE. Wind SBW, SSW, SW]
Seamen & tradesmen Variously Employ'd. At 4 AM Sent up the topsail and Squarsail Yards, & Set the Topsail & flying Jib.
Dist pr log 39 Knots

September 25th, 1795
[Course SBW. Wind NW, NE, ENE]
Light winds and pleasant. Seamen making robins [robands].[44] At 3 PM In foresail. Set ye Squarsail. Jib'd

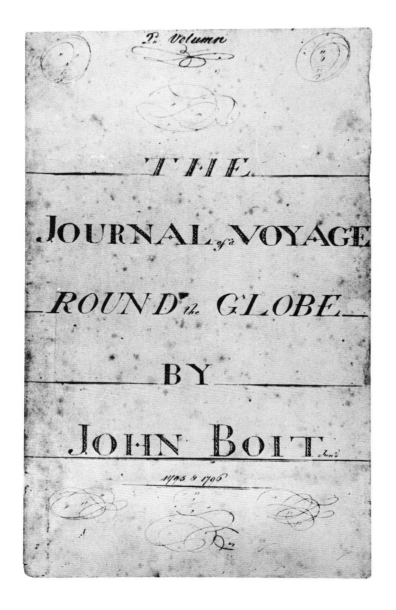

John Boit's hand-lettered title page for the second half of the Log of the *Union*.

Sloop. Saw two Dolphin. Owhyhee bears N39°W Dist 1330 Miles.
Lat Obsd 38°31′N Long 138°56′W
Dist pr log 53 Knots

September 26th, 1795
[Course SBW. Wind ENE, NE]
Fresh breezes & cloudy with frequent squalls, took in and set sail occasionally. People variously employ'd.
Dist pr log 125 Knots

September 27th, 1795
[Course SBW. Wind NEBS]
Steady breezes & cloudy weather. Variously employ'd.
Dist pr log 104 Knots

September 28th, 1795
[Course SBW. Wind NNE]
Lively breezes & pleasant weather with a following sea. All sail out, with a fine breeze. Saw Tropic birds & fly'g fish.
Dist pr log 125 Knots

September 29th, 1795
[Course SBW. Wind NNE, NEBN]
Lively breezes and pleasant. Employ'd making Spun Yarn. Kill'd a Hog. All hands employ'd mak'g rope.
Dist pr log 119 Knots

September 30th, 1795
[Course SBW. Wind NE, ENE]
Steady breezes, all hands employ'd making rope out of the Old Cable Yarns. Owyhee S49°W Dist 900 Miles.
Dist pr log 108 Knots

October 1st, 1795
[Course SBW. Wind EBN]
Lively breezes & close sultry weather. People employ'd making rope & pricking Spun Yarn. At 1 AM In Squarsail & set the foresail.
Dist pr log 78 Knots

October 2nd, 1795
[Course SBW. Wind East, NE, EBS]
Cloudy warm weather. All hands employ'd making Rope
etc. All sail out.
Lat Obsd 28°7'N Long 144°30'W
Dist pr log 48 knots

October 3rd, 1795
[Course SBW. Wind EBN, NEBE, EBS]
Light breezes & flattering weather. Parted ye Clue of the
topsail. Midnight some showers of rain. All hands em-
ploy'd making rope, & cleaning Furs etc. *This day took the
NE trade winds.*
Dist pr log 67 Knots

October 4th, 1795
[Course SBW. Wind EBS, SEBE]
Light winds and pleasant. Employ'd cleaning out the Fore-
castle etc.
Dist pr log 67 Knots

October 5th, 1795
[Course SBW. Wind SEBE, EBS]
Flattering weather with frequent squalls. At 10 PM In
topsail & flying jib. At 4 AM Set ye Topsail & flying jib.
All hands employ'd Stowing ye spare sails & Spars in ye
hold, cleaning Skins etc.
Lat Obsd 25°8'N Long 146°4'W
Dist pr log 84 Knots

October 6th, 1795
[Course SSW. Wind SEBE]
Moderate breezes and cloudy. All hands employ'd as
yester'y. Noon light winds, & exceeding warm close
weather.
Dist pr log 75 Knots

October 7th, 1795
[Course SSW. Wind ENE]
Light breezes and pleasant agreeable weather. All sail out.
All hands employ'd cleaning Skins & making Robins.
Dist pr log 121 Knots

October 8th, 1795
[Course SSW. Wind East]
Fresh breezes with a high sea. Carried away ye After leach
rope & repair'd it. Midnight fresh gales. Parted another of
our Chain bolts. All hands employ'd cleaning skins and
making caskets. Saw a Dolphin.
Dist pr log 123 Knots

October 9th, 1795
[Course SW, WSW, NNE. Wind NE, East]
Steady breezes with flying clouds. Unbent ye Mainsail, &
brought another too. At 6 Saw ye appear'ce of land to ye
West'd. At 5 Bore away to ye W'd. All hands employ'd
mounting ye Cannon & clean'g Muskets etc.[45] No land in
sight. Owyhee bears W'd 289 Mi.
Dist pr log 104 Knots.

October 10th, 1795
[Course W¾S. Wind EBN]
Lively breezes and pleasant with a tumbling sea. All sail
out. At 8 In Squarsail. Midnight pleasant breezes. At 5
AM set the Squarsail.
Lat Obsd 20°17'N Long 152°44'W
Dist pr log 116 Knots

October 11th, 1795
[Course W¾S. Wind EBS]
Moderate breezes and pleasant. Many tropic birds round.
At 8 PM In Squarsail. Caught a Dolphin. People employ'd
clean'g out the Fore Castle & smoking it.
Dist pr log 90 Knots

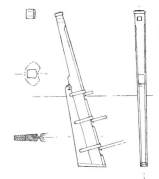

The *Union*:
Rudder details.
(Hewitt Jackson)

October 12th, 1795
[Course W¾S. Wind ESE, SE]
All sail out, struck a porpoise. Some dolphin round. *Begins pleasant weather, rolling away wing and wing. At 6 AM saw the island of Owhyee [Hawaii] one of the group of Sandwich [Islands] bear'g WBS 30 leagues [distant]. Excessive high land.*
Dist pr log 97 Knots

October 13th, 1795
[Course SW. Wind SE]
Brisk breezes with flying clouds attend'd with dist't thunder, many smoaks on shore. At 6 TK of Shore. *Many fires on the land, the extreemer of this isle from WBN to WBS. 3 or 4 leagues from nearest shore. Midnight pleasant. At daylight we where visited by plenty of canoes filled with natives. They brought a great quantity of hogs & fruit which they readily parted with in exchange for nails & iron hoops. The females were quite amorous.*
Dist pr log 39 Knots

October 14th, 1795
Pleasant agreeable weather, laying of & on the NE pt of Owhyhee.[46] Vast many canoes with natives along side with abundance of Vegetables, but with the disagreeable intelligence that Hogs was taboo'd (by Tama-maaah the King)[47] and only to be purchas'd for guns & ammunition. At 6 PM The extreems of Owhyee extend'd from SE to WBN. Employ'd steadily in trafic with the natives.

October 15, 1795
Light winds & pleasant, still laying of & on. The natives brought me 5 small pigs, which I purchased for Iron & [also purchas'd] many fowls. *However the indians did not forget to ask for fire arms & ammunition but I thought it proper to refuse. This Island from our present view off the NE point made a delightful prospect & the shore was crowded with people.*

October 16th, 1795
[Wind ESE]
Light winds and exceeding pleasant weather. Standing along shore towards Toy Yah Yah bay. At 8 PM Many of the Natives came of, & brought a large supply of Vegetables. At 10 Two large double canoes came of & brought 9 large Hogs & 6 Pigs, all which belong'd to a Cheif who had staid on board the preceding night, all the Hogs I purchas'd for a single Muskett & the pigs for a few chizzels. At 2 PM a very large double canoe came of & in her I was suppriz'd to see an English man. *From this man by the name of John Young,[48] I procured much information, the purport of which, was as follows, in regard to himself;* he said that he had formily been Boatswain on the Snow *Elenora* belonging to Newyork Capt. Metcalf & was detain'd by the Natives when that Vessell lay at Karakakooa bay, in this Isle while [he was] on shores, a recreating himself, & had been a resident here seven Years, during which time he had been treated by the King, Tamaa-maah [Kamehameha], with the greatest friendship & hospitality, & that he never as Yet had entertain'd a single wish ever to leave this delightfull Isle; *that in February 1794 Capt. Brown anchor'd in Fair haven harbor, Isle of Whoahoo[49] [Oahu] with two English sloops call'd the* Jack Hall [Jackal] *&* Prince La Boo [Lee Boo], *command'd by Capt. Gordon* & that he proceeded to alter one Vessell into a Ship, & the small one into a Cutter for so to make them handier for cruizing the NW Coast, in which trade he meant to embark, that while he was thus employ'd the Cheifs of Whoahoo made him a formal present of the Island with all its contents, of which he accordingly took possecion. & that on the 3'd of Dec' Capt. John Hendrick [Kendrick] in the Snow *Lady Washington* of Boston arriv'd at Fairhaven & [was] met with a very freindly reception by Capt. Brown, & on the 6th of ye same month in consequence of a long quarrel between the Cheifs of Whohaoa & Atooe (an Island to leeward) [Kauai] a battle was fought, & [victory] was

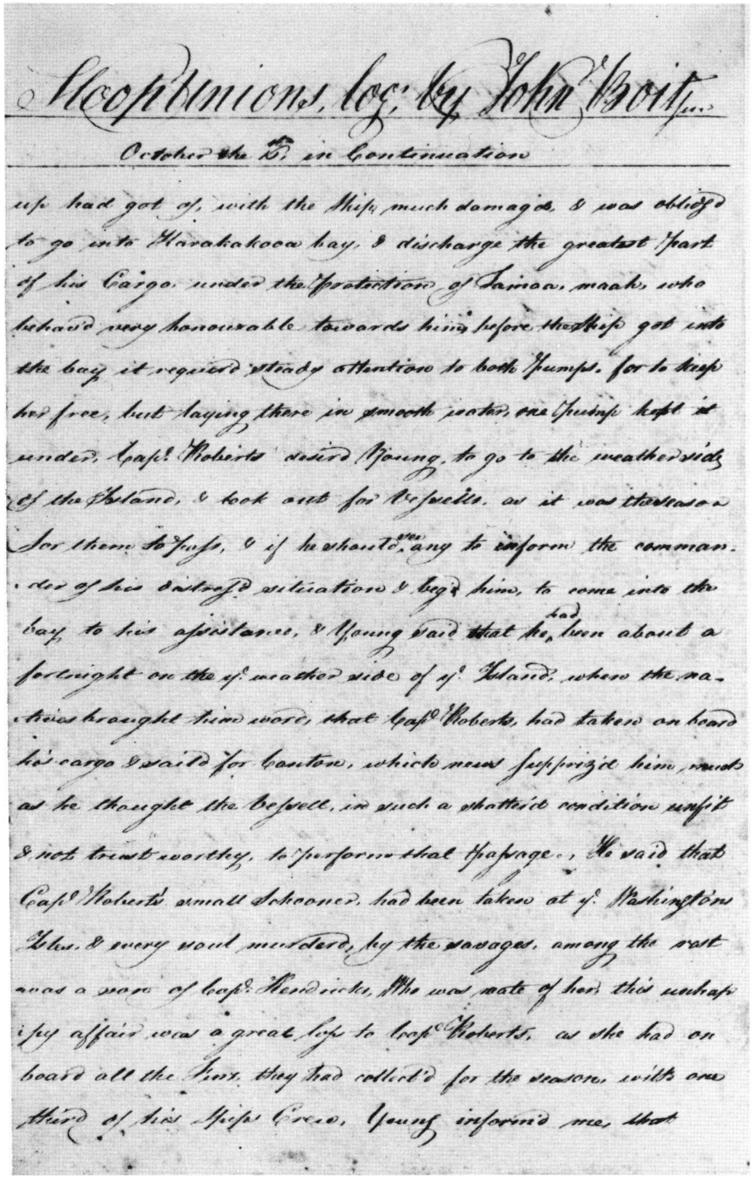

October the 16. in Continuation

[handwritten manuscript — left page]

[handwritten manuscript — right page]

On 16 October 1795, while in the Hawaiian Islands, John Boit, Jr., penned the longest entry in the Log of the *Union*. The entry recounts the the ship's arrival off Hawaii and his meeting with John Young, an Englishman who had taken up residence there and who was friendly with King Kamehameha I (Boit misspelt the name with an initial T). Young described the islands' situation for Boit in what was probably a veiled warning to stay clear of them. Boit wrote in this entry: "After mature consideration & suming up All the information into a point, which I got from Young, I came to a conclusion that it was not safe to run down among the Islands, with my small Vessell, at least without a good stiff breeze, & indeed I had no sufficient inducement to tarry any longer among them."

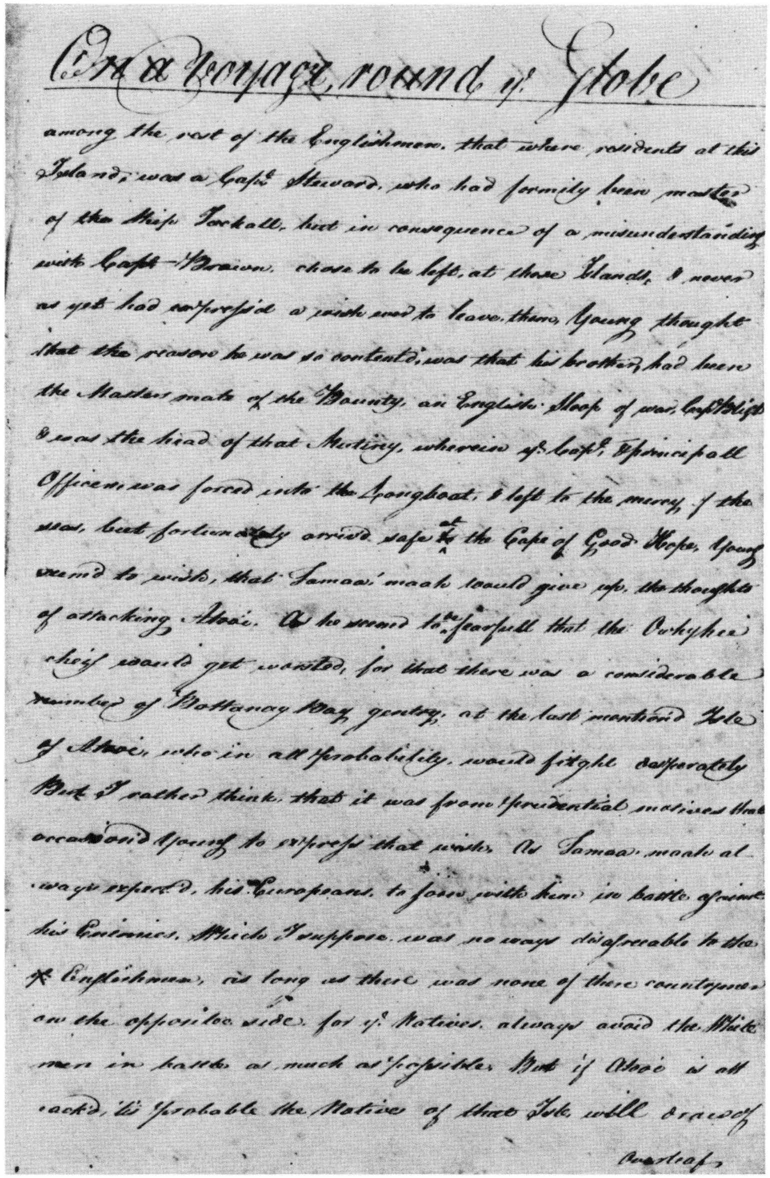

gain'd by the King of Whahooa, by the assistance of Capt. Hendrick. Who immediately inform'd Capt. Brown that on the morrow he should cause the Flag of the United States to be hoisted, & fire a federal salute, which he beg'd might be answer'd by the two Englishmen & it was accordingly agreed too, & Capt. Brown order'd three guns to be unshotted for that purpose & about ten the next morning, the ship *Jack hall* began to salute, but on coming to the 3'd gun it was discover'd not to be prim'd. So ye Apron of ye 4th Gun was taken of, which was fir'd, & being shoted with round & Grape Shot, it peirced the side of ye *Lady Washington* & kill'd Capt. Hendrick as he sat at his table, & kill'd & wound'd many upon deck, & that shortly after that the Snow put to sea bound to Canton under the command of Mr. Howell, & that in a few weeks after this unfortunate affair happen'd the Cheifs of Whoohoa order'd a great quantity of Hogs & Vegetables to be brought to the landing place, as a present to Capt. Brown & sent word on board the *Jack'all* for the Captain to send the boats for the above present. He [Capt. Brown] having always liv'd in the strictest freindship with the Natives & considering the Island as his own, & not at all suspicious of their intentions, Very imprudently sent all his boats, with every man out of the Ship but himself, & order'd Capt. Gordon of the *Prince Laboo* to do the same but Capt. Gordon only sent one boat, & kept an Islander, who had been employ'd on board as Cook, with him. Soon after a large double Canoe, full of men, rang'd up along side the *Prince Laboo* & struck her small boat that lay along side & somewhat damag'd her upon which Capt. Gordon run to ye gangway to blame them for it, & the Indian on board taken that advantage pitch'd him overboard, & there they immediately dispatch'd him. They directly repair'd alongside the *Jack'all* where Capt. Brown was walking the poop, by himself, when one of ye Savages gets up on the poop, & made a pass at the Good old Captain with an Iron dagger, which he fend'd of & seized a Swivell worm & drove the

fellow of, he was soon follow'd by a number more which the captain likewise beat of, but at last he was overpower'd by numbers, & receiv'd a fatal stab in the back of the neck & was pitch'd from the poop on to the main deck where he soon expir'd, & so by there savage artfulness they got possession of both Vessells, without the loss of a man on there side, in the mean time they had seiz'd the Boats & People that where on shore, & then the Cheifs held a conference together about what was most prudent to be done, some where for killing all the people & destroying the Vessells So as the horrid deed never should be found out. But at last it was determin'd that ye Officers & people [crew] should go on board, under a proper guard of Islanders & that they should finish riging the Vessells & when they was ready for sea, they should take on board a large quantity of Islanders & proceed to the Island of Owhyhee, & there try to decoy the King of that Isle, & reduce it. But the Officers and people of the above Vessells had sworn one and all that the night they put to sea, they would retake the Vessells from the Natives or lose there lives in the attempt. Accordingly, the very night they dropt out of the harbour they put their scheme in execution, & soon retook both Vessells, with a great slaughter of the Natives and only losing one man in the attempt, and after getting refreshments at the Windward Islands, they sail'd for Canton;

John Young (which is the name of the Man) from whom I receiv'd this information, likewise said that there was two Englishmen residents at the Windward Islands, besides himself, who had been left there by different Vessells, & that Tama-maah King of Owyhee had taken all the Islands in ye Groupe except Atooi & Owehow & laid most of them waste & that he, with most the other Owyhee cheifs, & 1500 War Canoes & above ten thousand men was then at Whahoo, meditating an attack against Atooi. He said that they had 5000 prime Muskets with them & many swivels & Cannon one of which was a four

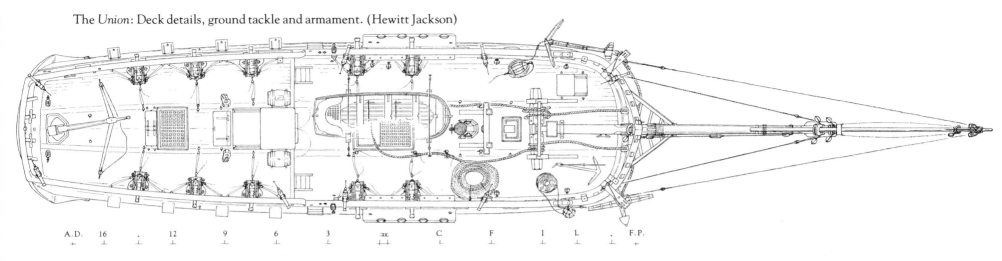

The *Union*: Deck details, ground tackle and armament. (Hewitt Jackson)

A.D.　16　.　12　　9　　6　　3　　xx　　C　　F　　I　　L　.　F.P.

pounder, & that the greater part of the Natives understood the using of Firearms equal to any men he ever saw. Young was the only European at present, that staid at Owhyhee, the rest being at Whahoo with Tama-maah where they was building a small Vessell for the king. Young said that he had only been at Ow'hee a few weeks, & was sent there for the sole purpose of informing all Vessells crews of the Freindly intentions of Tamaa-maah towards all Europeans, & to purchase Naval Stores for the Vessells they then had, & which they intended to build. Upon my asking him what vessels they had, he said Capt. Vancouver had caus'd one to be built, as a present to ye King in consideration of the freindly treatment he had receiv'd from him, while at the Island, & that she was 35 foot keel, the other was a small Schooner, formily own'd by Capt. Metcalf, it appear'd that Capt. M. had purchas'd this small Vessell at Macao, after his arrival at that port in the *Elenora* from the NW coast, & did there fit her out with the Snow, for the Coast again, & gave the command of her to his oldest Son. The two Vessells was to keep company, but in a gale of Wind of ye Coast of Japan, they got separated. It seems the Younger Metcalf made the quickest passage on to the Coast, & made purchase of a Valuable Cargo of Furs & Then not being able to find his

father on the Coast he push'd on towards Canton. He made the Island of Owyhee & was imprudent enough to come to an anchor, in Karakakooa bay, in order to procure refreshments. He had not been long in that situation, when an old Cheif, by the name of Ka'oo, came on board, & present'd the Capt. with a feather Cap & Cloak & beg'd permission to put it on, which was granted, but his savage heart being void of any human feelings, & thinking it good opportunity, seiz'd & threw ye Young man overboard, where he was soon murder'd by those alongside & the Natives immediately kill'd all on board except one man, who is now at the Island Whoahoa & this was the manner they got possest of their second Vessell.

Young further said that Capt. Roberts, the last year in a Ship from Boston, had run her on shore, upon the weather side of Owhyee, but fortunately by the help of a land breeze spring'g up had got [her] of, with the Ship much damag'd, & was oblig'd to go into Karakakooa bay, & discharge the greatest part of his cargo, under the protection of Tamoa-maah, who behav'd very honourable towards him, before the Ship got into the bay it requir'd steady attention to both pumps, for to keep her free, but laying there in smooth water, one pump kept it under. Capt. Roberts desir'd Young to go to the weather side of the Island, & look out for Vessells, as it was the season for them to pass, & if he should see any to inform the commander of his distress'd situation & beg'd him, to come into the bay to his assistance, & Young said that he had been about a fortnight on the weather side of ye Island when the natives brought him word, that Capt. Roberts had taken on board his cargo & sail'd for Canton, which news Suppriz'd him much as he thought the Vessell in such a shatter'd condition unfit & not trustworthy to perform that passage. He said that Capt. Robert's small Schooner had been taken at ye Washington's Isles [Queen Charlotte Islands], & every soul murder'd by the savages, among the rest was a son of Capt. [K]endricks, Who was mate of her. This unhappy affair was a great loss to Capt. Roberts, as she had on board all the Furs they had collect'd for the season, with one third of his Ships Crew. Young inform'd me that among the rest of the Englishmen that where residents at this Island was a Capt. Steward who had formily been master of the Ship *Jackall*, but in consequence of a misunderstanding with Capt. Brown, chose to be left at these Islands, & never as yet had express'd a wish ever to leave them. Young thought that the reason he was so content'd was that his brother had been the Masters mate of the *Bounty*, an English Sloop of war, [commanded by] Capt. Bligh & was the head of that Mutiny, wherein ye Capt. & principall Officers, was forced into the Longboat, & left to the mercy of the seas, but fortunately arriv'd safe at the Cape of Good Hope. Young seem'd to wish that Tamaa-maah would give up the thoughts of attacking Atooi. As he seem'd to be fearfull that the Owyhee cheif would get worsted, for that there was a considerable number of Bottanay Bay gentry, at the last mention'd Isle of Atooi, who in all probability, would fight desperately. But I rather think that it was from prudential natives that occasion'd Young to express that wish. As Tamaa-maah always expect'd his Europeans to join with him in battles against his Enimies. Which I suppose was no

ways disagreeable to the Englishmen, as long as there was none of there countrymen on the opposite side, for ye Natives always avoid the White men in battle as much as possible. But if Atooi is attack'd, 'tis probable the Natives of that Isle will draw of there White men to oppose Tamaa-maah's. Which I suppose will be contrary to the wishes of both party's, & I rather think that ye Botany men would fight desparately for ye generallity of ye Convicts sent to Botanay are desparate fellows. Young did not rightly know what Vessell had left them at Atooi. But he said that he heard that it was an American Ship that brought them. Young likewise inform'd me, that Old Capt. Metcalf in a Brig from the Isle of France had been cut of at Coyars, in ye Queen Charlotte Isles by ye Natives of that place, & ev'ry soul murder'd except one man, who got up in ye Main top, & was taken alive. Capt. Metcalfs younger son was mate of the Brig. This man, whom ye Natives took alive, was afterwards bought of by ye Master of a Boston ship who pass'd here about a fortnight since. 'Twas from this man that Young got his intelligence, the purport of which was as follows. That some time in the year '94, Capt. Metcalf came to an anchor in his Brig at Coyars Sound, & began a freindly traffic for furs with the Savages, but not being much suspicious of them, let a great number come upon his decks, & the natives taken advantage of there superiority in number, clinch'd and stab'd ev'ry man on board except ye one that sprung up the Shrouds.[50]

This horrid Massacre was executed in the space of a few minutes, with no loss, on the side of the natives. The man said that after they had insulted the body's of ye dead as they thought sufficiently, they told him to come down, which he accordingly did, & deliver'd himself up to them, at the same time beging for mercy. They immediately took him on shore at the Village, where he was kept in the most abject slavery for above a twelve month, in winter, & in the worst of weather, amide Snow & ice, they would drive

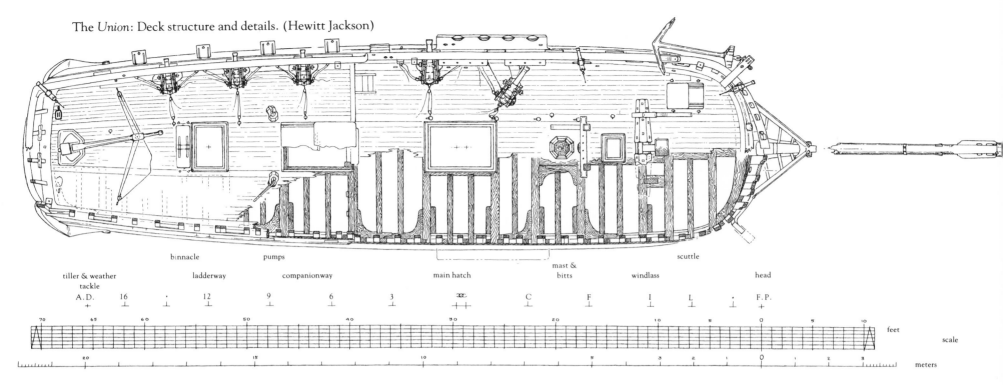

The *Union*: Deck structure and details. (Hewitt Jackson)

binnacle   pumps   mast &   scuttle
                           bitts

tiller & weather   ladderway   companionway   main hatch   windlass   head
tackle

him into ye Woods to fetch logs & when he had got most to ye Village with his load, he would be met by his task masters who would there disburthen him & drive him back after more, & when any Vessell came into the harbour, they would lash him hand & foot to a tree & keep him in that situation, with a scanty allowance, till she again sail'd for fear that he might run away. Ye man told Young that Coyar had in his possession ye riging of a large Ship, whose shroud Hawser was above 9 Inches, it appear'd to be french riging, it might have [come from] one of those French Frigates which was out on discovery, & went in with the people all sick with Scurvy or else some french privateer, who had run down ye Coast of new spain with there Vessell, & went into Coyars with the same predicament. In either case ye natives of that sound would have been powerfull enough to have conquer'd them. How fortunate I must have been, to have escap'd the dilligence of this savage tribe, for 'twas in that very Sound, in June last they meant to have taken my Vessell, but fortunately they perceiv'd, that I was very suspicious of there intentions, & in all probability that was all that sav'd me from destruction, & I could never reconcile it to myself, till I heard this news, why the natives came possess'd of so many Ships bolts, & Hooks, a great number of which, they had the audacity to bring along side of my vessell for sale, some of which I purchas'd. This poor man, that was taken with Metcalf, was at times delerious, owing entirely to the cruel treatment he had receiv'd, while among the Savages.

Young inform'd me that two Vessells had pass'd the Islands from ye NW Coast, bound to Canton, this season before me. One an English snow from Bengall, Capt. Moore, who pass'd the last of Sep'r, the other, a Boston Ship, call'd the *Dispatch*, formily command'd by Capt. Newbury. But that Captain was, unfortunately, & accidently kill'd by an Indian, it seems this indian must have been a favorite for he was allow'd into the Cabin, where Capt. Newbury was showing him a pistol as he lay in his birth, the Captain snap'd the pistol sev'rall times not knowing it was load'd, at last he hand'd it to the Indian for him to look at it, which he soon begun to Snap, & at last it unluckely went of, & being pointed toward the captain, the ball enter'd his breast, of which wound he soon expir'd. This Ship pass'd Owhyhee Oct 3d, under the direction of Mr. Caswell. She staid at ye Island two days, & left a good recommendation with Young, advising all Masters of Vessells who should call this way to put entire confidence in him.

Young had likewise good recommendations from Capt. Vancouver, commander of his Britannic Majesty's Ships ye *Discovery* & *Chatham*, out on a voyage of discovery, who had winter'd at Karakakooa Bay,[51] in these recommendations. Tamaa-maah was Spoke highly of, as a Cheif in whom all Europeans might put the greatest confidence, without ye least fear of being betray'd & that any Vessell might anchor in Karakakooa bay with the greatest safety, while under the protection of Tama-maah. Young said that Tianna a very turbulant Owhyhee cheif, & a man that had caus'd a great deal of uneasiness upon ye Island, was fortunately Kill'd at ye taken of Whohooa while fighting against his own sovereign. I was sorry to hear that Hogs could only be purchas'd at Owhyhee for Muskets, however this canoe having brought of five very large ones, induced me to part with an indifferent Blunderbuss for them. Young seem'd to be suppriz'd at my keeping at such a distance from ye Island, indeed, I must own that I was timid of keeping very nigh it, & then allowing no woman to come of, made me suspicious that it was a concerted plan to draw me nearer in shore. However I had not the least reason to suspect Young, in any bad designs against mine or any other Vessells that touches at these Islands, on the contrary, I beleive that he would do his utmost to serve any Masters of vessels that touches

The *Union*:
Jib stay details.
(Hewitt Jackson)

here both in procureing refreshments, & persuadeing the natives, as much as lay in his power, to behave freindly towards them. Indeed the recommendations that he show'd me, both from Capt. Vancouver, and ye Master of the *Dispatch*, would have induced any man that want of a suspicious make, to have gone in with the Island & put entire confidence in him.

But for my own part, I concluded that though Young may be a very good man, which no doubt he is, Yet I never could think, that one Englishman or even fifty would have any weight with so powerfull a Chief as Tamaa-maah, in frustrating any plan that he proposed, either in regard to taking of Vessells, or any other, of consequence & very likely that the rest of the Englishmen are not so well disposed men, as Young is; & Although Capt. Vancouver thought fit to recommend Tamaa-maah as a man in whom entire confidence might always be put, & no doubt he thought so, but perhaps did not consider, at ye same time, that it was good policy in the King of Owhyhee to keep in strict freindship with him for two substantial reasons. One was because he knew that Capt. Vancouver was a midshipman with Capt. Cook at the time when that great commander & circumnavigar was murder'd at Karakakooa Bay, by the hand of one of the Savages of Owhyhee: [the other] he knew the Ships was of considerable force, with plenty of men, & consequently that if he acted amiss, that it was in the power of Capt. Vancouver to do him considerable damage, for I suppose he well remember'd the damage the Island had receiv'd after the death of Capt. Cook and very likely suppos'd that Capt. Vancouver would improve upon the means taken after that unfortunate affair, if there should be a call for harsh methods to be taken with them. For revenge seems to be innate with savages, & very likely they suppose Europeans to be like themselves, in that particular.

But though ships of war might be safe in Karakakooa bay Yet I humbly am of opinion that small Merchantment

76

have no business to venture themselves there at all. For I shall always think that no man is safe in ye hands of savages, any longer than he holds himself independent of them; for when once he gets in there power, depend upon it, his life is always in a very critical situation, & for the least error, perhaps is totally undone. For who can suppose that a set of men, brought up in a state of nature, without the advantages of Civilization or any kind of education, should be grac'd with any of those humane and finer feelings which adorn the most civiliz'd nations. I have heard people pretend to advance the thought that the Sandwich Islanders where not to be reckon'd a savage nation. To be sure they are bless'd, with a frank, chearfull, countenance which helps, to endear them so much to strangers, but I hold them among the worst of savages, for if they had that savage appearance, which is so strongly pictur'd in the face of the NW Indians, they would not be so likely to deceive so many Europeans, who have trusted too much to appearances & have been artfully murder'd. I think Europeans having been left at these Islands, is a great damage to all Vessells that in future will touch here for refreshments, for they have put the Natives up to many things, that otherwise they never would have thought of, in particular there refusing any thing for their Hogs except arms & ammunition, which the englismen well knew that the Masters of Vessells would give rather than pass, without procuring so nessescary a refreshment. But for my own part, though it was my intention at first to have procur'd a vast many Hogs, if Iron would have purchas'd them, but rather than humor them so much as to sell them Muskets, although I could have very well spared them, made me determine to purchase no more than just was nessescary to last me to Canton.

Young inform'd me that among the Europeans resident at ye Windward Isles there was two Carpenters, & a Blacksmith, who was now actually building a small Vessell at Whohooa & had got her [construction] considerable

forward, & he said Tama-maah wish'd to purchase copper for her bottom, for the worms had done his other Vessels great damage. I question'd Young about ye *Bounty*, which I once heard had been at these Islands, but he said that she never had been there, while he had been a reside[nt] upon them. But added, if she should come, there they should certainly take her & restore ye Ships & pirates to the first english man of War, that should touch there after.

I offer'd to give Young his passage to Canton but he excus'd himself from excepting it, mentioning at ye same time, that this was the only Country that he was ever in, where he could be allow'd so many privelidges as he here enjoy'd, for 'twas at Owhyhee he said, that peace & contentment seem'd to go hand inhand, & ev'ry one seem'd to be perfectly happy, with the portion, that was allotted to him. For poverty was a stranger, in this land of liberty, and Slavery was a term, they did not understand, & for his own part, he had a very good plantation allotted to him, by the Cheif, & as many Wifes as he chose to take. The regulation of wifes is very good in this Country, for when either party gets displeas'd with ye other, they have an undoubted right to draw of without ye trouble of applying to a justice of the peace for a disvorce, but one law that they have among them, I think is the most cruel that perhaps ever exist'd, that is, wherin ev'ry man is

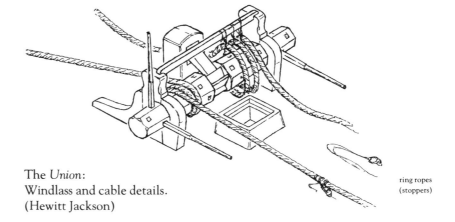

The *Union*:
Windlass and cable details.
(Hewitt Jackson)

ring ropes
(stoppers)

77

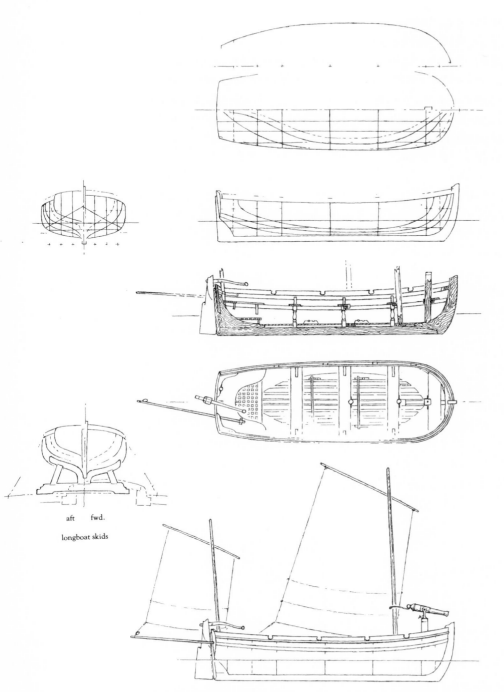

The *Union*: Longboat studies, showing lines, profile, structure, sail plan and longboat on skids. (Hewitt Jackson)

countenanc'd in doing as he pleases with what he deems to be his own & they carry it so far as to murder there own children. Young told me of one instance of the kind which was shocking; he said that it was a rule among them that all Male children should belong to the Father & ye female to the wife, & upon a dispute of this kind that happen'd upon his plantation, wherin ye mother claim'd ye male child, & the father getting exasperated at this presumtion of his wife, seiz'd the child, & with ye fury of a savage, broke its back across his knee & threw it in her face.

Young left me about 10 in ye evening after I made him **a present of such articles as I thought** might be most usefull to him, but promis'd to return on the morrow, and assist me in trafficking with the Natives, but after he had got into his Canoe to depart, he return'd on board again, & very kindly inform'd me that one of my people had secreted himself away in the Canoe. I immediately call'd the fellow out, & Young left us. It seems this sailor of mine, by the name of John Barton, was one of those kind of people, that sometimes come into this transitory world merely by chance, or as Seamen term it born along shore without ever knowing who there Father or mother was, or perhaps even thinking that they ever had any. Such a man as this, it might be expected, would readily take up with those Islands, as a place of residence, as any part of the Globe whatever. Perhaps for this very reason, that lasiness was very much countenanc'd by the inhabitents of the Sandwich Isles. However I only had recourse to threats, not having the heart to flog the poor illitterate devil, although he so richly deserv'd correction.

After mature consideration & suming up All the information into a point, which I got from Young, I came to a conclusion that it was not safe to run down among the Islands, with my small Vessell, at least without a good stiff breeze, & indeed I had no sufficient inducement to tarry any longer among them, having on board 16 large Hogs, 10 Small pigs, 2 doz Fowls, & a large supply of Water &

78

Musk melons, breadfruit, Plantains, Sweet potatoes, Yams, Taro, Sugar Cane & Cocoa Nuts, besides a good lot rope & line. At Midnight a fine breeze spung up at SE, Upon which I haul'd upon a wind to the N & E with a determination, to pass to the N of the Island Mowee & so run down to the Northward of all the Islands. Noon pleasant.

Lat Obsd 21°8′N

October 17, 1795
[Course NW. Wind ENE]
Light winds and pleasant weather. At 5 PM the Isle of Morotay[52] bore SWBW½W, Kanai SW½S & ye South'st pt. of Mowee bore SBE Dist. 12 leagues, from which I take my departure, it lying in Lat 20°54′N & Long 155°56′W from Greenwich Observa'ry.

Dist pr log 60 Knots

The Hawaiian Islands
to
Canton, China

18 October 1795 to 10 January 1796

October 18, 1795
[Course NW, NWBW, WBN. Wind NE, ENE]
Dark squally weather with a following sea, at 8 Single reef'd the Mainsail. Sent down ye Topsail Yard, to fit a new parell & repair the sail.
Dist pr log 107 Knots

October 19, 1795
[Course W½S, WBS. Wind EBN, NE]
Lively breezes with frequent rain squalls. At 2 PM In fore-sail & set squarsail. Unbent ye Old mainsail it being split. Many Bonnetto round of which we caught one.
Dist pr log 110 Knots

October 20th, 1795
[Course SWBW. Wind East, NBE]
Light breezes with pleasant agreeable weather. All sail out. Sail maker repairing the Old Mainsail. At 6 AM Jib'd Ship, Seamen breaking out ye Hold for fresh water etc.
Lat Obsd 22°57'N Long 160°50'W
Dist pr log 51 Knots

October 21st, 1795
[Course SW. Wind NBE]
Pleasant breezes. At 4 PM Discover'd an Island[53] bear'g NWBW 10 leagues dist. It appear'd to be pretty high land, its Lat. by estimation is 23°10'N & Long. 161°32'W bear'g N30°W Dist. 107 miles from the Isle of ye Tahoura [One of the Sandwich Islands]. Being pretty certain that I am the first discoverer of it, I saw fit to name it Hatch's Isle, in honour of Crowell Hatch Esq., my principall owner.
Lat Obsd 21°52'N Long 162°28'W
Dist pr log 113 Knots

October 22nd, 1795
[Course SW. Wind EBN, ENE]
Fresh breezes and squally disagreeable weather. Sail maker repair'g ye Topsail. At 10 sent up ye Tops'l Yard & set ye sail. People picking Oakum, killed & salt'd 2 Hogs.
Dist pr log 146 Knots

October 23rd, 1795
[Course SW. Wind ENE]
Moderate breezes with frequent rain squalls. Men of war & tropic birds round. All hands variously employ'd. Unbent ye new Mainsail & brought ye Old one too.
Dist pr log 112 Knots

October 24th, 1795
[Course SW. Wind ENE]
Squally with heavy showers of rain, parted ye strap of the top in lift block & again repair'd it. Midnight heavy thunder, & sharp light'g.
Dist pr log 119 Knots

October 25th, 1795
[Course SWBW. Wind ENE]
Brisk breezes with frequent heavy rain squalls. Bent & Set the Squars'l. Many Men of War birds, & Gannets flying round; Strong indications of the vicinity of land.
Lat Obsd 17°26'N Long 170°5'W
Dist pr log 134 Knots

October 26th, 1795
[Course SWBW. Wind EBN]
Lively breezes. All hands employ'd eating fresh pork, & some other nessescary business, all sail out.
Dist pr log 148 Knots

October 27th, 1795
[Course WSW. Wind EBS]

Very squally with much rain, all sail out. Fitted a new long preventer pennant to ye Boom. Saw a gannett & many sheerwaters. Midnight fresh gales.
Dist pr log 152 Knots

October 28th, 1795
[Course WSW. Wind EBS]
Pleasant breezes, put ye Cannon below & unbent ye cables. Carpenter to work on the Yawl, Sail maker on ye Spare sails. Unbent the Foresail & Jibs, & brought Old ones too. Got ye spare sails up to dry, fitted new crotch ropes, etc.
Dist pr log 137 Knots

October 29th, 1795
[Course WBS½S. Wind East]
Moderate breezes & pleasant weather. Many tropic birds round. Caulker employ'd caulking the quarter deck Stantions. Seamen cleaning furs.
Dist pr log 134 Knots

October 30th, 1795
[Course W¾S. Wind EBN]
Brisk winds with frequent rain squalls. Kill'd & salt'd three Hogs. Found one of the after shrouds parted. In Mains'l, & got it down to repair.
Lat Obsd 15°31'N Long 182°27'W
Dist pr log 157 Knots

October 31st, 1795
[Course WBS½S. Wind East]
Lively breezes & pleasant. At 4 PM Set all sail. Seamen cleaning furs. Sail maker upon ye Spare sails.
Dist pr log 164 Knots

November 1st, 1795
[Course WBS½S. Wind EBN]

Brisk breezes & pleasant weather. Some Tropic birds & flying fish round the Sloop. All sail out, with a steady breeze.
Lat Obsd 15°33′N Long 187°52′W
Dist pr log 148 Knots

November 2nd, 1795
[Course WBS½S. Wind EBN]
Moderate breezes and pleasant weather. Seamen cleaning Otter skins. Caulker on ye Main deck. Tinian bears W¼S. Dist 1368 Mi.
Dist pr log 132 Knots

November 3rd, 1795
[Course WBS½S. Wind ENE]
Light breezes and pleasant. All sail out with a following sea. Gannetts & Sea Guls flying round with large flights of Sea birds.
Dist pr log 116 Knots

November 4th, 1795
[Course WBS½S, W¾S. Wind EBN]
Moderate breezes & pleasant weather. Caulker & Carpenter steadily employ'd, caulking ye Main deck. Vast many tropic birds round. Seamen brushing furs, & repairing the riging.
Dist pr log 154 Knots

November 5th, 1795
[Course W¾S. Wind EBN]
Fresh breezes & clear weather. Seamen cleaning furs, Caulker as yesterday.
Lat Obsd 15°22′N Long 197°49′W
Dist pr log 174 Knots

November 6th, 1795
[Course W¾S. Wind EBN]

Brisk breezes & pleasant weather. All sail out. All hands employ'd cleaning furs, picking Oakum, Caulking decks etc. A following sea.
Dist pr log 177 Knots

November 7, 1795
[Course WBS½S. Wind ENE]
Fresh gales & pleasant, with a high sea, which caus'd ye Sloop to labour exceedingly. All hands variously employ'd. At 4 AM Split the squarsail & unbent it.
Dist pr log 187 Knots

November 8th, 1795
[Course SWBW. Wind EBS]
Lively breezes & pleasant with a rolling swell. Jib'd Sloop, finished caulking ye Main deck. Finish'd cleaning ye Furs. People employ'd cleaning out ye Forecastle.
Dist pr log 141 Knots

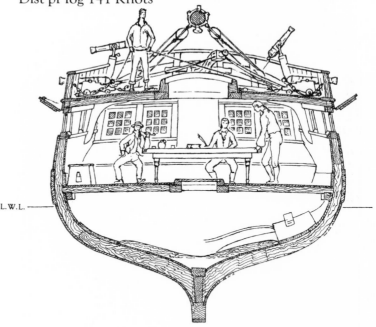

The *Union*: Cross section at 12 (see profile on p. 19) showing great cabin and bread room. (Hewitt Jackson)

November 9th, 1795
[Course W¾S. Wind NE]
Brisk breezes & pleasant weather with a tumbling swell. Caulkers caulking ye Forecastle. All hands employ'd breaking out the hold for boards & fresh water.
Dist pr log 100 Knots

November 10th, 1795
[Course West, WBS. Wind NE]
Lively breezes with a smooth sea. Finish'd caulking ye Fore peak. Seamen variously employ'd.
Lat Obsd 15°2'N Long 211°15'W
Dist pr log 179 Knots

November 11th, 1795
[Course WBS. Wind ENE]
Pleasant gales. Caulker, employ'd caulking ye Cabin flour

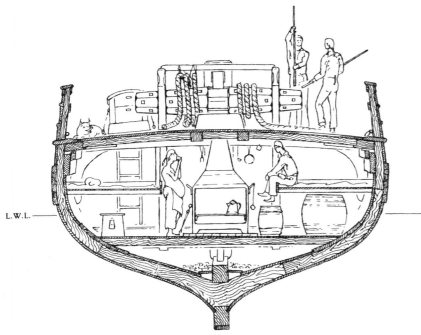

L.W.L.

The *Union*: Cross section at F (see profile on p. 19) showing windlass, galley and forecastle details. Note the all-important dog on the deck. (Hewitt Jackson)

deck. Saw a Booby, many porpoises round. Employ'd weaving mats.
Dist pr log 166 Knots

November 12th, 1795
[Course WBS. Wind EBN]
Hard squalls with heavy rain. At 1 PM In topsail, single reef'd ye Mains'l. All hands employ'd as Yesterday. At 10 In Squars'l. At 5 AM Set ye Squarsail & topsail. At 6 Split ye Squars'l, so bad, as to be irreparible, saw a flock of Gannets.
Dist pr log 169 Knots

November 13th, 1795
[Course W½S, up North of NNW, up ESE of SE, WSW. Wind NE, NNE, East]
Fresh breezes & squally with rain. Many Gannets & Booby's round. At 5 PM Saw the Isl's of Tinian, Saypan & Aguiguan, three of the Mariano Isl's,[54] extend'g from West to NWBW 10 leagues dist. At 6 PM The S. pt. of Aguinan bore WBS. At 7 Hove too under a double reef'd Mains'l & Jib. At Midnight wore to ye S'd. Ship'd a sea, & Stove in part of ye waste boards. At 8 Bore away & ran through between Tinian & Aguinan, distant from Tinian two miles.
Dist pr log 101 Knots

November 14th, 1795
[Course WBN½N. Wind ENE, NBE]
Moderate breezes & pleasant. At Meridian, Tinian bore E. 8 leagues, Aguag SE & Saypan NEBE. Set ye Fores'l for a Steering sail. Many tropic birds & Albacore round.
Dist pr log 114 Knots

November 15th, 1795
[Course WBN½N. Wind ENE, NNE]
Squally weather with plenty of rain. Seamen & tradesmen

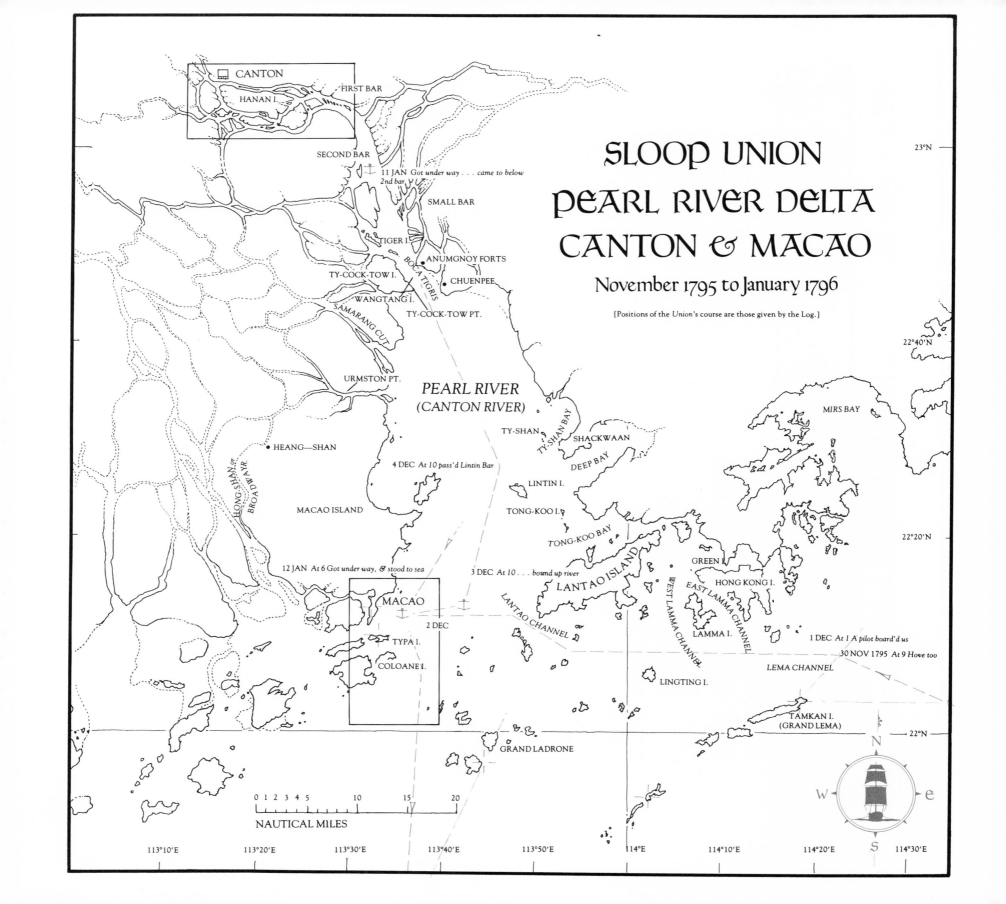

CANTON

FIRST BAR

HANAN I.

SECOND BAR

11 JAN *Got under way . . . came to below 2nd bar,*

SMALL BAR

TIGER I.

ANUMGNOY FORTS

TY-COCK-TOW I.

BOCA TIGRIS

CHUENPEE

WANGTANG I.

TY-COCK-TOW PT.

SAMARANG CUT

URMSTON PT.

PEARL RIVER
(CANTON RIVER)

TY-SHAN

MIRS BAY

TY-SHAN BAY

SHACKWAAN

DEEP BAY

HEANG—SHAN

4 DEC *At 10 pass'd Lintin Bar*

LINTIN I.

HONG SHAN or BROADWAYR.

TONG-KOO I.

MACAO ISLAND

TONG-KOO BAY

LANTAO ISLAND

GREEN I.

HONG KONG I.

WEST LAMMA CHANNEL

EAST LAMMA CHANNEL

12 JAN *At 6 Got under way, & stood to sea*

3 DEC *At 10 . . . bound up river*

LANTAO CHANNEL

LAMMA I.

1 DEC *At 1 A pilot board'd us*

30 NOV 1795 *At 9 Hove too*

MACAO

2 DEC

TYPA I.

COLOANE I.

LEMA CHANNEL

LINGTING I.

TAMKAN I.
(GRAND LEMA)

22°N

GRAND LADRONE

SLOOP UNION
PEARL RIVER DELTA
CANTON & MACAO

November 1795 to January 1796

[Positions of the *Union's* course are those given by the Log.]

23°N

22°40′N

22°20′N

0 1 2 3 4 5   10   15   20

NAUTICAL MILES

N

W   E

S

113°10′E   113°20′E   113°30′E   113°40′E   113°50′E   114°E   114°10′E   114°20′E   114°30′E

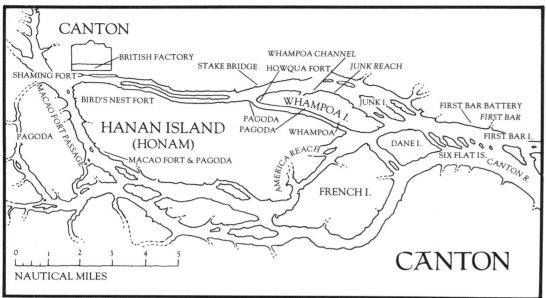

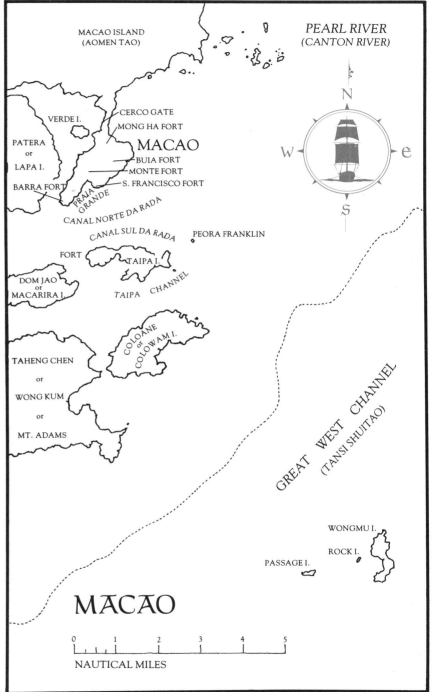

variously Employ'd, fish round. People employ'd cleaning
out the Fore Castle etc.
Lat Obsd 16°19′N Long 222°7′W
Dist pr log 119 Knots

November 16th, 1795
[Course WNW. Wind NE]
Gentle breezes & pleasant weather with a smooth sea.
Caulker caulking ye long boat. Seamen picking Oakum &
repairing ye riging.
Dist pr log 108 Knots

November 17th, 1795
[Course WNW. Wind ENE, variable]
Light winds & pleasant with a large swell from ye North'd.
At 2H 21′30″ Ap Time I had two sights of ye sun & moon
near't limbs, which gave long 142°58′E. Noon pleasant.
Caught a Bonnetto & Shark.
Dist pr log 70 Knots

November 18th, 1795
[Course WNW. Wind variable, EBN]
Light winds & pleasant warm weather with a rolling swell from ye North'd. All hands variously employ'd. Many fish, & Tropic Birds round.
Dist pr log 68 Knots

November 19th, 1795
[Course WNW. Wind ENE]
Moderate breezes & pleasant with a tumbling swell from ye North'd. At 1H 37'10'' I had three sights of ye sun & moon nearest limbs which determin'd ye Long to be 140°22'E. Porpoises round. Parted one of ye Cross trees, & fish'd it. All hands employ'd weaving Mats etc.
Dist pr log 100 Knots

November 20th, 1795
[Course WNW. Wind ENE]
Gentle breezes & fair weather with a large swell from ye North'd. At 2H 42'50'' Apparant time I had two sights of the sun & moon nearest Limbs, which determin'd ye Long to be 138°43'E. Scrap'd & paid ye bottom of ye Yawl.
Lat Obsd 19°14'N Long 229°11'W
Dist pr log 127 Knots

November 21st, 1795
[Course WNW. Wind NE]
Gentle gailes & pleasant. Sail maker on the old Mainsail. Three sights of ye sun & moon nearest, which determin'd the Long to be 135°15'0''E from London. All hands employ'd cleaning Small arms.
Dist pr log 127 Knots

November 22nd, 1795
[Course NWBW. Wind NE]
Moderate breezes & pleasant weather with a confus'd sea.

Albacore, and many birds round. Sail maker repair'g ye spare Mains'l.
Dist pr log 112 Knots

November 23rd, 1795
[Course NW½W, West. Wind NE, NNE]
Fresh breezes & pleasant. Unbent ye Old Mainsail, & bent another. Many fish round, but are very shy. Painted ye Yawl. Billy repair'g ye MSail. Mounted two fourpounders.
Dist pr log 130 Knots

November 24th, 1795
[Course WBN, West. Wind NE, WBS]
Brisk breezes with dark low'ry weather & rain. Albacore round. Split ye Topsail. Unbent it & brought another too. Sailmaker repari'g the Old one.
Dist pr log 135 Knots

November 25th, 1795
[Course WBN, West. Wind NBE, NE]
Fresh gales attend'd with dark rainy weather. Skip Jack & Albacore round. At 11 PM Hove too under a double reef'd Mainsail & jib. At 6 AM Weather as before. Bore away to West'd & set all sail. Saw a Man of war bird.
Dist pr log 114 Knots

November 26th, 1795
[Course West, NNW. Wind NE, West]
Lively breezes with dark rainy weather. At 6 PM Double reef'd ye Mains'l. At 5 Out reefs. Saw a flock of ducks & a Hawke.
Lat Obsd 21°49'N
Dist pr log 128 Knots

November 27th, 1795
[Course WNW, West. Wind NBE, NE]

Fresh gales with dark rainy weather. At 6 PM Short'd sail. Down Yards. At 11 Hove too under a double reef'd Mains'l & foresail. At ½ past Saw ye Isles of Bottle Toba-go Lema[55] bear'g NBE 3 leag's. At 6 Saw ye Island of Formosa bear'g W½S. At 10 Abrest ye South't pt. within 2 Miles. At Noon ye South pt bore E½S, Six leagues.
Dist pr log 114 Knots

November 28th, 1795
[Course West, WBS. Wind NE, NW]
Gentle breezes & pleasant. Passed many strong tide rips, a number of smoaks on shore. **Mounted ye quarter deck** guns. Unbent ye Old Mains'l & brought another too. At 10 PM Split ye Mainsail; Sail maker reparing it. At 5 AM Set ye Mainsail. Strong gales with a mountanious sea. Painted ye Cannon. Saw a peice of wood adrift.
Dist pr log 104 Knots

November 29th, 1795
[Course WNW, West. Wind NBE, NE, ENE]
Strong gales & hazy weather with a mountanious sea. Midnight do. weather. Sound'd in 40 fm water. At 4 AM Sound'd, 37 fm fine grey sand. At 6 Above 40 sail of fisher-man in sight. A very high sea runing.
Dist pr log 154 Knots

November 30th, 1795
[Course West; Up NNE of North, drift 3 miles pr H.; up NE of NNE, drift 2 mi pr H. Wind ENE, North]
Heavy gales with a high sea. Many Chinese fishing boats laying too in sight. At 1 PM Hove too, with our head to ye North'd. At 4 bore away, more moderate. At 7 lay too, with our head as before. Midnight fresh breezes & pleas-ant. Soundings from 25 to 30 fm soft mud. At 1 AM wore to ye south'd. At 3 Bore away to ye West'd. At 7 Saw ye Grand Lema[56] bear'g west five leagues. At 9 Hove too for a

pilot, fir'd a gun & hoisted ye Colours. 20 fm water. Noon hazy, a pilot boat in sight.
Lat Obsd 22°15'N
Dist pr log 42 Knots

December 1st, 1795
[Wind NE, North]
Lively breezes. At Meridian ye Grand Lema bore SWBS 2½ leagues, Linting WBS. At 1 A pilot board'd us, & I agreed with him for 40 dollars, to carry ye Sloop to Macao roads.[57] At 2 He took charge, made all sail & bore away to ye West'd. At 9 Came too in Macao roads, in 4½ fm water, muddy bottom, the Fort at Macao bearing WBN 2 leagues. Typa Island SW. S Ends.

December 2nd, 1795
[Wind North'ly, NBW]
Pleasant breezes. At daylight hove out ye boats, & hog'd ye Barnacles of ye bottom. Scrap'd & Slush'd down ye mast. At 9 I went on shore to visit the Governor, & pro-cure a river pilot. I was met at the landing by a number of ye English Supercargoes, who very politely went with me to Governors house & likewise put me in a way how to proceed in procuring a pilot. I met with no difficulty in procuring a pilot, & getting what refreshment I stood in need of.

December 3rd, 1795
[Wind NE]
Fine pleasant weather. At 2 PM I left Macao & at 5 Ar-riv'd on board, ye pilot came on board, & took charge. A Macao boat came along side & I sold a small Anchor for 13 dollars. At 10 Got under way, bound up the river.[58] At 11 Came too, with ye small bower.

December 4th, 1795
[Wind SSE]

Fresh breezes & pleasant. At 1 Came to Sail. At 10 pass'd Lintin bar, spoke a Ship bound to Newyork, Capt. Forrester. Put some letters on board of him. Pass'd a vast quantity of Chinese fishing boats.

December 5th, 1795
[Wind South]
Pleasant breezes. At 9 PM It being dark, We came to anchor below the Shiping. So Ends with fine pleasant weather.

December 6th, 1795
[Wind ESE]
Pleasant. At daylight Weigh'd [anchor] and ran up above ye Shiping, & moor'd with ½ a Cable each way. Found riding here 7 Sail of American ships & 8 or 10 of other Nations. People employ'd Cackling ye Cables & striping the Sloop. I went to Canton & return'd in the evening with a number of Chinese merchants, to look at the skins.[59] *Many visitors on board. Was sorry to find that sea otter skins fell 100 dollars in value since I was here in the* Columbia *which is a disastrous circumstance to my voyage. However, as fortune is fickle it's no use to repine at our ill luck. Pleasant weather generally. We laid in this river till the 12th Jan'y 1796, during which time I gave the sloop a complete over haul. Sold the cargo tolerable well so as to make a saving voyage for the owners. Invested the return in nankeins[60] & pelts which enabled me to take some freight & French passenger to the Isle de France* [Mauritius] *which helped the voyage very much. A number of my people having took the samll pox at Canton* [I] *was obliged to leave them behind as 'tis death for any commander to take the small pox to Mauritius knowlingly.*

December 7th, 1795
[Wind ESE]
Pleasant agreeable weather. Purchas'd a quantity of riging & Blocks from ye Swedes, also a bb [barrel] of Tar. Hir'd a

Cooper to repair the water Casks, & a Blacksmith to repair our Iron work. So Ends with pleasant weather. *Moored in ye River of Canton.*

December 8th, 1795
[Wind NNE]
Pleasant agreeable weather. All hands employ'd, breaking out the hold & repairing riging & sails.

December 9th, 1795
[Wind NNE]
Fine pleasant weather. Carpenter on ye Channels. Caulker on ye Sloops sides. Seamen on ye riging. So Ends.

December 10th, 1795
[Wind NE]
Weather ye same as Yesterday. All hands employ'd in there various departments. So ends.

December 11th, 1795
[Wind NNE]
Pleasant agreeable weather. Carpenter fitting a New topmast. Sail maker making a New Top Gt. Sail.

December 12th, 1795
[Wind NE]
Still pleasant. Land'd the ballace [ballast]. Seamen &

THE *UNION* NEARING THE BOCA TIGRIS AT THE MOUTH OF THE PEARL RIVER ON THE SOUTH COAST OF CHINA (opposite)

On 4 December 1795, the *Union* with its load of furs, approached the Boca Tigris, having "at 10 pass'd Lintin bar, spoke a Ship bound to Newyork, Capt. Forrester. Put some letters on board him. Passed a vast quantity of Chinese fishing boats." In Canton, Boit was dismayed to find the price of otter skins much reduced since his last voyage. He added in his Remarks: "*However, as fortune is fickle it's no use to repine at our ill luck.*"

tradesmen employ'd in there various departments.

December 13th, 1795
[Wind NNE]
Pleasant weather. Finish'd Caulking. Seamen upon the riging & scraping ye Sides. Sail maker as yesterday.

December 14th, 1795
[Wind NNE]
Pleasant. Hog'd Ship & clean'd ye bottom. Some straping blocks. Sail maker as yesterday.

December 15th, 1795
[Wind NNE]
Pleasant. Finish'd the repairs of the riging. All hands employ'd Bootoping & scraping.

December 16th, 1795
[Wind NE]
Cloudy weather attend'd with small showers of rain. Pay'd the sides & bends. Carpenter making a new Cross jack y'd.

December 17th, 1795
[Wind NNE]
Cloudy disagreeable weather. Got ye hold ready for receiving Cargo. Carpenter upon the Spars.

December 18th, 1795
[Wind NBE]
Rainy disagreeable weather. Seamen straping blocks. Tradesmen in there departments.

December 19th, 1795
[Wind North]
Fine pleasant weather. I came down from Canton. The Grand Hoppo[61] came down & measur'd ye Sloop. All hands variously emp'd.

December 20th, 1795
[Wind NNE]
Pleasant weather. Employ'd painting the Sloop, & blacking the Spars, finish'd the Sails.

December 21st, 1795
[Wind NE]
Still pleasant. Got the riging over head. Employ'd painting & various other jobs. So Ends.

December 22nd, 1795
[Wind NNE]
Got the yards at work & Set up ye riging, finish'd painting. Employ'd variously.

December 23rd, 1795
[Wind NE]
Pleasant agreeable weather. Seamen & tradesmen variously Employ'd. Deliver'd a long boat load of wood to ye *Fliza.*

December 24th, 1795
[Wind NBE]
Still pleasant. A Chop came down from Canton for ye Furs, I having sold them to Mr. Monqua, one of the Hong merchants. Deliver'd the Cargo & sent an Officer & two men to guard them.

December 25th, 1795
[Wind NE]
Pleasant weather. Carpenter putting up bulkheads in the Hold. Seamen upon the riging. So Ends.

December 26th, 1795
[Wind NNE]
Pleasant. The Chinese stole both boats from along side owing to ye Negligence of the watch. Gave the hoppo

man 20 doll'r for to recover them. Bought a small boat for 25 doll'r.

December 27th, 1795
[Wind NBE]
Pleasant. The Hoppo man brought the boats. Made the watch pay the expense, which amounted to 30 doll'r. Sold the long boat for 65 dollars to Capt. Reed.

December 28th, 1795
[Wind North]
Pleasant. I agreed with Mess'r John Howell & Co., Compadore, for sea Stock [cargo] for to be deliver'd by the Ship *John Jay* below the Boca. A Chop came along side, laden with Sugar, Nankeen & China, dischar'd her & stow'd it away.

December 29th, 1795
[Wind NBE]
Pleasant. Sent four of the people to Canton, to be innoculated for ye small pox. Capt. Howell of ye *America*, gave me 15 Casks water.

December 30th, 1795
[Wind NE]
Pleasant, people matting the hold, a Chop came along side, loaded with Sugar, Nankeen, & China. So Ends.

December 31st, 1795
[Wind North]
Discharg'd the Chop & stow'd it away. Clear'd hawser. Found the small Bower [anchor line], cut ½ of by ye Chinese, bore it in.

January 1st, 1796
[Wind ENE]
Fine pleasant weather. Seamen & tradesmen employ'd in there various departments. So ends.

January 2nd, 1796
[Wind NE]
Pleasant weather. Bent the sails. Rec'd on board two Bullocks, & a quantity of flour, as a present, from the Grand Hoppo.

January 3rd, 1796
[Wind ENE]
Pleasant. People employ'd making wads & Cartridges. S Ends.

January 4th, 1796
[Wind NNE]
Pleasant. Seamen cleaning muskets and Pistols. Tradesmen in there various departments.

January 5th, 1796
[Wind NE]
Pleasant weather. All hands variously employ'd. So ends.

January 6th, 1796
[Wind EBN]
A Chop Came down from Canton, borrow'd 10 Lascars from ye *Anna Country* Ship.

January 7th, 1796
[Wind NE]
Pleasant. Sent all the people to Canton on liberty. Discharg'ed the Chop & stow'd it [cargo] away. Sent ye Lascars on board there own Ship.

January 8th, 1796
[Wind ENE]
Pleasant. The Chow chow Chop[62] came along side &

brought all the Liberty people. Discharg'd ye Chop & Stow'd ye goods away.

January 9th, 1796
[Wind NNE]
Pleasant. Employ'd unmooring & getting ready for Sea. Edward Usher, the Carpenter, ran away, & took with him his Cloaths & broad Axe. So Ends.

January 10th, 1796
[Wind NBE]
Unmoor'd, & dropt below the fleet. Employ'd clearing decks. Three french gentlemen came on board, to take passage, to the Isle of france. I settled my business at Canton. Got my [clearance] Grand Chop, & came down on board.

Canton
to
Boston, Massachusetts

11 January to 8 July 1796

January 11th, 1796
[Wind ENE]
Fine pleasant weather. Got under way in company, with ye Ship *John Jay* & [at] 6 Came to below 2d bar.

January 12th, 1796
[Wind NNE]
Pleasant agreeable weather with a fresh breeze, rec'd on board our Stock from the *John Jay*, which her Compadore supply'd us with. At 6 PM got under way, in company with ye *Jay* & pass'd through the Boca Tigris & was join'd by Ships *India Packet*, *Eliza*, & *Dispatch*, Capts. Harris, Gibaut & Caswell. Made all sail & stood towards Macao roads. I was oblig'd to discharge & leave behind My people who was down with the Small pox, it not being possible to take them to ye Mauritius, it being death to any Comman-

der, who knowingly takes that disorder there. At 6 All ye fleet[63] came too in Macao roads, the Ship *Sampson*, Capt. Seward, of New York pass'd us bound out. We all met on board of *Eliza*, & agreed to keep Company through ye China Sea, & appoint'd Capt. Gibaut our Commadore. At 6 Got under way, & stood to sea. At 10 We where abrest the Grand Ladrone.[64]
N.B. [this entry] contains 36 hours.

January 13th, 1796
[Course SSE, SBE, SBE½E. Wind NE]
Fresh gales with showers of rain. At Meridian the Grand Ladrone bore NNE 6 or 7 leagues, from which I take my departure, it lying in Lat 21°57′N & Long 113°58′E. Latter part strong gales, still in company with the fleet. At 8 Down Yards.
Dist pr log 154 Knots.

January 14th, 1796
[Course SBE½E, South, SBE. Wind NNE, ENE]
Strong gales & thick weather. At 2 PM double reef'd the Mains'l. In foresail. A high sea runing. Split the Mains'l. Unbent it and brought another too. The Fleet all in company.
Dist pr log 160 Knots

January 15th, 1796
[Course SBE, SWBS. Wind NE]
Moderate breezes, sent up the Yards & set all sail & 10 Hove too and sound'd, but got no bottom. A swell from the Eastward. Pulo Condore bears from Sapata S61°W, 162Mi.
Lat Obsd 14°54'N Long 114°1'E
Dist pr log 139 Knots

January 16th, 1796
[Course SWBW. Wind ENE]
Steady breezes & pleasant weather. All hands variously employ'd. All sail out. Unbent the Old mainsail & brought another too. Seamen employ'd on ye riging etc.
Dist pr log 139 Knots

January 17th, 1796
[Course SWBS, SE, SSW. Wind ENE, NE]
Gentle breezes & very pleasant. Set up the riging. Bore up, & spoke ye Commodore. At 3 AM Set the squarsail. All hands employ'd on the riging etc. Still in company with the fleet. Pulo Sapata⁶⁵ bears S58°W Dist 123 miles.
Dist pr log 142 Knots

January 18th, 1796
[Course SSW, SWBS, WBS. Wind NNE]
Fresh gales with a high sea. At 2H 14'40'' Ap. time by two sights of ye sun & moon I determin'd ye Long to be

111°38'E. of London. Jib'd ship & split the squarsail. Still in company with fleet. At 11 Got bott'm in 25 fm water. Sandy bottom.
Dist pr log 157 Knots

January 19th, 1796
[Course SW, SWBS, West, SSW. Wind NE]
Brisk breezes, round'd too & got bottom with 25 fm line, brown sand. By two sights of the sun & moon, I determin'd the Long to be 109°2'40''E. Still in company with the fleet. Pulo Aore bears S30°W dist 360 Miles.

January 20th, 1796
[Course S½W, South, SBW. Wind NNE]
Squally with rain. At meridian got bottom in 19 fm water. Spoke the Commodore. All sail out. A strange sail to ye North'd.
Lat Obsd 5°13'N Long 107°44'E
Dist pr log 166 Knots

January 21st, 1796
[Course SSW, SWBS. Wind NE, NNE]
Gentle breezes & pleasant weather. Sound'd & got bottom with 44 fm line, Soft mud. At 4 The Ship *Sampson*, Capt. Seward join'd the fleet from Canton. Found the Jib stay parted, employ'd repairing of it, in company with ye fleet.
Dist pr log 155 Knots

January 22nd, 1796
[Course SBE, SSE. Wind NNE, ENE]
Pleasant breezes. At 1 PM Saw the Islands of Pulo Timon, Pissang, & Aore, bear'g from S. to West. At 6 Pulo Aore bore NWBW 9 leagues. Still in company with the fleet. All sail out. Pass'd much drift wood.
Dist pr log 153 Knots

January 23rd, 1796
[Course SBE, South, SWBS. Wind ENE, NE]
Gentle breezes with a smooth sea. 19 fm water. At 3 AM, Saw the Island of Pulo Taya bear'g WBS 2 or 3 leagues. At 8 The Seven Islands, extend'd from ENE to SE 4 or 5 leagues. Soundings 10 fm Clay. Noon rainy, saw Banca Isle.⁶⁶
Dist pr log 109 Knots

January 24th, 1796
[Course SSW, SW, SWBS. Wind NNE, NEBN]
Light breezes with rain squalls. Soundings from 10 to 15 fm Clay. A Strong tide, setting to the South & East'd. Came too in 19 fm water, with the small bower. At 2 The Sloop drop't let go the best bower, At 6 Got under way in company with ye fleet, saw Monopin hill bear'g SE & the Sumatra shore from NW to WSW 3 or 4 leagues. Pass'd a Ship & many proas [native boats].
Dist pr log 60 Knots

January 25th, 1796
[Course SEBE, EBS, ESE. Wind NE]
Steady breezes & pleasant. At 1 PM having got to the West'd of Fred. Hendrick we bore away through the straits of Banca⁶⁷ [Selat Gelasa] pass'd a Ship & many Proas. At 6 The 4th Pt. bore SEBE. At 7 The fleet came to anchor in 12 fm water. Midnight rainy. At 6 Hove up & came to sail in company with the fleet & stood down the Straits. At Meridian saw 1st pt.
Dist pr log 75 Knots

January 26th, 1796
[Course SSE, SEBE, ESE. Wind NNE]
Pleasant breezes with strong tides. At 5 pass'd 5th Pt. within 3 mile & bore away to the South'd. Soundings from 6 to 10 fm. At 6 The Isle of Lucepara bore NEBE 4 or 5

mile. Midnight pleasant, 10 fm water. All hands variously employ'd.
Lat Obsd 4°26'S
Dist pr log 110 Knots

January 27th, 1796
[Course SBW½W, SBE, NWBN. Wind NW, SW]
Light winds, attend'd with much thunder & Lightning over Sumatra. Soundings from 10 to 15 fm water. At 7 PM The tide being against us, we came too in company with the Fleet. At 3 AM Got under way. Saw the Sumatra shore bear'g SSW. Two high lumps looking like Isl's bore SSW½W to WBS. The Sisters bear'g SW½S, 8 or 10 leagues to be seen from the Mast head.
Dist pr log 30 Knots

January 28th, 1796
[Course SSW½W]
Light winds & pleasant weather with a remarkable smooth sea. Sound'g from 8 to 10 fm. Hoisted out the Yawl & I went on board the *John Jay*. Much thunder & Lightning over Sumatra. At 8 PM Came too in company with ye fleet. At 4 AM Got under way. At 5 Saw ye Sisters bear'g SW½S 3 or 4 leagues. At 8 Pass'd the Sisters within 2 mile of them, and Stood for North Isle *where we intend to fill up with water.*

January 29th, 1796
[Course SWBS, SW. Wind NW, WBN]
Light winds & pleasant with strong currants. Setting to the SE. At 6 PM Pt St. Nicol bore SWBS 6 or 7 leagues. At 7 Came too in 12 fm water. Midnight dark & rainy. At 5 AM Got under way, in company with the fleet. At 8 saw N. Isle bear'g SW & a large Ship laying in ye road. We soon found it to be a Sweedish ship. At 9 Came too in North Isle roads.⁶⁸ Noon pleasant, sent a boat after water. *Light airs, pleasant weather & strong tides setting to the SE. At*

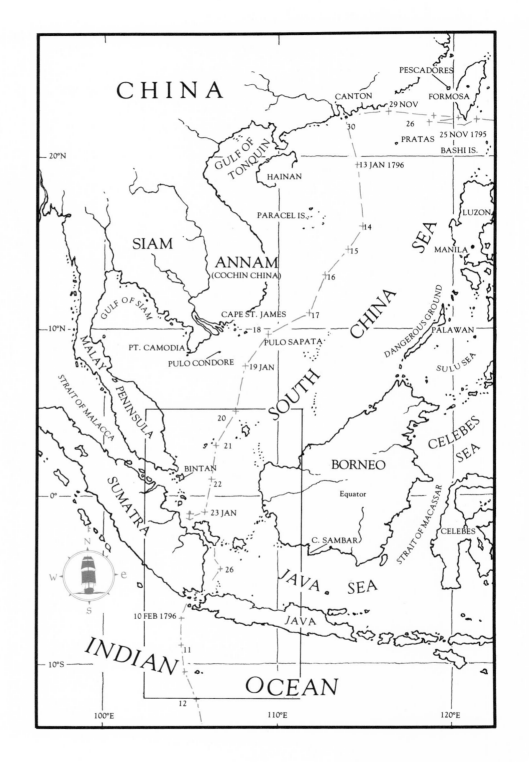

SLOOP UNION
POSITIONS & COURSE
THROUGH
SOUTH CHINA SEA
&
SUNDA STRAIT

November 1795 to February 1796

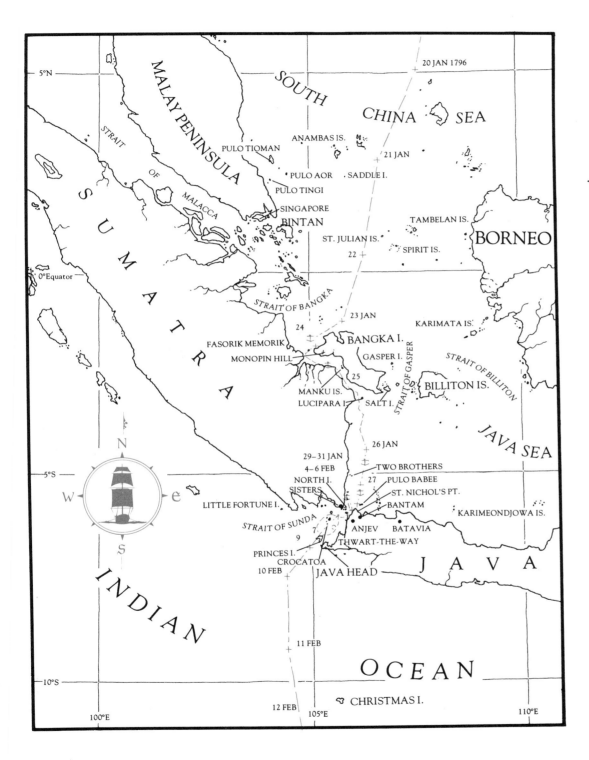

SLOOP UNION
POSITIONS & COURSE
THROUGH
THE STRAITS
OF
BANGKA AND SUNDA

January to February 1796

97

6 PM St. Nicholas on the Isle of Java bore SWBS 7 leagues. At 10 came too in the Roads of North Isle & commenc'd watering. Many Malays on the beach.
Dist pr log 38 Knots

January 30th, 1796
Light variable winds with some showers. Our boat return'd with a load of water. Employ'd starting it in the hold, & repair'g the riging. Sent the boat on shore after more water. At 4 She return'd. 3 Malay Pro'as & a Stray Ship in the Offing. Standing into the roads. Noon warm & Sultry.

January 31st, 1796
Fine, pleasant weather. *Having fill'd up our water this day got underway & stood for the Strait of Sunda.* [69] At 1 PM The Sweed got under way, but the wind dying, she soon came too again. The Malay proas came into the roads, and inform'd us by letters from Batavia, that the french had got possession of the Cape of Good Hope. At 4 AM We got under way in company with the fleet. The Ship that was in sight proved to be a french Sloop of war, mounting 34 Guns. She examin'd us all & let us pass.

February 1st, 1796
[Wind from WNW to SWS]
Light breezes & pleasant weather. At 6 PM The SE point of Crocatore [70] SEBE, the NW pt. WBS. Saw a sail, standing towards us. At 10 The French Sloop of war Spoke her, & let her pass. She hoisted American colours.

February 2nd, 1796
[Wind WNW]
Hard squalls with heavy rain & a high sea. A Strong currant setting to the North'd & Eastward. The Ships *John Jay* & India packet, weather'd away Princes Isle & bore away to the South'd. At 6 PM The S. pt. of Princes Isle bore SW 5 or 6 leagues, the W. pt. of Crocatore NW½N. Midnight dark & squally. Fresh winds, turning to windward. Endeavouring to weather princes Isle.

February 3rd, 1796
Heavy squalls of wind & rain with a high sea & a strong currant setting to ye N & E. At 6 PM Princes Isle [71] bore SWBW. TK to the North'd. At 9 TK to the East'd. Midnight exceedingly squally with rain. At 2 AM TK to the North, thick & rainy. At 8 More clear, one sail in sight, the S. pt of Crocatore bore NNW 4 leag. Noon squally five sail in sight.

February 4th, 1796
[Wind WNW]
Heavy squalls with rain & a high sea with a strong currant to East'd. At 5 PM Stood over; under the East end of Tamineis Isle, & came too in 17 fm water, sand & Clay, in company with the Sweedish Ship, & *Samsson*, the S. pt of Crockatore SSW & the S. pt of Tamn'e WBS. I went on board the *Sampson*, & was inform'd that the Sweedish Ship had run down the *Dispatch* of Boston & carried away her Bowsprit & Cutwater, & the *Samspon* had run down the *Eliza* & carried away his Jib boom & Sprits'l yard.

February 5th, 1796
[Wind West]
Fresh gales with heavy rain squalls. All hands variously employ'd. The winds variable. At 6 AM Hove up the Anchor, & run under the Sweeds quarter & came too in 12 fm water. Sent the Yawl, with the boats crew on shore at St. Taminis. At 8 She return'd load'd with Cocoanuts.

February 6th, 1796
[Wind from West to WNW]
Light breezes with heavy showers of rain, laying wind bound. Hove in slack Cable. At 5 AM got under way in

company with the *Sampson* & *Sweed* & stood to the E. of Crockatore. Light winds. Some showers. Noon pleasant, abrest Crocatore Isle.

February 7th, 1796
[Wind West, variable]
Light winds with exceeding strong currants to the S & E. At 6 PM The S. pt. of Princes Isle bore SW½W, the peak of Crocatore N½E, the W'd Extreme NNW. At 3 Set the squars'l, at 4 In ditto. Strong South East currants. Noon the W. pt. of Princes Isle bore S., the peak of Crockatore NBE.
Lat Obsd 6°16′S

February 8th, 1796
[Wind NNW]
Moderate breezes & pleasant, the *Sweed* & *Sampson* in sight to the E. At 6 Princes Isle bore SBW & the Peak of Crocatore NBE. At 8 Heavy squalls. At 6 TK to ye North'd. At 7 Out reefs & set all sail, four Ships in sight.

February 9th, 1796
Light breezes & pleasant. Saw the Ship *dispatch* with a jury bowsprit out, & the *Commodore* to the North'd. At 6 the S. pt of Crocatore bore E½S, Stone Isle NE 3 miles. Stand'g to the SW. Light winds, weather'd away the W'd. pt. of Princes Isle in company with ye *Commodore, Dispatch,* & *Sampson,* the *Sweed* could not weather. Noon Java Head bore SEBS 3 or 4 leagues. *At length, thank God, we weather'd away of Princes Isle in Co with* [the rest] *of the fleet.*

February 10th, 1796
[Course South, SW, SBE. Wind WSW, West, SW]
Light winds & pleasant, with a strong currant to the S & E. At 5 The *Sampson* TK She not being able to weather

prin's Isle. At 6 PM Java head bore ESE 4 or 5 leagues. The W. pt. of Princes Isle EBN½N. Midnight squally. Spoke the Ship *Eliza,* Capt. Gibaut. People employ'd unbending the Cables & Stowing the Anchors. Some fish & Birds round.
Lat Obsd 7°41′S
Dist pr log 53 Knots

February 11th, 1796
[Course South, S½E, SBW. Wind WSW]
Steady breezes & pleasant with a smooth sea. All hands employ'd knoting yarns & repair'g the riging. Spoke ye *Dispatch.* Latter part fresh breezes, in top g[allan]t Sail. Many boobies round.
Lat Obsd 9°26′S Long 104°30′E
Dist pr log 91 Knots

February 12th, 1796
[Course South, SBW, SSW. Wind WSW, WBS, West]
Brisk winds & cloudy, in company with the *Dispatch* of Boston. At 5 PM Saw Chrismas Isle[72] bear'g SBW 12 leag. At 6 The S. pt. bore SBW½W 7 or 8 leags. At 5 PM Chrismas Isle bore NW. People employ'd making sinnett & points etc.
Dist pr log 111 Knots

February 13th, 1796
[Course SEBS½S, South. Wind SWBS, WSW]
Light winds & pleasant weather with a large swell from the South'd. All hands variously employ'd. At 8 Down Top G[allan]t Yard, the *Dispatch* in sight to the East'd.
Dist pr log 78 Knots

February 14th, 1796
[Course SBE½E, SSE. Wind SW, SWBS]
Moderate breezes & pleasant weather. All hands variously employ'd, some small Dolphin round. Latter part fresh

breezes with a head beat Sea. At 10 AM In flying jib. The *Dispatch* in sight to leeward.
Dist pr log 82 Knots

February 15th, 1796
[Course S½E, South. Wind WSW, SWBW]
Brisk breezes with a head beat sea. By the Mean of three distan's of the sun & moon nearest limbs, I determin'd the Long to be 105°52′15″ E. of Green'. Midnight ditto, do. The *Dispatch* out of sight to leeward. A Ship in sight which I take to be the *Sampson*. Dolphins round.
Dist pr log 72 Knots

February 16th, 1796
[Course S½E, South. Wind SWBW, WSW]
Brisk breezes & pleasant weather with a head beat sea. Down flying Jib, fitt'd New topsail haulyards & flying jib sheets the Old ones being worn out. Midnight flattering with rain. Latter part as before, with no likelyhood of a change for the better. Some Men of war birds on the wing. A ship in sight to leeward.
Dist pr log 77 Knots

February 17th, 1796
[Course South, SBW. Wind SWBW, WSW]
Steady breezes with a high head beat sea. At 5 AM Set all sail. Dolphin & Men of war birds round. A Ship in sight to leeward.
Dist pr log 69 Knots

February 18th, 1796
[Course South, SBE, West. Wind SWBW, SW, SSW]
Moderate breezes & pleasant, employ'd making Hanks & cleaning Muskets. Dolphin round. Employ'd picking Oakum. The Ship *Dispatch* in sight to leeward.
Dist pr log 52 Knots

February 19th, 1796
[Course SBE, SSE. Wind SWBW, SW]
Light winds & pleasant with a head beat sea. Employ'd picking Oakum. At 8 PM TK to the Westward. Latter part pleasant with a damn'd plenty of rain. People variously Employ'd. The *Dispatch* in sight to leeward.
Dist pr log 66 Knots

February 20th, 1796
[Course WNW, WBN, WBS. Wind SW, SBW, SBE]
Squally with rain. At 2 PM In fly'g jib. At 5 Set the Squarsail. Split the tops'l, unbent it, & brought another too. All hands employ'd on the repairs of the Sails & riging.
Lat Obsd 17°14′S Long 104°54′E
Dist pr log 107 Knots

February 21st, 1796
[Course W½S, WBS. Wind SBE]
Fresh gales & squally with rain & a tumbling sea. Many flying fish round. Saw a Man of war bird. At 5 AM Set the flying jib. Sail maker to work on the Spare sails. Pass'd many strong tide rips.
Dist pr log 146 Knots

February 22nd, 1796
[Course W¾S, WBN, West. Wind South, SSW, SBW]
Lively breezes with frequent showers with a head beat sea. Parted the strap of the Fore stay. Saw a Man of war bird. Midnight squally, out all sail. Albacore round. All hands employ'd fitting ye Forestay & Setting up the riging. Slush'd the Mast.
Dist pr log 120 Knots

February 23rd, 1796
[Course West, WBS, WSW. Wind SBW, South, SSE]
Lively breezes with frequent rain squalls. Set up the riging

fore & aft. Latter part pleasant. Sent up the top gall't Yard & set the sail. Sail maker repair'g the Spare sails.
Dist pr log 118 Knots

February 24th, 1796
[Course West, WBS, W½S. Wind SBW, South, SBE]
Fresh breezes & pleasant with a smooth sea. All sail out. People variously Emp'd. Latter part as before. Men of War & tropic birds round.
Dist pr log 128 Knots

February 25th, 1796
[Course West, WBS. Wind South, SBE, SSE]
Steady breezes & pleasant weather, all hands variously employ'd. Midnight exceeding pleasant. Unbent the flying Jib to repair. Employ'd pick'g Oakum.
Lat Obsd 18°13′S Long 93°47′E
Dist pr log 133 Knots

February 26th, 1796
[Course W½S, West. Wind SE, ESE]
Steady breezes & pleasant. Sail maker repair'g the Spare sails. Seamen variously employ'd. Unbent the Mainsail to repair, & brought another too. Got the Bower Anchor in to fresh pud[din]g.
Dist pr log 135 Knots

February 27th, 1796
[Course West. Wind SE, EBS]
Fresh breezes with frequent rain squalls. Employ'd fresh puddening the rings of the Bower Anchors. Split the Topsail, unbent it & brought another too. Sail maker repair'g the Spare Mainsail.
Dist pr log 181 Knots

February 28th, 1796
[Course West. Wind ESE]

Lively breezes with frequent rain squalls. Employ'd breaking out the Hold for fresh water. Sailmaker repair'g the Spare Mainsail etc.
Dist pr log 157 Knots

February 29th, 1796
[Course West. Wind SE, ESE]
Fresh gales with many flying clouds. Seamen variously Emp'd. Latter part fresh gales, found both trussell trees[73] at the Mast head parted, under the riging so as not to be come at without unriging. Noon fresh breezes & cloudy.
Dist pr log 178 Knots

March 1st, 1796
[Course W½S. Wind SEBE, ESE]
Fresh breezes & pleasant. Sent down the Topsail & top gall't Yard, and lash'd the Heel of the Topmast to the Mast head. Fitted slings to the Cross jack Yard. Splic'd the Small bower Cable, where it had been chafed, & various other jobs.
Lat Obsd 19°5′S Long 79°37′E
Dist pr log 157 KNots

March 2nd, 1796
[Course West. Wind SEBE, EBS]
Steady breezes. Many Tropic Birds round. By two sights of the sun & moon Nearest limbs, I determin'd the Long to be 80°38′45″E.
Dist pr log 158 Knots

March 3rd, 1796
[Course West. Wind ESE]
Fresh breezes & cloudy. Sailmaker repair'g the Old Mainsail. Latter part as before, Seamen & tradesmen variously employ'd in there departments.
Dist pr log 153 Knots

March 4th, 1796
[Course WBN½N, WBN. Wind EBS]
Fresh breezes & pleasant. Pep'l employ'd making Cable bends, points etc. Sail maker on the Old mainsail. Employ'd Spin'g Yarns, picking Oakum etc. Finish'd repairing the Mainsail.
Dist pr log 148 Knots

March 5th, 1796
[Course W½N. Wind EBS]
Lively breezes & pleasant. Seamen Spining Yarns & picking Oakum. Sailmaker on the Old Mainsail etc. Unbent the Squarsail to repair, & bent the Mainsail in its stead. Employ'd steadily as before.
Lat Obsd 19°35′S Long 68°38′E
Dist pr log 166 Knots

March 6th, 1796
[Course West, W½N. Wind EBS]
Steady breezes & pleasant. Seamen spin'g Yarns & picking Oakum etc. Squally. Set the Squarsail. Unbent ye topsail to repair, & Set the top Gall't jack. Sailmaker repair'g the Tops'l. Saw two Sea Guls, flying round.
Dist pr log 154 Knots

March 7th, 1796
[Course WBN. Wind ESE]
Gentle breezes with flying clouds. Seamen Spining Yarns. Sail maker repair'g the Topsail. Bent & set the topsail. Saw a flock of Land birds. Employ'd as before. Flying clouds with a smooth sea.
Dist pr log 142 Knots

March 8th, 1796
[Course WNW, WBN. Wind ESE]
Saw sevrall flock sea larks. Fresh breezes & cloudy weather.

Employ'd spining Yarns & pricking Spunyarn etc.
Dist pr log 146 Knots

March 9th, 1796
[Course WBN. Wind EBS]
Gentle breezes & pleasant weather, many birds flying round. Employ'd as yester'y.
Dist pr log 146 Knots

March 10th, 1796
[Course WBN½N, West. Wind ESE, SE]
Brisk, pleasant weather and fresh trades. Have experienced a windward current. Plenty of birds & porpoises round. At 1 AM saw the Isle of Martinique extend'g from W to WSW, 4 or 5 leagues. At 5 AM Saw the Isle of Rodirigue Extending from W to SWS 4 or 5 leagues. At 7 Unbent the Old sails & bent a fresh suit.
Lat Obsd 19°43′S Long 62°45′E
Dist pr log 141 Knots

March 11th, 1796
[Course West, WBN. Wind SEBE]
Fresh winds with frequent rain squalls. All hands variously Employ'd. Sail maker repair'g the Old sails. Seamen picking Oakum & drawing Shot from ye Guns. Mauritius 175 miles.
Dist pr log 136 Knots

March 12th, 1796
[Course WNW. Wind ESE, NE]
Light winds with warm pleas't weather. Caught a bonnetto. All hands employ'd bending the Cables & scaling the Cannon.
Dist pr log 84 Knots

March 13th, 1796
[Course WNW, WBN½N. Wind ENE, SE]

Light winds & pleasant. Many birds round, people variously employ'd. Some fish round. Employ'd scrubing & clean'g the Boats.
Dist pr log 55 Knots

March 14th, 1796
[Course WBN, EBS. Wind SE, SBE]
Steady breezes. Saw the Isle of France[74] bear'g West, 12 Leagues. At 2 PM Saw Ronde Isle bear'g W½S. At 2 PM *France Isle bore W½S & the extreme of Mauritins from W to SWBW. Lay'd off & on to windward through the night with some squalls. At daylight bore off. At 8 AM abreast of Stagoes de Still. Stood between this last mentioned Isle de Ronde & Flat Isles. At 10 were abreast Port Louis. A pilot came on board & took charge. At meridian got safe to at anchor in Port Louis Harbour. I went on shore with the passengers. Found riding* [there] *a number of American sail & a great number of Danish & Sweedish & French merchantmen. Remained at this place til 28th March during which time* [we] *give the sloop a good overhaul; discharg'd the freight & fill'd up with coffee & pepper & took Mr. Bowen, a crazy man, as passenger.*
[At anchor, Port Louis, Isle of France]
Dist per log 45 Knots

March 15th, 1796
[Wind SE]
Pleasant weather with a strong breeze. Employ'd working up the harbour. We where visited by the Health boat. At 6 AM The Pilot had the Sloop Moor'd with both anchors ahead, & a Hawser out astern made fast to the Chains. So ends.

March 16th, 1796
[Wind SE]
Pleasant weather. Seamen employ'd stop'g the Sloop, for to get the Cross & truss'll down to repair. I found in the harbour that there was 7 sail of American ships.

March 17th, 1796
[Wind ESE]
Fine pleasant agreeable weather. People employ'd scraping & paying the Sides & Bends, etc.

March 18th, 1796
[Wind SE]
Pleasant warm weather. People employ'd repair'g the riging. Employ'd a Carpenter for to make new truss'l trees.

March 19th, 1796
[Wind SSE]
Fresh breezes & pleasant. Got the trussell trees over head & rig'd the Sloop complete. Bought two quoils of riging of Capt. Pierce.

March 20th, 1796
[Wind ENE]
Pleasant agreeable weather. Employ'd rattling down the riging. Discharg'd a part of the Cargo. Sev'rall vessells arriv'd in the harbour this day.

March 21st, 1796
[Wind ESE]
Still pleasant warm weather. All hands variously employ'd.

March 22nd, 1796
[Wind East]
Pleasant agreeable weather. All hands employ'd steadily as yesterday.

March 23rd, 1796
[Wind ESE]
Pleasant agreeable weather. Employ'd setting up the riging. So ends.

March 24th, 1796
[Wind ENE]
Still pleasant, rec'd on board a quantity of Pepper & Coffee—& stow'd it away.

March 25th, 1796
[Wind SE]
Fine weather, rec'd on board a few bags of Coffee. Employ'd filling up our water.

March 26th, 1796
[Wind variable]
Employ'd, bending sails, fill'd up the remainder of our water, & stow'd it away.

March 27th, 1796
[Wind NE]
Pleasant weather. Unmoor'd & haul'd out of the teir. A guard of soldiers came on board.

March 28th, 1796
[Wind ENE]
Pleasant agreeable weather. At 9 the pilot came on board & took charge. Rec'd on board Mr. Bowen, as a passenger. He came on board in Chains, & was genneraly supposed to be a Mad man. At 10 Cast of our fasts. At 11 The pilot left us, in boat & [we] bore away to the westward. *Mr. Bower, appearing to be tolerable rational; [I] had the irons taken off him to make his [condition] more comfortable, however, kept a guard over him.*

March 29th, 1796
Pleasant breezes.
(NB) There was a mistake of one day in the harbour log, therefore the occurrences of Yesterday belongs to this days work.

March 30th, 1796
[Course SWBW, SW½W. Wind SEBE]
Fresh breezes & squally. At 5 PM The West end of the Isle of France bore SEBE 8 leagues dist. At 10 In tops'l & single reef'd the Mainsail. At 6 AM Saw the Isle of Bourbon bear'g W. 8 leagues. Set all sail.
Dist pr log 95 Knots

March 31st, 1796
[Course WSW, WBS½S. Wind SE]
Fresh breezes & pleasant weather. At 1 PM the W. pt of Bourbon bore NNW 10 leagues. The E. do. NE. At 11 Carried away one of our Chain bolts, in topsail. At 5 AM Drove a new Chain bolt, set up the shroud & set all sail. I find Mr. Bowin to be quite rationall.
Lat Obsd 23°9'S Long 51°57'E Dep[arture taken] from Bourbon.
Dist pr log 146 Knots

April 1st, 1796
[Course WBS, West. Wind SE]
Lively breezes with frequent showers. All sail out, with a smooth sea. Latter part as before, caught a Bonnetto. Employ'd securing the Cannon. Put ye swivels in the hold.
Dist pr log 129 Knots

April 2nd, 1796
[Course West. Wind SEBE, EBS]
Steady breezes & pleasant weather. People variously employ'd. Sail maker repairing the Old tops'l. Unbent the New fores'l & brought another too. Cape of Good Hope S70°W, dist 1710 miles.
Dist pr log 141 Knots

April 3rd, 1796
[Course West, WBS. Wind East, ENE]
Lively breezes and pleasant weather with a smooth sea.

Some Albatrosses round the Sloop. At 6 AM Saw the South pt. of Madagascer Isle, bear'g NNW 10 or 12 leagues dist. The water somewhat coloured.
Lat Obsd 26°32′S Long 44°30′E
Dist pr log 168 Knots

April 4th, 1796
[Course West, WNW. Wind ENE, ESE]
Steady breezes and pleasant weather. The water much colour'd, many birds round, & some fish. Latter part squally with rain. A smooth sea. Some Bonnetto round.
Dist pr log 145 Knots

April 5th, 1796
[Course WNW, WBN. Wind NNE, North]
Light breezes and pleasant, caught two Bonnetto, struck a porpoise. Birds round. Latter part light variable winds. Some whales round. People making Mats etc.
Lat Obsd 27°28′S Long 40°37′E
Dist pr log 77 Knots

April 6th, 1796
[Course SWBW, NWBN. Wind WNW, WBS]
Light winds & pleasant weather with a smooth sea. Fish & Birds round. Latter as before, all sail out. Albacore round.
Cape of Good Hope S68°W, dist 1190 miles.
Dist pr log 48 Knots

April 7th, 1796
[Course WBN, West. Wind NBE, North]
Gentle breezes & pleasant with a smooth sea. At daylight, We discover'd a bad spring in the lower mast, 4 feet above ye deck. Down Yards & Topmast. Woulded[75] ye Mast, & got preventer Backstays up to the Horse piece.
Dist pr log 124 Knots

April 8th, 1796
[Course WNW, West. Wind North, NNW]
Fresh breezes & flying clouds. At 9 PM In squarsail, set the foresail. At 10 Single reef'd the Mainsail. Latter, fresh breezes with a head beat sea. Pitch'd away the Jib boom. Sail maker repairing the squarsail, etc.
Dist pr log 123 Knots

April 9th, 1796
[Course WBS. Wind South, SSE]
Fresh breezes & pleasant weather. Albatrosses round the Sloop. Employ'd making a jib boom. Set the Squarsail. Seamen overhauling & setting up the riging.
Dist pr log 91 Knots

April 10th, 1796
[Course WBS, WSW. Wind SE, ENE]
Lively breezes & pleasant with a smooth sea. Latter part fresh breezes. Jib'd Ship. A following sea. Got a New Jib boom out. *Bower more rational.*
Lat Obsd 31°2′S Long 31°37′E
Dist pr log 138 Knots

April 11th, 1796
[Course WBS. Wind ENE, NW]
Brisk breezes & pleasant with a following sea. At 8 PM Single reef'd the Mainsail. At 6 AM Split ye Bonnet of the Squarsail, Out reef, Sailmaker repairing the Squarsail.
Dist pr log 162 Knots

April 12th, 1796
[Course West, NNE, WNW. Wind North, WNW, SWBW]
Light winds with a high sea. Some Albatrosses & black Pettrel round.
Corr[ecte]d for 2 d'ys—Lat Obsd 34°10′S Long 28°2′E
Dist pr log 98 Knots

April 13th, 1796
[Course WBN, W½S. Wind East, E½N]
Fresh gales with flying clouds & a high following sea.
Many Albatrosses, & Black Pettrel flying round. At 2 AM
Jib'd, Double reef'd the Mainsail. In squaresail.
Dist pr log 165 Knots

April 14th, 1796
[Course NNW, NWBW. Wind West, SW]
Light winds & pleasant. All hands variously employ'd.
Latter part rainy, with heavy thunder and sharp lighting.
Albatrosses round.
Dist pr log 44 Knots

April 15th, 1796
[Course NWBW. Wind ESE, calm]
Light winds & pleasant weather with a rolling swell.
Pass'd many strong tide rips. A swell from the SW.
Lat Obsd 35°4'S Long 23°38'E
Dist pr log 41 Knots

April 16th, 1796
[Course NW, NWBW, WNW. Wind NE, SE, NWBW]
Light winds and pleasant weather. Out Yawl, & try'd the
Currant & found it setting to the West'd. In Boat. At 6
Foggy. Sound'd & got bottom in 70 fm. Coarse sand, with
broken shells. At 11 Sound'd 85 fm same ground. Many
Gannets round.
Dist pr log 45 Knots

April 17th, 1796
[Course West, WNW. Wind SBW, SSW]
Still foggy. At 4 The Fog clear'd of; Saw the land extending from NW to NE 8 leagues, St. Brass Mountains[76]
bear'g North. 65 fm water. Many gannets & Albatrosses
round. At daylight, Saw four Ships, standing in shore
upon a wind.
Dist pr log 62 Knots

April 18th, 1796
[Course NWBW, West. Wind WSW, ESE]
Light winds & flattering weather. Many Gannets & Alba-
trosses round. Sounding 65 fm fine Sand. Midnight do.
weather. Light winds jib'd Sloop. Seven sail in sight to the
East'd. 53 fm Coarse sand.
Dist pr log 52 Knots

April 19th, 1796
[Course NWBN, NNW, WSW. Wind WBS, West, NW]
Fresh breezes & cloudy, plenty birds round. At 6 Saw
Cape Vaccas[77] bear'g North 12 leag. 49 fm water, course
sand with red specks. Midnight fresh breezes & pleasant.
TK off Cape Vaccas 4 leagues dist. At 6 AM Saw Cape
Agullas bore NBW½W 14 or 15 leagues dist. Fresh gales
& a high sea.
Dist pr log 76 Knots

April 20th, 1796
[Course WBS, WBS½S. Wind NWBW, NW]
Fresh breezes. At 4 PM Single reef'd the Mainsail, at 5 In
2'd reef & foresail. At 8 Ballenc'd reef'd, in jib & set the
Foresail. Midnight heavy gales. At 4 Split the foresail,
unbent it & brought another too. Pass'd a ship standing in
shore, upon a wind under reef'd courses. At 9 Wore in
shore.
Dist pr log 44 Knots

THE *UNION*, WITH SAILS REEFED, DURING THE STORMY
PASSAGE AROUND CAPE OF GOOD HOPE, APRIL 1796
(opposite)

The *Union* rounded Cape of Good Hope 19-25 April 1796, in stormy
weather. On 22 April Boit recorded: "Stiff gales with an exceeding
high sea runing, one of which at 3 PM Broke on board of us, which
stove in 2/3 of the Waste on the Starboard side, broke 4 Stantions &
Split 8 feet of the plank sheer, & wash'd away the Boats Oars & mast
& one hen Coop."

April 21st, 1796
[Course N½E, NNE. Wind NWBW, NW]
Heavy gales with squalls of rain & a mountanius sea. At 2 Wore ship. In Jib & fores'l & hove too with her head to the North'd. At 6 Out 2 reef'd of the Mains'l, set ye Jib. At 8 Ballenc'd reef'd, Down Jib & hove too, with her head to the Southward. Latter hard gales, lying too, with a mountanious sea, 58 fm water rocky bottom.
Dist pr log 11 Knots

April 22nd, 1796
[Course WSW, SSW, NNW. Wind WNW, West, WBN]
Stiff gales with an exceeding high sea runing, one of which at 3 PM Broke on board of us, which stove in 2/3 of the Waste on the Starbord side, broke 4 Stantions & Split 8 feet of the plank sheer, & wash'd away the Boats Oars & masts & one hen Coop. Got the quarter guns below, & secur'd the things on deck, in the safest manner possible. Set the Fores'l & ballenc'd Mainsail. Noon pleasant.
Lat Obsd 36°11′S Long 19°35′E
Dist pr log 2 Knots

April 23rd, 1796
[Course NNW. Wind West]
Since the 19th have been laying too with a heavy gale of wind from the westward. Fresh gales, two sail in sight standing to the North'd & West. At 4 PM Out 2d reef of the Mains'l. Set the Jib. At 10 Out all reefs, set the foresail. Latter part moderate breezes two sail still in sight. 75 fm water, mud & sand. A large swell from ye S. Noon lively, breezes, employ'd repair'g the riging & waste.
Dist pr log 58 Knots

April 24th, 1796
[Course NNW, SWBS. Wind West, WNW, SW]
Steady light breeze from SW. At Sunsett saw the land towards

Cape of Good Hope from NNW to NNE 10 or 12 leagues, 45 fm, pebble stones. Midnight, 53 fm, sand like pepper & salt. At 6 AM 63 fathoms, same bottom. At noon pleas't, land in sight from NW to NE & find the sloop to the eastward of her reckoning since last lunar observation.
Dist pr log 73 Knots

April 25th, 1796
[Course WBS, West, WBN. Wind South, SE, SEBS]
Lively breezes with frequent rain squalls. Wind at length comes fast from SE. At 1 PM Got sight of land bear'g NWBN 7 or 8 leagues. Pass'd many Currant rips & vast flights of Gannets & Albatrosses together with some Kelp. At 8 sound'd 92 fm, rocks. At 6 AM Sound'd. No bottom with 100 fm of line. Jib'd Sloop & haul'd to ye North'd.
Lat Obsd 35°16′S Long 17°45′E (Fresh dep[artu]re from Agullas.)
Dist pr log 144 Knots

April 26th, 1796
[Course NNW, NWBN. Wind SSE, SE]
Lively breezes & pleasant weather. Employ'd repairing the waste. Latter part steady breezes. Few birds & porpoises round. Got the Jib boom out. Isle of St. Helena bears N 47°W, Dist 1480 Miles.
Dist pr log 142 Knots.

April 27th, 1796
[Course NNW. Wind SSE]
Gentle breezes & pleasant, with a rolling swell. Got the Jib boom rig'd & various other nessescary jobs. Midnight pleasant gales. Some Porpoises round, & a few birds. Seamen variously employ'd. Varnish'd the Jib Boom etc.
Dist pr log 150 Knots

April 28th, 1796
[Course NNW, NBW. Wind SSW, WBN]

Steady breezes & pleasant weather. Employ'd repair'g the Jib sheets etc. A few albertrosses round.
Dist pr log 113 Knots

April 29th, 1796
[Course NBW, NNW. Wind WBN, SSW]
In squars'l & set the foresail. A few birds round. At 10 PM In flying jib. Midnight cloudy, with small rain. Latter part fresh gales. Double reef'd ye Mainsail. A large following sea.
Dist pr log 135 Knots

April 30th, 1796
[Course NNW. Wind SSE, SEBS]
Steady gales & dark low'ry weather. Scudding under a double reef'd Mainsail & head of the Squarsa'l. A high sea runing. Latter part as before. Out 1 reef of the Mainsail, caught a flying fish. Albertrosses & Pettrel flying round. St. Helena bears N49°W, dist 1010 Miles
Dist pr log 180 Knots

May 1st, 1796
[Course NNW, NBW. Wind SSE, SBE]
Steady breezes with a high following sea, scudding under a single reef'd Mainsail, & head of the Squarsail. Porpoises round the Sloop, & a few Sea hens. Seamen making twine & various other jobs. Double reef'd ye Mains'l.
Lat Obsd 24°38'S Long 6°13'E
Dist pr log 170 Knots

May 2nd, 1796
[Course NBW, NNW. Wind SBE, SSE]
Brisk gales & dark cloudy weather, scuding as Yesterday, a high following sea, a few birds round. Latter part pleasant, pass'd a turtle. People variously employ'd, a high sea runing. Few Black hallets round.
Dist pr log 177 Knots

May 3rd, 1796
[Course NNW. Wind SSE]
Lively breezes with flying clouds with a high following sea. At 8 PM Out 2nd reef of the Mainsail. At 3 Out all reefs. On Bonnets, more moderate, with a smoother sea. People employ'd on the riging. St. Helena bears N54°W, Dist 500 miles.
Dist pr log 168 Knots

May 4th, 1796
[Course NNW. Wind SSE]
Lively breezes with flying clouds. Split the Squars'l. Sail maker repairing it. At 11 AM Set the squarsail. Employ'd Variously, a rolling sea.
Dist pr log 144 Knots

May 5th, 1796
[Course NNW. Wind SSE]
Gentle breezes & pleasant weather. Seamen & tradesmen variously employ'd. Some flying fish round. Latter part pleasant. Sent the Top mast aloft, & rig'd the Topsail Yard & black[ed] it. Hazy weather.
Lat Obsd 17°23'S Long 1°11'W
Dist pr log 126 Knots

May 6th, 1796
[Course NNW. Wind SSE]
Moderate breezes & pleasant weather with a smooth sea. Seamen & tradesmen variously employ'd. Latter part as before. Cut up the Spare Squarsail Yard, to make Oars with. Flying fish round. St. Helena bears WBN¾N, dist 195 miles.
Dist pr log 113 Knots

May 7th, 1796
[Course NNW. Wind SSE]
Gentle breezes & pleasant. People variously employ'd, all

sail out. Saw a Dolphin. Latter part as before, variously emp'd. Saw a large Shark. Assencion bears N57°W, 730 miles.
Dist pr log 123 Knots

May 8th, 1796
[Course NNW. Wind SSE]
Lively breezes & pleasant weather. Employ'd variously. Saw a Man of war bird. Latter part as before, with a following sea, caught a flying fish. Assencion[78] bears N61°W dist 580 miles.
Dist pr log 156 Knots

May 9th, 1796
[Course NWBN. Wind SEBS]
Steady breezes & pleasant weather with a following sea. Many flying fish round. Latter part as before. All hands employ'd cleaning muskets etc. A following sea.
Dist pr log 158 Knots

May 10th, 1796
[Course NW. Wind SE]
Fresh breezes & pleasant, with a following sea. Caught a noddy. Latter part as before. Saw a man of war bird. Employ'd breaking out the fore peak for provisions. *Have had generally, since leaving the Cape, very fresh gales [from] SW. Birds & fish the whole time round.*
Lat Obsd 9°50′S Long 9°38′W
Dist pr log 143 Knots

May 11th, 1796
[Course NW. Wind SE]
Brisk breezes & pleasant. Seamen & tradesmen, variously employ'd. Men of war birds round. Latter part, as before, porpoises round. Squally with light rain. Flying fish round, saw a Booby.
Dist pr log 116 Knots

May 12th, 1796
[Course NW. Wind SEBS]
Moderate breezes & warm pleasant weather. Sent the topsail yard aloft & set the sail. Latter part, as before. Employ'd on the repairs of the riging. Porpoises & Many birds round.
Dist pr log 119 Knots

May 13th, 1796
[Course NW. Wind SE]
Steady breezes & pleasant weather. All hands variously employ'd. Many birds round. Midnight cloudy. Latter part as before. Employ'd repairing the Yawl etc. Tropick & other birds round.
Dist pr log 132 Knots

May 14th, 1796
[Course NW. Wind SEBS]
Brisk breezes and pleasant weather. Seamen variously employ'd. Many birds round. Latter part as before. Men of War & tropics birds round, likewise Gannets.
Dist pr log 135 Knots

May 15th, 1796
[Course NW. Wind SE]
Lively breezes & pleasant weather. Many birds, of different species, round the Sloop. At 3H19′50″ Ap't time, I had three sights of the sun and moon Nearest limbs, which determin'd the longitude to be 14°13′W.
Lat Obsd 4°57′S
Dist pr log 144 Knots

May 16th, 1796
[Course NW½W. Wind SE]
Lively breezes & warm pleasant weather. Saw a Booby. Vast flights of flying fish round. Employ'd on the repairs of the riging. Latter part, as before, found one of the Main

shrouds parted, just below the seizing. Employ'd fitting a preventer for etc.
Dist pr log 138 Knots

May 17th, 1796
[Course NWBN. Wind SE]
Lively breezes & squally with some rain. At 1 PM Jib'd Sloop. Saw a Booby & a Noddy. Squally weather, saw a Booby. Split ye squars'l, repair'd & set it again.
Dist pr log 138 Knots

May 18th, 1796
[Course NWBN. Wind SE]
Moderate breezes & warm pleasant weather. Booby's round. People variously employ'd. Latter part, as before. Vast many flying fish round.
Dist pr log 129 Knots

May 19th, 1796
[Course NNW½W. Wind SSE]
Light winds with a rolling sea & hazy weather. People variously employ'd. Saw Boobies. Unbent the Mainsail & brought another too. Sail maker repair'g ye Spare one.
Dist pr log 79 Knots

May 20th, 1796
[Course NBW½W, NNW. Wind SBE, SSE]
Light winds & pleasant. Sail maker repair'g the Mainsail. Seamen as usuall. Bonnetto & Porpoises round.
Lat Obsd 0°56'N Long 25°44'W
Dist pr log 60 Knots

May 21st, 1796
[Course NW. Wind variable, SW]
Light winds & a smooth sea with a currant to the NW.

Bonnetto round. Employ'd on the Spare S'ls. Latter part pleasant with strong currant rips. Fish round. Employ'd on the riging.
Dist pr log 46 Knots

May 22nd, 1796
[Course NW. Wind SWBS, SBW]
Light winds with frequent rain squalls. Caught a Shark. Albacore round. Strong currant rips. Latter part, as before. Employ'd making Brooms & Scrubing brushes. Fish round. Sail maker on ye Mains'l.
Dist pr log 65 Knots

May 23rd, 1796
[Course NWBN. Wind SSW, SSE]
Gentle breezes with pleasant weather. Albacore round the Sloop. A smooth sea. Latter part squally with thund' & rain. Sharks round.
Dist pr log 48 Knots

May 24th, 1796
[Course NWBN. Wind from South to SW]
Squally with rain. Sharks, Albacore & Bonnetto round, but are very coy. Latter part light winds, caught a Noddy, porpoises round.
Dist pr log 49 Knots

May 25th, 1796
[Course NW½N. Wind variable, South]
Light winds with dark low'ry weather. Sail maker repair'g the Mainsail. Seamen as usual. At 4 AM, A violent gust of wind struck the Sloop, from the NE, Which split the Squars'l & tops'l, & damaged the Mainsail, heavy rains. Pass'd a dead Negro & a crue of rice. Land to ye NW.
Lat Obsd 3°43'N Long 28°59'W
Dist pr log 54 Knots

May 26th, 1796
[Course NW. Wind variable, SE]
Light winds & pleasant. The topsail being so badly split, was oblidg'd to condemn it, sail maker repair'g the squars'l. Caught a Dolphin. Got out the boat & scrap'd the Barnacles of the bottom. Dolphins round. Sailmaker as Yesterd'y. At Noon hoisted in the boat.
Dist pr log 24 Knots

May 27th, 1796
[Course NW. Wind calm, NBE, NE]
Squally with rain. Caught a porpoise. Dolphin & Albacore round. Finish'd the squarsail. At 8 PM In topsail. At 11 Set do. & the Squarsail. At 19H34'20''AP time I determin'd the Longitude by Celestial Observations to be 31°45'W of Greenwich Observatory. Seamen repairing the riging.
Dist pr log 66 Knots

May 28th, 1796
[Course NWBN, WNW. Wind NE, North]
Pleasant breezes, all sail out. People variously employ'd. Squally with light rain. Seamen on the riging etc. Albacore round.
Dist pr log 70 Knots

May 29th, 1796
[Course WNW, NWBN. Wind North, NEBN]
Light winds & cloudy with frequent showers of rain. Seamen & tradesmen employ'd in there various depart's. Latter part as before with a confused Sea.
Dist pr log 55 Knots

May 30th, 1796
[Course NNW, NWBN. Wind NE, NEBN]
Squally weather with a confused sea. At 4 PM In foresail. Set the Squarsail. Porpoises in sight. Latter part squally.

At 21H23'50'' Apt. time I determin'd the Longitude by celestial Observations to 34°10'0''W of Greenwich. In Squarsail, a pitching sea.
Dist pr log 104 Knots

May 31st, 1796
[Course WBN, NW½N. Wind NBW, NEBN]
Fresh breezes with a high sea & frequent rain squalls. Unbent the Squars'l. In flying Jib & topsail. Midnight more moderate, Set do., do. At 22H10'0'' Apt. time I determin'd the Lo'g by four sights of the sun and moon Distance to be 36°41'47''W of Green' Obser'.
Dist pr log 109 Knots

June 1st, 1796
[Course NWBN. Wind NE]
Fresh breezes with frequent rain squalls. Unbent the Mainsail & brought another too, a cross sea. At 10 PM In topsail & flying jib. Midnight squally. Sent down the topsail & Squars'l Yards, the topsail being split, sail maker repairing it. Repair'd the riging on the Cross jack Yard.
Lat Obsd 10°32'N Long 35°40'W
Dist pr log 127 Knots

June 2nd, 1796
[Course NWBN. Wind NE]
Lively breezes with frequent rain squalls. Sail maker on the topsail. Seamen on the riging. Midnight do. weather. Latter part as before, with a confused Sea. New Serv'd the ties. Vast many fish round. Noon cloudy. Granada NE point bears West, 1337 miles.
Dist pr log 125 Knots

June 3rd, 1796
[Course NWBN. Wind NE]
Steady breezes with frequent rain squalls. Sail maker repair'g the Old Mainsail. A confused sea. Latter part

fresh breezes with a smooth sea. Sent the Yards aloft & set the topsail. The S. pt. of St. Lucia bears West 1200 miles.
Dist pr log 114 Knots

June 4th, 1796
[Course NWBW. Wind NE, NEBE]
Brisk breezes & pleasant. Sail maker repairing the Mainsail, & Seamen in there various departments. Latter part squally with light rain & a smooth sea, flying fish round. St. Iago N. point (E. South'y) dist 1120 Miles. Martinice NE pt. bears W. south'y, 1120 Miles dist.
Dist pr log 123 Knots

June 5th, 1796
[Course NNW½W. Wind NEBE]
Fresh breezes with frequent squalls. Took in, & set sail occasionally. A rough sea. No fish to my sorrow. Latter part pleasant. Employ'd painting the Sloops stern & other nessescary Jobs.
Lat Obsd 16°58'N Long 40°43'W
Dist pr log 127 Knots

June 6th, 1796
[Course NNW½W. Wind NEBE]
Fresh breezes & cloudy with a smooth sea. Employ'd painting, blacking, & taring, & other nessescary jobs. Latter part pleasant, all hands employ'd as Yesterday. No fish & a few birds round. SW Pt of Burmudas bears N53°W Dist 1310 mi. Isle Sable bears N28°W dist 1710 Miles.
Dist pr log 130 Knots

June 7th, 1796
[Course NNW½W. Wind NEBE]
Steady breezes with warm, pleasant weather, pass'd much Gulf weed. Employ'd painting the Sloop etc. Employ'd

break'g out the hold for fresh water & for the better arrangements of it.
Dist pr log 120 Knots

June 8th, 1796
[Course NNW½W. Wind NEBE]
Pleasant breezes. Employ'd painting & Still continue to pass Gulf weed. All Sail out. Midnight squally with some rain. Latter part employ'd as before, good breezes. At 23H29'20'' Apt time I determin'd the Long by the Mean of four distances of the sun and moon nearest limb to be 45°35'20''W of Green'. Bermudas bears N58°W Dist 1140 Miles. Georges Bank Bears N46°W Dist. 1600 Mi.
Dist pr log 118 Knots

June 9th, 1796
[Course NNW½W. Wind ENE]
Lively breezes & pleasant warm weather. Employ'd painting the Sloop & other nessescary Jobs. Latter part, as before. Some tropicks. At 23H40'0'' Apt time I determin'd the Long to be 46°34'15''W of Green' by Celestial Observations.
Dist pr log 116 Knots

June 10th, 1796
[Course NNW½W. Wind EBS, EBN]
Fresh breezes & pleasant. Seamen & tradesmen variously employ'd. Pass'd much Gulf weed, tropicks round. Latter part pleasant. Employ'd painting the Mouldings & head. Seamen straping blocks.
Dist pr log 114 Knots

June 11th, 1796
[Course NNW½W. Wind SEBE, SE]
Moderate breezes & pleasant weather. At 1H55'10'' Apt time I determin'd the Long by Celestial Observation's to be 47°34'0''W of Green'. Employ'd painting etc. Latter

part pleasant, painted a spread Eagle on the Sloops stern. Employ'd lacing on Mats & other Jobs. Pass'd much weed. Burmudas bears N68°W. Dist 850 Mi. Cape Cod bears North 49°W, dist 1370 Mi.
Dist pr log 96 Knots

June 12th, 1796
[Course NWBN. Wind East]
Pleasant breezes. Finish'd painting etc. At 2H43'0'' Apt time I determin'ed the Long by the sun & moon to be 48°18′W. of Greenwich. Latter part as before Found one of ye Chain bolts on the larbord side parted. Employ'd making Spun Yarn etc. Isle Sable bears N29°W. Dist. 1060 Miles. Nantucket N52°W Dist 1270 Miles.
Dist pr log 109 Knots

June 13th, 1796
[Course NWBN. Wind ENE]
Lively breezes & pleasant weather with a smooth sea. All hands employ'd Spining Yarns etc. Latter part as before. Seamen employ'd in there various departments.
Dist pr log 117 Knots

June 14th, 1796
[Course NWBN. Wind ENE, EBS]
Moderate breezes with a smooth sea. Porpoises round, saw a Booby. Still continue to pass much Gulf weed. Midnight pleasant. All sail out. Gulf weed still passing. The East End of St. George's Bank bears N54°W 980.
Dist pr log 91 Knots

June 15th, 1796
[Course NWBN. Wind SE]
Pleasant breezes with a Swell from the SE. Still continue to pass much Gulf weed. People variously employ'd.
Lat Obsd 32°20′N Long 51°57′W
Dist pr log 70 Knots

June 16th, 1796
[Course NWBN, NNW. Wind SEBE, SSE]
Light winds with a smooth sea. Bent & set the Top gallent sail, part'd one of the Shrouds & knoted it. Employ'd fleeting [overhauling] the dead eyes of the shroud & setting up the riging etc. Some Gulf weed. Noon pleasant.
Dist pr log 46 Knots

June 17th, 1796
[Course NWBN, North. Wind WBS, WNW]
Light winds & pleasant weather. People variously employ'd. At 6 PM pass'd two Schooners, bound to ye South'd. At 4 AM A ship pass'd us, bound to the North'd & Eastward. A strong currant to the South'd. Georges bank East part bears N54°W, 820 Dist.
Dist pr log 43 Knots

June 18th, 1796
[Course NNW, NBW½W. Wind West, WSW]
Light breezes & flying clouds. At 3 PM In top gall't sail, & sent the Yard down. Saw a sail to ye North'd. Latter part as before, little Gulf weed seen. Employ'd making Caskets [shortline to attach sail to yard] etc. A head beat sea.
Dist pr log 45 Knots

June 19th, 1796
[Course North, NBE. Wind WNW, NWBW]
Light breezes with flying clouds with a swell from the North'd. Latter part, some showers with a smooth sea. Some weed passing.
Dist pr log 40 Knots

June 20th, 1796
[Course West, NNE, WBN. Wind NNW, NW]
Light winds & cloudy. At 2 PM Pass'd a Snow, bound to the North'd & East'd. She show'd Danish colours. Latter part, fresh breezes. In topsail & flying jib. Georges East

point—N53°W Dist 700 miles.
Dist pr log 58 Knots

June 21st, 1796
[Course West, NWBW. Wind NNW, NBE]
Fresh breezes with a pitching sea & heavy rains, Accompanied with Sharp lightning & hard thunder, a hawk flying round. Plenty of Gulf weed passing. Latter part pleasant with a damnable currant setting to the South'd. Noon a steady North'y trade wind.
Lat Obsd 33°22′N Long 55°34′W
Dist pr log 63 Knots

June 22nd, 1796
[Course West, NE, W½S. Wind NNW, NWBN]
Light winds & pleasant. Employ'd variously. Saw a Booby & a Tropic bird. Broach'd a bag of Sugar & a bag of Coffee for Ships men. Latter part, more flattering with a smooth sea. Gave ye people tea for Supper ev'ry night as I am nessesciated to shorten their allowance of Meat & bread.
Dist pr log 50 Knots
[The ship tacked three times against the W and NW winds]

June 23rd, 1796
[Course NNW, NWBN. Wind WBS, WSW]
Lively breezes with a confus'd sea which made the Sloop labour much. Two Shooners & a Ship in sight, stand'g to the S & E. At 6 Spoke the French Sloop of war *Scipio* from New York bound to the West Indies, out 8 Days. Reckon'd himself in 61°W Long from London. Her boat boarded us & examin'd my papers & let me pass after treating me very politely. Made sail.
Dist pr log 76 Knots

June 24th, 1796
[Course NWBN, NW. Wind SW, SSE]

Squally with thunder & Lightning with a confus'd sea. Unbent the Old fore sail, & brought another too. Latter part squally with rain. Sent the Yards down & single reef'd ye Mains'l. A high sea runing. Sloop of war [visible] Long 62°30′W.
Dist pr log 104 Knots

June 25th, 1796
[Course NW½W, NW. Wind NEBE, NNE, NBE]
Fresh gales with a high sea. At 5 PM More moderate. Set the topsail & squars'l. Out reef. At 8 In squars'l, set the flying jib. Latter part as before. Employ'd scraping & mounting the cannon. At 19H46′40″ Apt time I determin'd the Long by Celestial Observation to be 63°43′0″W. Sloop of war Long 64°W.
Lat Obsd 35°48′N
Dist pr log 84 Knots

June 26th, 1796
[Course North, NBW. Wind WNW, WBN]
Light winds with frequent squalls. Two whirlwinds pass'd us. A confus'd sea runing, a sail in sight to ye NE. Latter part strong breezes with a strong currant, much gulf weed. In topsail & flying jib. Flying fish round. Noon, a high sea.
Dist pr log 94 Knots

June 27th, 1796
[Course NNW, NEBN. Wind WBS, NNW]
Fresh gales with a high sea. Unbent the Old jib & brought another too. Sent the yards down from aloft. Midnight, a pitching time. Latter part, more smooth, caught two large Dolphin. Sent the Y'ds down & set the Topsail, painted the cannon. At 22H4′0″ Apt time I determin'd the Long by Celestial Observ. 66°30′W.
Dist pr log 74 Knots

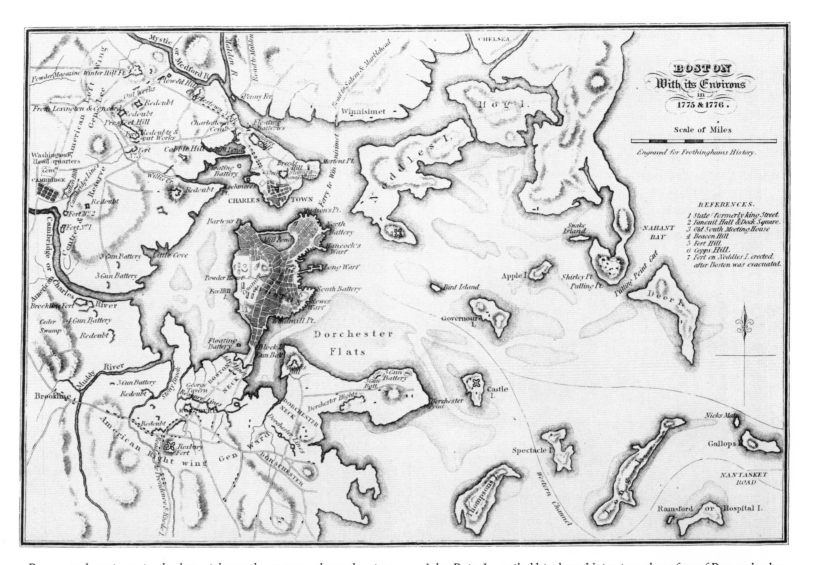

Boston and environs in the late eighteenth century, about the time John Boit, Jr., sailed his sloop *Union* into the safety of Boston harbor.

June 28th, 1796
[Course NW. Wind calm, WSW]
Calm & pleasant. Dolphin round. Two Whales in sight, & some Gulf weed. Employ'd painting the boat etc. Latter part as before, caught a large Dolphin. A strong NE Current. The South Shoal bears WNW 180 Mi. Dist. The West End Georges Do. NWBW½W 118 miles SW. Dist pr log 49 Knots

June 29th, 1796
[Course NWBW, NWBN. Wind SWBW, WSW]
Fresh gales with dark rainy weather & a mountanious sea.

At 5 PM Spoke ye Brig *Ranger*, Capt. Frazier, from Philadelphia bound to Cowes, out 6 days. Reckoned himself in ye Long of 65°W. At 2 AM Sound'd, no bottom. At 19H5′0″ I determin'd the Long by Celestial observations to be 67°26′W. Noon flying scud.
Dist pr log 90 Knots

June 30th, 1796
[Course West, W½S, North. Wind NNW, WNW]
Fresh breezes & cloudy. All hands variously employ'd. The water colour'd. Pass'd Cape Ann moorings, Gulf weed etc. At 9 Spoke a Snow, from Limirick bound to New York, Capt. Hay, reckoned himself in 66°W Long.
Lat Obsd 40°42′N Long 63°46′W
Dist pr log 55 Knots

July 1st, 1796
[Course North, NNW, NBW. Wind NNW, West, WBN]
Light winds & pleasant weather with a smooth sea, birds round. Midnight pleasant, no bottom. Pass'd a Ship bound to ye East'd. At 9 Got soundings on Georges bank in 50 fm Grey sand. Noon pleasant. Employ'd on ye rig'g.
Dist pr log 44 Knots

July 2nd, 1796
[Course North, NWBW. Wind calm, WNW, variable]
Calm with a smooth sea & pleasant weather, 50 fm water. Grey sand with yellow specks. Caught two Haddock. Employ'd cleaning small arms. Caught a haddock & two Dog fish. 40 fm water, few birds round.
Dist pr log 23 Knots

July 3rd, 1796
[Course NW½W, NW. Wind NNE, calm, NBE]
Light airs & pleasant with a smooth sea. Caught 5 haddock, & ten Dog fish. 42 fm water, fine grey sand. Midnight pleasant. 37 fm water. At 8 AM 30 fm fine black &

white sand. Latter part foggy at times with strong tide rips. At noon 23 fm.
Dist pr log 31 Knots

July 4th, 1796
[Course WNW, North, NE. Wind SW, SSW]
Moderate breezes & pleasant weather. Three sail in sight. Irregular sound'gs from 14 to 25 fm water, fine sand with red specks which I suppose to be ye E. edge of Nantuck shoals. Midnight pleasant. 24 fm water. Latter part, a thick fog. At 8 28 fm water. Pepple stones. At 9 35 Do., at 10 60 fm, sand. Many whales & Manheaden round. Noon a thick fog.
Dist pr log 69 Knots

July 5th, 1796
[Course W½N, WBN. Wind SBW, SWBS]
Thick foggy weather. No ground with 100 fm line, which determine ye shoal water yesterday to have been on Georges Bank. Vast many whales playing round, & shoals of Mackerell, a sail in sight. Latter part light winds & pleasant, two schooners in sight. Sail maker & sailors repairing the sails & riging.
Lat Obsd 42°26′N Long 66°7′W
Dist pr log 49 Knots

July 6th, 1796
[Course SWBW, WBS, W½N. Wind North, South, SBW]
Light airs from north. Spoke a schooner from Plymouth bound to the Grand Banks, out 24 hours, Capt Hyland. [He] told me Cape Cod bore W. 25 leagues. At midnight breeze from SW. Saw a sail stand'g towards us. Shortly after she fired ten musketts & two 18 pound shot at us, one of which went through the foresail; they then hail'd me & order'd all our sails to be taken in. Their boat boarded & took me on board with my papers. She proved to be the Engligh Frigate Reason. John

117

Berriford Captain from Halifax on a cruize. Finding they could not make a prize of the sloop, suffer'd us to pass after treating me in a rough, ungentleman like manner. Bad luck to him!
Dist pr log 35 Knots

July 7th, 1796
[Course W½S, WBN, SSW. Wind SSW, SW, West]
Foggy disagreeable weather. Two sail in sight. No ground with 80 fm line. At Sunset clear & pleasant. Struck ye ground in 60 fm water. At daylight saw Cape Cod bor'g from SSE to SW, 5 or 6 leagues. At 10 Spoke a fishing schooner bound to Plymouth. Took one of her hands as a passenger to Boston, told us ye light [Boston] bore W. 10 leagues. 10 sail in sight.
Dist pr log 58 Knots

July 8th, 1796
Light winds & pleasant. Vast many fishing boats in sight. At 4 PM A pilot took charge of the Sloop to take her to Boston, the Lighthouse bear'g WBN 3 leagues. At 8 PM Abrest the light, the wind very Bafling. The pilot brought us to an Anchor at 9 In Nantasket roads. My passenger went to town in a fishing boat. In the morning got under way & soon anchored of the Long Wharf—& in a few days discharg'd this Cargo.

THE *UNION* ENTERING BOSTON HARBOR, 8 JULY 1796 (opposite)

After a remarkable voyage around the world, the *Union*, its young master and crew enter Boston Harbor, finishing a voyage of nearly two years. With a salvo the *Union* salutes the fort on Castle Island (background). In his Remarks, Boit wrote: *I believe the Union was the first sloop that ever circumnavigated the globe. She proved to be an excellent sea boat & was a very safe vessel, still I think it too great a risque for to trust to one mast on such a long voyage when a small Brig would answer on the East Coast as well.*

N.B. saluted Castle William, with fifteen Guns which was Return'd with 11 Guns.

At noon anchor'd abreast the town. Saluted the town was return'd with their welcome huzza.

So ends this voyage.

Having sail'd round the globe to the westward, have lost one complete day, it being Saturday at Boston & only Friday with us. Thank God, I found all my relations in health & the tender embraces of an affectionate & honored father made up for all the troubles & anzietys incident to such long voyages.

During this voyage which was performed in 22-1/2 months, the crew enjoy'd good health. No doubt the care that was taken to keep them clean & fumigate their berths was the best prevention for the scurvy that could possibly have been adopted.

I believe the Union was the first sloop that ever circumnavigated the globe. She proved to be an excellent sea boat & was a very safe vessel, still I think it too great a risque for to trust to one mast on such a long voyage when a small Brig would answer on the East Coast as well.

The cargo came out in fine order & I receiv'd great satisfaction in the idea that my conduct through the voyage had been very satisfactory to the owners and although my voyage was not so lucrative as was contemplated at the commencement, owing to the rise [in cost] of skins on the coast & fall [in price] of the same at Canton, still, upon the whole, it was a saving voyage. No vessel that left Canton in Co. with the Union had so quick a passage, although we was detain'd a fortnight at the Isle of France. I believe we was the first that arriv'd in America except the Eliza of Boston, who arriv'd two days before us.
So ends the Remarks on the Union's voyage.

Notes

1. This is the distance the vessel sailed each day. According to dead reckoning the international nautical mile has been defined as 1,852 meters, or about 6,076 feet.

2. Properly spelt, *sennit*. A kind of flat, braided cordage made by pleating together several strands of rope, yarn or coarse hemp. Old rope was reconstituted in this manner.

3. Nautical term. To change course of ship to bring wind on opposite side of vessel in tacking to windward.

4. To avoid chafing of lines against the shrouds.

5. Fresh fish and porpoises were often caught by the crew of the *Union* to vary their diet and prevent scurvy. Diet was much more important for the crew's health than fumigation (which is frequently mentioned).

6. Isles of Sol, Bonnavista, Mayo and St. Jago were all islands of the Cape Verde group, which consists of ten islands and five islets. Sailing ships from New England ports bound for Cape Horn usually passed close to these islands.

7. Waist nettings were rigged on each side of the vessel and above the rails to keep the natives from boarding during an attack.

8. One of the Falkland Island group that lies northeast of the southern tip of South America. These islands were the last port of call for sailing ships going around Cape Horn from east to west. Good water, wood and a plentiful supply of game provided well-needed stores and refreshment for the difficult passage.

9. A swivel gun was the lightest stationary gun on the vessel, swiveling on an upright post (usually on the rail). It threw a one- or two-pound ball. At times a swivel gun was mounted in the bow of the ship's boat. The *Union* had eight of them.

10. Brush-like device used to clean the ship's bottom. It is made of twigs held between pieces of timber.

11. After reaching the Pacific Ocean the cabin and deck spaces forward (waste) were reconstructed to afford more room below deck.

12. Columbia's Cove. A small, well-protected harbor frequently used by the *Columbia* on her two voyages to the Northwest Coast. It is located near the entrance to Nasparti Inlet (known to Boit as Bulfinch Sound) on the east side of Cape Cook (called Woody Point by the trading vessels).

13. Two of the most important supplies on the *Union* were water and wood for cooking. It was a remarkable accomplishment to have sailed from the Falkland Islands to Columbia's Cove without any replenishment en route.

14. A mixture of linseed oil and tallow was used to grease the mast, which allowed easier movement for the parrels (mast hoops).

15. These were boiled and the brew drunk by the crew to prevent scurvy, a practice originated by Captain Cook.

16. To paint with tar, pitch, tallow, etcetera, to prevent weathering.

17. An important native village even today, located on the southeast corner of Flores Island, Clayoquot Sound and probably approached by the *Union* through Brabant Channel.

18. The most southerly point of the Queen Charlotte Islands and named by the French voyager La Pérouse in 1785.

19. In 1708, a report appeared in a British magazine that an admiral, Bartholomue de Fonte, had penetrated a river on the Northwest Coast in latitude 53°N and after several days he met a ship from Boston that, supposedly, came through a northwest passage. This was placed on a chart of the period and immediately revived interest in finding such a passage.

20. Chief Usak, alias Ugah or Ukers, as Boit called him, was a raven chief of the area now known as Skincuttle Inlet located on the eastern side of Moresby Island. This chief's main village was in the present Jedway Bay. In 1791 the fur trade vessels *Columbia* and *Hope* were in this bay which had about 10 villages. Bishop Rock, at the mouth of this inlet, is named after Charles Bishop, captain of the trading vessel *Ruby*. Port Ucah was the name given to Skincuttle Inlet by Ingraham in 1791. It was in this inlet, in 1862, that the first outbreak of the smallpox decimated the Haida tribe, resulting in a mass migration to Alaska.

21. Conaswaks Village (also Cumswah and Cumshewa). Boit's *Remarks* 31 May 1795: *Abreast Cumswah's village. A vast many canoes came off with Chief Cumswah among them. Purchased an excellent lot of furs. Chiefly for iron & cloth but it coming on to blow fresh down the strait & rather on shore—had to stand off towards Cape Haswell* [Cape St. James].

In the papers of Leonard Clay: "This village was named after the Eagle Crest Chief Go'mshewa. The main village was located inside the entrance on the north side of the Cumeshewa Inlet. This was the location of the attack on the schooner *Resolution* by Chief Koyah with the help of the Cumshewa tribe. Ten crew men were killed. Attacks were also made on the ships *Sea Otter*, *Phoenix* and the *Alexander*, in which seven crew men were killed."

22. Coyea Harbor (Kuya) located near Anthony Island at the west end of Housten-Stewart Channel which separates Kunghit Island from Moresby Island. (A more detailed description will be found in footnote 26.)

23. Tadent's Village. This village, also called Altatsef, Tasen and Tadense, was located on the southeast point of Lagara Island and facing Lucy Island. It was destroyed by fire shortly after the fur trade era.

24. Housten-Stewart Channel, between Prevost Island and Moresby Island of the Queen Charlotte Islands was named Barrell's Sound by Captain Gray in the *Columbia* in honor of Joseph Barrell, the principal owner of that vessel.

25. Port Montgomery is referred to in Boit's Log of the *Columbia*, 20 September 1792: "We stood into Port Mongommery, a small harbour to the north'd of Barrell's Sound which the *Adventure* had visited before and her captain [Haswell] named after our famous American general who fell before Quebec while gloriously fighting in the defence of our liberties."

26. Island. This is Anthony Island located at the extreme southern end of the Queen Charlotte Islands and at the western end of the Housten-Stewart Channel which separates Moresby and Kunghit islands. This was the location of Koya's village, and was one of the most populated and warlike of any of the Queen Charlotte Islands.

Wilson Duff and Michael Kew, in an article in the 1957 annual report of the Provincial Museum, Victoria, B.C., state: "The traders knew the village as Koyah's Village, following the usual practice of naming the place after its chief, who conducted the trade. Koya, Coyea, Skoich Eye (there are many different spellings). Sometimes they anchored directly off the village or in the channel nearby, but often, too, they stopped on the east coast of Moresby Island, near the other end of Houston Stewart Channel, where they found some of the villagers dispersed to their summer camps. Wherever the traders stopped, the word soon spread and canoes converged on the ship" (*Anthony Island, A Home of the Haidas*).

Koya was a very powerful and ruthless chief who ruled his tribe with an iron hand during the latter part of the Eighteenth Century. Following his death, the name of the village was changed to Ninstint after a later chief. The first contact with Koya's village by a trading vessel was recorded by Robert Haswell in the log of the sloop *Lady Washington*, under the command of Captain Robert Gray. She visited the village 11 June, 1789, and carried on a brisk trade with Koya and his tribe without any untoward incidents. Two years later the same vessel under the command of John Kendrick made two stops at this village, the second on 13 June, 1791. At this time Koya and his tribe attacked the crew of the *Lady Washington* but were repulsed; forty natives, including Koya's wife and two children, were killed. Koya participated in four recorded attacks on trading vessels, two of which were successful, and two disastrous. In the last attack, on the *Union*, he was killed by Boit, together with 50 to 70 members of his tribe. He was probably the most warlike of any of the Haida chiefs. These Haida tribes migrated to southern Alaska over the years and by 1880 the last survivors moved to Skidegate, Alaska.

27. This vessel was a tender to the ship *Columbia* on the latter's first voyage to the Northwest Coast (1 October 1787–9 August 1790). Later she was practically commandeered by Captain John Kendrick for his own use in a voyage from China to the Northwest Coast. Kendrick was accidentally killed aboard the *Washington* in the Hawaiian Islands in 1795 and the vessel was wrecked in the Straits of Malacca shortly thereafter.

28. This island, at the entrance to Clayoquot Sound, was originally called Observatory Island but later changed to Lennard Island, the present location of a lighthouse.

29. Port San Juan, just inside the entrance of the Strait of Juan de Fuca; called by the Indians Pachenat and by the fur traders,

Poverty Cove. It was originally named by Manuel Quimper, commanding the sloop *Princess Royal*, June 1790.

30. Probably Cloose but called Nitinate among many other spellings. This must have been a large village nearby, as the trading ships often mention it.

31. Tatoosh Island lies half a mile northwest of Cape Flattery. It was mentioned by John Meares on 30 June 1788, and is an important landmark at the south entrance to the Strait of Juan de Fuca.

32. The entrance to the Strait of Juan de Fuca is a stormy place at best, even in the summer. Strong NW and SW winds create heavy seas against the rapid outgoing tides. The seamanship of John Boit and the seaworthiness of the little *Union* must have been sorely tested while cruising these waters, the shores of which had many villages and furs.

33. Golintah Island, most likely Destruction Island. The natives in the nearby villages were extremely warlike and had previously attacked trading vessels. It was probably near this island, on 12 July 1775, that the Spanish explorer, Juan Francisco Bodega y Quadra in the *Sonora*, lost a boatload of seven men sent ashore to secure water.

34. On 17 August 1775 Bruno Hezeta, a Spanish voyager, noted the mouth of the present Columbia River and although he was unable to enter it, named the north cape San Rogue and the south cape, Frondosa. Captain John Meares, in 1788, named the north cape, Disappointment because he failed to see the river behind it. Captain Robert Gray entered the Columbia River on 12 May 1792 and named it after his ship. It must be assumed that he also named the north cape, Hancock, which accounts for its use by Boit. However, the name Disappointment has endured.

35. Boit's attempt at crossing the Columbia River's bar exemplified the great difficulties involved even in the middle of summer. He spent nine days trying to enter the river, recalling that in the same passage by the *Columbia* three years earlier, a fine collection of sea otter skins had been secured.

36. Named by Captain Robert Gray in the sloop *Lady Washington*, consort to the ship *Columbia* on her second voyage to the Northwest Coast. She was probably the first American ship to

make a recorded landing on the Oregon coast (at Tillamook Bay). On 16 August 1788, Captain Gray's servant, Marcus Lopins, was murdered when on shore by the natives, which accounts for the name.

37. Nootka Sound was a world-renowned name during the latter part of the eighteenth century, owing to the bitter dispute between Great Britain and Spain over the right each had to the area, a dispute that nearly led to war. The sound was discovered and named Nootka by Captain James Cook in April, 1778. It was occupied by the Spaniards from 1789 to 1795, when, in the presence of the British and Spanish commissioners, the British flag was hoisted in token of possession and the Spanish troops embarked. In 1792 Vancouver and Quadra met at Friendly Cove regarding the lands to be restored by the Spaniards to the British. Friendly Cove was used extensively by fur-trading vessels as a refitting and rendezvous point.

38. "Maguinna, the well known Indian chief of Nootka Sound, who gained notoriety by being the contemporary of Vancouver, Quadra, Martinez, Eliza, Meares and other British and Spanish seamen who were prominent characters towards the close of the eighteenth Century in the history of the Northwest Coast of America. Maguinna was the chief from whom Captain John Meares, of the merchant vessel, *Felice*, purchased, in 1788, the land, little better than a garden plot, in Friendly Cove, on which the British claim to a portion of this coast against the Spanish claim to the whole coast of Northwest America was first founded. Maguinna was the chief who, in 1803, captured the American ship *Boston* at anchor in his domain of Nootka Sound, and massacred the whole crew with the exception of two men. The unforeseen result of the purchase of the land by Captain Meares brought Nootka into prominence before the whole civilized world and Maguinna was in close contact with British and Spanish naval diplomats; while his celebrated and successful attack on the *Boston* made his name detested and feared by the whole of the fur trading seamen frequenting these shores" (Walbran, *British Columbia Place Names*, p. 317).

39. De Fonte.

40. Haswell's Isles. These are probably the Scott Islands at the northwest corner of Vancouver Island.

41. Woody Point. In 1778, Captain James Cook called this broad promontory on the northwestern coast of Vancouver Island, Woody Point. Its name was subsequently changed to Cape Cook by Captain George H. Richards, H.M. surveying vessel *Plumper*.

42. Bulfinch Sound (Nasparti Inlet), on the east side of Woody Point, was named after a prominent Boston physician. It was very familiar to Boit from his voyage in the *Columbia*.

43. Owyhee. One of many variant spellings of Hawaii during the eighteenth and early nineteenth centuries.

44. Robands. Small lengths of line passed through the eyelet holes at the head of a sail to attach it to the yard or jackstay.

45. Boit was very careful to keep the armament in good condition and ready for use when approaching a possible anchorage. The *Union* was equipped with ten carriage cannons and eight swivel guns, which were relatively heavy armament for a vessel of her size.

46. The *Union* was "hove to" 9 to 12 miles off the northeast tip of the large island of Hawaii. Because of the small size of his vessel, Boit avoided being surrounded by countless large canoes in shore, which (with their crews of from 20 to 30 men) could easily overpower the small craft.

47. Tama-Maah, the king, is Boit's spelling for Kamehameha I ("The Very Lonely One"). He was born at Kohala, on the island of Hawaii, in 1758 and died 8 May 1819 at Kailua. In 1779, as a young chief, he directed negotiations between his uncle, King Kalamiopuu, and Captain James Cook, European discoverer of the Island. He initiated the conquering and unification of the islands in 1790 when, with the help of the castaway English sailors John Young and Isaac Davis, he invaded the Island of Maui. In 1792 he completed the conquest of the Island of Hawaii and by 1795, overcame Maui, Lanai, Molokai and Oahu. Kaui was brought under his control in 1809. By 1810, Kamehameha had united all of the Hawaiian Islands. He was a strong ruler and maintained his kingdom's independence through the difficult period of European discovery.

48. John Young. This young beachcomber became one of Kamehameha's chiefs of staff and it is evident that he was giving a

veiled warning to Boit that the *Union* was in grave jeopardy of being taken over and confiscated if she came closer to the beach.

49. Whoahoo is Boit's phonetic romanization of Oahu, the present site of Honolulu. Fair Haven was the principal harbor and anchorage for that island.

50. Young's description of repeated native attacks on fur-trading vessels both on the Northwest Coast and the Hawaiian Islands was another evidence that he was warning Boit of the great danger that the latter was exposed to in coming ashore at Hawaii.

51. Karakakooa Bay was the first anchorage of Captain Cook when he discovered the Hawaiian Islands on his third voyage to the Pacific. It is also where he was killed by the natives in a shore incident. The shoreline back of the bay and also that of Kona, further north, were thickly populated during the late eighteenth century and were visited frequently by ships of that period.

52. Morokay. Probably the island of Mokokai.

53. This island is difficult to identify from Boit's description. It could be one of a group near the island of Niihau to the west of Kauai.

54. Mariana (Ladrone) Islands.

55. These islands must be the Hungton (Lanyu) group.

56. Lamma Island is directly southwest of Hong Kong. Here Boit took aboard a pilot for the 30-mile sail to Macao. Until 1840, when England gained control, Hong Kong was an inhospitable, barren island, with few inhabitants and was a lair for pirates.

57. Macao was and is a Portuguese settlement located at the southwestern entrance to the Pearl River flowing out of the Canton estuary. A full description is given in the Introduction.

58. After taking on a river pilot, the *Union* left Macao on December 3rd. On December 4th, she passed Lintin Bar and anchored near the second bar on the 5th. The following day she reached an anchorage at Whampoa, some 12 miles below the factories at Canton.

59. Usually the furs were unloaded at the Whampoa anchorage and lightered up to the factory at Canton where they were stored until sold. This was not done in the sale of the *Union*'s furs until December 24th when they were sold to a Mr. Mongua (see entry for that date).

60. Nakeen, nankin, a buff-colored, durable cloth, originally made in Nankin, China.

61. Harbor master.

62. Small sampans supplied by the interpreter.

63. The voyage from Canton into the Indian Ocean via the South China Sea and the Strait of Sunda was made dangerous by pirates and privateers working out of Malaya, Indonesia and other small countries bordering on these waters. Some of these vessels were of considerable tonnage and posed a real threat to merchant ships in the area. It was for this reason that trading vessels usually grouped themselves into small convoys for self-protection.

64. Grand Ladrone. An island that was an important landfall off the mouth of the Pearl River leading to Canton.

65. Pulo Sapata. One of a multitude of islands in the South China Sea whose names have been changed on modern charts.

66. Banca Isle. This is present Bangka Island approximately 200 miles northwest of the Strait of Sunda.

67. Straits of Banca. Between Bangka Island and Sumatra.

68. North Isle Roads. This must have been on the Java side of the entrance to the Strait of Sunda. Vessels going through the strait could take on water and wait for favorable tidal and wind conditions.

69. The *Union* entered the Strait of Sunda with a convoy on 31 January 1796 and struggled with adverse winds and contrary tides until February 9th, when she finally weathered the southwest point of Princess Island and broke free into the Indian Ocean.

70. Crocatore (Krakatau) Island. An island volcano in the western end of Sunda Strait which posed a serious obstacle to sailing vessels entering the Indian Ocean.

71. Panaitan (Prinsen) Island. Another island that was an obstacle at the western end of Sunda Strait.

72. Christmas Isle. Appeared on a Dutch chart of 1666 as Moni. Renamed by Captain James Cook; Cook stopped here on Christmas Day 1777 for turtles, "perhaps as good as any in the world."

73. Trussell trees (Trestle trees). A very important part of the masting of any sailing vessel. The trees were two strong pieces of timber placed fore and aft and resting on the cheeks at the head of the mast. The rigging and sails of the *Union* were beginning to show extreme wear and weakness after her long time at sea. This created a wearisome problem for John Boit during the rest of the voyage.

74. Isle of France, later renamed Mauritius. Portuguese navigators discovered this island in 1505. Subsequently taken over by the Dutch, Isle of France was abandoned by them in 1710, and held by the French from 1715 to 1810. Its capital, Port Louis, also administered the smaller island dependencies including Rodriquez, 350 miles east, and scattered groups, 250 to 580 miles away.

75. Woold. To reinforce a mast or spar by winding several close turns of rope tightly around it.

76. St. Brass Mountain. On the extreme tip of the Cape of Good Hope.

77. Cape Vaccas. Located approximately 200 miles east of the Cape of Good Hope.

78. Assencion. Ascencion. A 34-square-mile island, 750 miles northwest of the Island of St. Helena in the South Atlantic. Discovered by Portuguese navigator da Nova in 1501. The British took possession in 1815. It remains an important navigational and tracking station.

Research on the Sloop Union

Hewitt R. Jackson

The contemporary material for details of the sloop *Union* are extremely limited. There are her specifications in the Federal Archives and Records Center at Waltham, Massachusetts; two small profile drawings in John Boit's Log—one of her at anchor in Friendly Cove, Nootka (*see* p. 48), and the other under sail and saluting the fort as she returned to Boston (*see* p. xxxi). Captain Boit reported that she was a good sea boat but a dull sailer. This, with a few scant log entires, constitutes what we had to go on for our reconstruction. Fortunately, I had made an extensive study of the *Lady Washington*, the sloop that had sailed as consort to the *Columbia Rediviva* on her voyage to the Northwest Coast in 1787. She was also "of 90 tons" and was a fine sailer according to the journals surviving that venture. There is one surviving drawing of her at anchor.

The first problem was to arrive at a probable set of dimensions for a 90-ton sloop that would have the characteristics of a good sea boat and be reasonably fast and weatherly. My old copy of *The Merchants and Shipmasters' Manual, Ship Builders' and Sailmakers' Assistant — Enlarged* of 1865 carried a great deal about the measuring of ships by both the "old" and "new" methods. The "Manual of Admeasurement" (a portion on measurements) section also has many examples of these methods. A set of dimensions in the middle range was selected as being somewhat probable for the vessel we had in mind. I avoided the tubs at one extreme and the "sharp built" flyers at the other.

With the basic dimensions more or less determined, a search was made for lines of a vessel that would meet the other requirements of the voyage that had been stated so well by captains Cook and Vancouver. The first was a relatively shoal-draft vessel to navigate the rivers and inlets of the Northwest Coast; secondly, the ability to

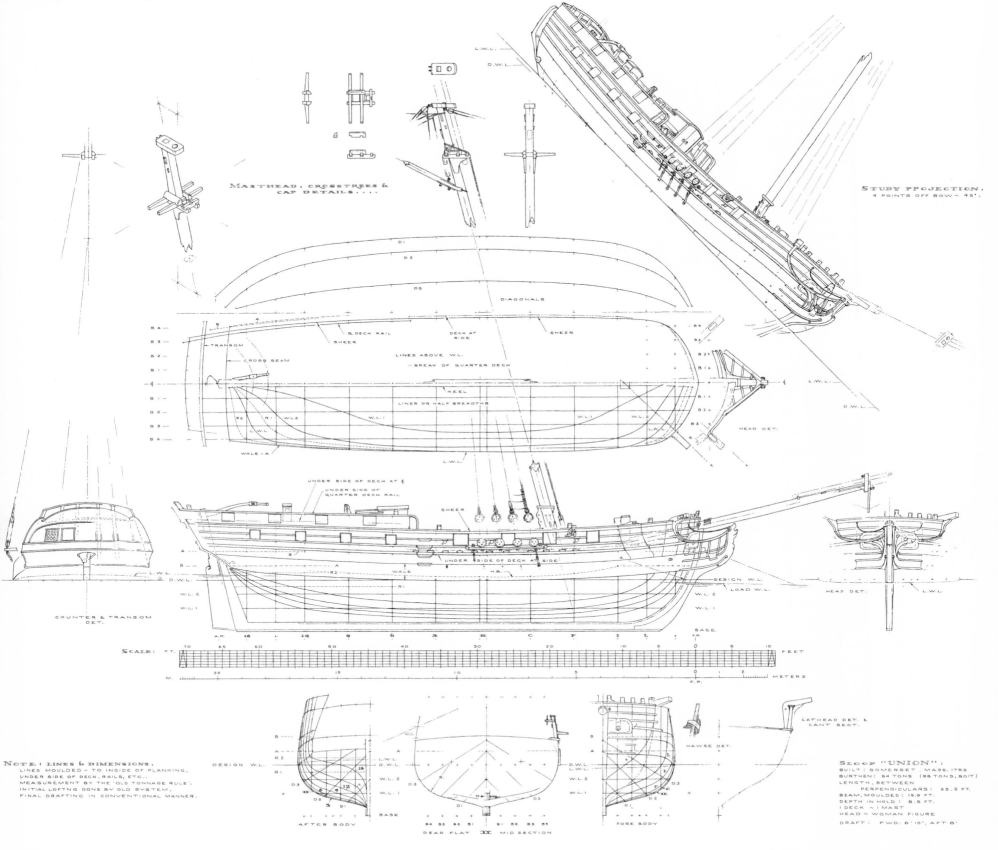

MASTHEAD, CROSSTREES & CAP DETAILS....

STUDY PROJECTION.
4 POINTS OFF BOW ~ 45°.

D 1
D 2
D 3
DIAGONALS

LINES ABOVE W.L.

B 4
B 3
B 2
B 1

Q. DECK RAIL
DECK AT SIDE
SHEER
SHEER

TRANSOM
CROSS SEAM
BREAK OF QUARTER DECK

KEEL

LINES OR HALF BREADTHS

R2 R1 W.L.2
W.L.1
L.W.L.

B 1
B 2
B 3
B 4

W.L.I
W.L.2
L.W.L.
D.W.L.

HEAD DET.

WALE ~ A

L.W.L.

COUNTER & TRANSOM DET.

UNDER SIDE OF DECK AT ₵
UNDER SIDE OF QUARTER DECK RAIL
SHEER

UNDER SIDE OF DECK AT SIDE

A
B
R2
R1

WALE
H.B.

L.W.L.
D.W.L.
W.L.2
W.L.1

DESIGN W.L.
LOAD W.L.
W.L.2
W.L.1

HEAD DET.
L.W.L.

A.P. 18 15 12 9 6 3 II C F I L BASE
F.P.

SCALE: FT. 70 65 60 50 40 30 20 10 5 0 5 10 FEET

M. 20 15 10 5 0 1 2 METERS

NOTE: LINES & DIMENSIONS.
LINES MOULDED ~ TO INSIDE OF PLANKING,
UNDER SIDE OF DECK, RAILS, ETC.,
MEASUREMENT BY THE 'OLD TONNAGE RULE'.
INITIAL LOFTING DONE BY OLD SYSTEM,
FINAL DRAFTING IN CONVENTIONAL MANNER.

DESIGN W.L.

B
A
R2
R1
D3
D2
D1
BASE

AFTER BODY

L.W.L.
D.W.L.
W.L.2
W.L.1

DEAD FLAT II MID SECTION

B4 B3 B2 B1

B
A
D3
D2
D1

D.W.L.
L.W.L.
W.L.2
W.L.1

FORE BODY

CATHEAD DET. & CANT SECT.

HAWSE DET.

SLOOP "UNION":
BUILT: SOMERSET, MASS. 1792
BURTHEN: 94 TONS (98 TONS; BOIT)
LENGTH, BETWEEN
  PERPENDICULARS: 65.5 FT.
BEAM, MOULDED: 19.9 FT.
DEPTH IN HOLD: 8.5 FT.
1 DECK ~ 1 MAST
HEAD ~ WOMAN FIGURE
DRAFT: FWD. 6'10", AFT 8'

PROFILE, LINES, BODY PLAN & DETAILS.

SLOOP "UNION" SHEET 5

"stand on her feet" if grounded, dictated a full mid-section and firm bilges. She would have to be somewhat full in her lines to accommodate the storage of water, provisions and cargo for a voyage far beyond the ordinary.

The dimensions, roughly laid down, were 65'6" length between perpendiculars, beam moulded 21'6" and depth of hold, 7'6". A study of published lines and data was then made to determine a suitable starting point.

Fred H. Chapman's *Architectura Navalis Mercatoria* (1768) was the first to be consulted as it contains a wide selection of lines and dimensions; also the plates are splendid examples of the drafting of the period. Steele's *Naval Architecture* of a slightly later date was also consulted as it was logical to assume that the English source would provide more typical examples.

The various works of Howard I. Chapelle and correspondence with him turned up some unpublished (at that time) plans that were useful, particularly in detail. The most helpful of his work was the discussion of old prints and paintings that depicted Colonial sloops, though none of these featured the vessel as a major component of the picture. Among the miscellaneous material in my studio files was an article by C.H. Davis pertaining to the Hudson River sloops, a distinctive American type. While the article was principally concerned with the fully developed sloops used on the river at a later date, the lines, deck and sail plan of the *Experiment* were presented as are notes on the development of the sloop type. The *Experiment* is described as a Hudson River packet, built in 1780 and handsomely fitted for the passenger trade. She made a voyage to China and return in 1785-1786 under a Captain Dean. Her length was 60', beam 20' and depth of hold 7'6" with a tonnage of 75 77/95 tons. The plans as presented were

drawn by Charles Davis and are drawn in the modern manner. Those of the later sloops were derived from half-models to which he had access.

Only one detailed painting of a sloop of this particular period was turned up. This is of an unidentified sloop (No. 190) in the collection of the Peabody Museum, *Marine Paintings and Drawings of the Peabody Museum* (Brewington-Salem 1968). This was attributed to Corné and was quite helpful.

In the period in question, vessels were not habitually described by rig, as we know it, but usually the service in which they were engaged and by hull form. Thus, a cutter was usually a fast and lightly built vessel carrying a sloop-like rig. A similar fast hull form was to be found in the luggers. A hoy was a type that must be considered; defined as "a small vessel, usually rigged as a sloop, employed in carrying passengers and goods, particularly in short distances on the sea-coast."

Ships were designed in this period with a system of tangential arcs. The compass was the principal tool of design. The system worked well through the mid section of the vessel but as the ends were approached, the planks had to be faired in. This is where the "art and mystery" of the master shipwright came in. It was this reliance on "rule of thumb and eye" that made it virtually impossible to reproduce an outstanding hull. It should be remembered that this method of design was ancient and preceeded both the builder's model and the mould loft in the shipyards. The drawn set of plans and details is a recent innovation.

A step-by-step exposition of the reconstruction is not required, so it will suffice to say that an incredible amount of time was spent at the drawing board. Upon completion it was decided to make a comparison with the small profile of the *Lady Washington*, which was drawn on board the ship by Robert Haswell. The rendering is minute and comprises only a small part to the extent that this is possi-

---

One of the many preliminary studies (opposite) produced by maritime illustrator and scholar, Hewitt Jackson; part of the long and arduous job of assiduously reconstructing the sloop *Union* for this volume.

ble. It has been used as a guide and reference throughout the reconstruction process. (It turned out to be a scale profile, in all probability drawn from the ship's spar and sail plan, and the same proved to be true for the two drawings of the *Union*.)

The document of the *Union* states that she was built at Somerset, Massachusetts in 1792 and was of 94 tons burthen, length 65'5", beam 19'9" and depth of hold 8'5". She had one deck and one mast. The head was a "woman figure." There is no mention of galleries or badges, thus indicating their absence. From the Log and Remarks, we learn of ten carriage guns, six- and three-pounders, and of eight swivel carried on the rails. Entries tell of altering and raising the bulwarks and cutting in and framing the appropriate gun ports. There is little other detail given in the Log except that it is noted that a yellow spread eagle was painted on the stern shortly before she arrived home in Boston. In the matter of sails and rigging, a rather complete inventory can be arrived at from the Log entries.

This sloop is so close to the *Lady Washington* in dimension and tonnage that a direct comparison is possible. Spar and rigging details would be much the same and very little in the way of calculations had to be done. Study prints of the drawings were prepared and the photographic negatives brought out the detail in excellent shape. There is a greater rake to the mast on the *Union*, thus allowing it to be stepped further forward to gain more unobstructed deck space. The boom is lengthened and the gaff substantially shortened as a result of this. The sail plan, as a whole, coincides with that of the *Lady Washington*, though somewhat different in appearance. In short, we had a very workable point of departure for the reconstruction.

Some further remarks on the rigging of the *Union* may serve to clarify certain entries in the Log. The towering single mast and relatively few sails must have had some distinct advantages on shorter coastal voyages, but the size of the individual sails were greater than those on brigs and ships of much greater tonnage. They must have been real brutes to handle in a gale. The rig, as a whole, seems incredibly lofty as we first look at it. What must be realized is that in the regions of severe weather, the yards and top mast were sent down (on deck) and the jib boom was run in. Deprived of all these light "kites" the rig begins to look compact and manageable (*see* illustration on p. 107). The Log notes the enumerable times this was done.

Both the standing and running rigging were hemp, usually from the Baltic. This was not the manila stuff but rather a fine fiber that, when impregnated with Stockholm tar, was extremely durable and strong. When a piece of gear was worn beyond use, it was picked apart for its still usable fiber. This "picking oakum" was very much a part of shipboard life and mentioned many times in the Log. The present "marline" and "oakum," as we know it will give an idea of what it was like. Once a piece of line was picked apart, the fibers were spun into threads or spun yarn, then twisted into strands and laid into rope. On the voyage, the forward pair of shrouds were replaced with new lines and the former were picked apart to provide material for lighter gear and running rigging. This endless cycle of picking oakum through to the laying up of rope of various sizes and the plaiting of sennet and mats filled all the available time in ships of this period. When we realize that a rope walk ashore could often be up to a quarter-mile in length, the ingenuity of these seamen is realized.

The hemp rigging was of large dimension to allow for strength, wear and deterioration. The stay on the *Union* would have been a good nine inches in circumference and required a sixteen-inch deadeye. The shrouds would have

While preparing for the final color drawing reproduced in this book as the frontis, Hewitt Jackson produced this preliminary study of the *Union* with its boarding nets up to counter the Indian attack at Barrell's Sound. Annotations on the drawing were used by Jackson to aid in the construction of this late-eighteenth-century New England sloop.

A STUDY OF THE SLOOP "UNION",
CAPT. JOHN BOIT, W/ BOARDING NETS
RIGGED, BARREL'S SOUND.
19 TO 22 JUNE, 1795....

ANCHORAGE: LOCAATED - LOG, JOURNAL & L. CLAY. A VERY
      GOOD SITUATION. COULD GET OUT UNDER ANY
      EXPECTED WIND CONDITION...

BOARDING NETS: DERIVED FROM PAINTING OF SHIP "JASON"
      OF BOSTON - 1802 - ANTOINE ROUX, SEN. (C.G. WELD
      COLLECTION IN 1920).
      CREW WOULD BE PROTECTED AND THE SLOOP
      SAILED & MANOEUVRED WITH THIS SET UP.
      THE ADDITIONAL OR UPPER HEAD RAIL AND
      NETTING SHOWN IN BOIT'S DRAWINGS ARE
      DETAILS ALSO SHOWN ABOVE.

CANOES: 'HEAD' TYPE. SEE THE TITLE PAGE ILLUSTRATION
      OF ROBT HASWELL'S JOURNAL. "COLUMBIA" & BRIG
      IN 'HANCOCK'S RIVER, NORTH END OF WASHINGTONS
      ISLANDS' - CANOES SHOWN. (MASSET SOUND.
      N.E. GRAHM IS. Q.C. ISLANDS).. UNPUBLISHED
      PICTURE. REF. COPY FROM MASS, HIST. SOC.
      NEG. NO. B 5517 A.

been at least six feet with a ten- or twelve-inch deadeye. All of this standing rigging would have been "wormed, parcelled and served." In places of wear, pigskin would have been worked over it.

The standing rigging, while of great strength, was elastic to a degree and tended to stretch. Temperature and humidity affected it. The shrouds and stays of the *Union* might easily have stretched two to three feet in a short space of time.

Sails were linen or hemp, the latter having a distinct greenish tint when new and later weathering to a deeper tan. In the American ships, linen was preferred though not always in good supply. Some was of local manufacture, but most imported from Europe. This canvas was hand woven and soft. In reading the sailmakers' manuals, we get the impression of a very baggy sail. A good wetting and a stiff breeze would soon stretch it to a more functional shape. The better paintings of the period confirm this.

The drawing techniques used in the illustrations for this book are pretty much standard for this type of work when it comes to the more usual details. As the plans progressed, the same preciseness is retained but more of the techniques of the illustrator are used. There is some simplification of structural detail where warranted. Men have been added to give scale and a point of reference. Detailing in both the longitudinal and cross sections has been added to show the accommodations and stowage of stores, cargo and provisions, something not required for ship or model building. The intent is to be informative to the lay reader and helpful to the more advanced scholars.

John Boit's Navigation

For his time, John Boit was a most competent navigator, perhaps even an outstanding one.

The system of lunar navigation practiced at that time was quite new (though the principles of it had been known to astronomers for a long time). One must be struck with the rapidity with which the American mariners became aware of it and gained a high level of proficiency in its use.

J.C. Beaglehole, in his *The Life of Captain James Cook* (pp. 153-56), points out that the expedition astronomer on the first voyage, Charles Green, was disturbed to find out that no one on board was familiar with or capable of taking or working up a lunar observation. In 1768 he wrote to the Royal Society from Rio de Janeiro: "I thought it a little odd when I found that no person in the ship could either make an observation of the Moon or Calculate one when made."

Indications are that Captain Cook was not familiar with the system upon sailing, but that he rapidly became proficient in these observations and calculations as the voyage progressed. Before this it had not been a practical tool for navigators.

A complex and extensive set of tables and instructions had been worked up by astronomers for their use and for navigational purposes. There were several English versions of this material published and available in the closing decades of the eighteenth century. We have no way of knowing just what of this material was aboard the *Union*, but the Log gives ample evidence of its continuing and frequent use.

These materials lacked the refinement required for precise navigation and were replete with errors and geographical misinformation, but they were a vast improvement over anything known to the time. The old adage of "lead, latitude and lookout" was still appropriate and these "Three L's" of early navigation were to remain in force for generations to come.

The practical application of lunar navigation was almost coincidental with the development of the chronometer and, as both were effective in the determination of longitude, this was a significant advance in navigation.

In plotting the *Union*'s track around the world the log positions were used and directly entered upon the chart. Both lunar and dead reckoning calculations were made and they are readily followed in the *Union*'s Log as one goes along. By the standards of the times Boit's landfalls are good.

In the South Atlantic Ocean weather prevented good observations as the Falkland Islands were approached, but the sighting and recognition of Jasons Isles was in good order. In the Pacific Ocean most of the logged positions were to the westward of true position. The approach to the Northwest Coast was without incident and Columbia's Cove was entered after a series of good landfalls. The landfall at the Sandwich Islands was as expected though the "appearance of land" had been entered a few days previously. These islands provided a new point of departure on the route across the Pacific. When Tinian and Saipan were sighted the log positions were about six degrees or roughly 250 miles west of these islands. Boit calmly noted the true position, established a new point of departure, and was on his way. At the southern point of Formosa the landfall was in good order and the run to Macao was without incident. Again, in the Indian Ocean, the log positions placed the *Union* about 300 miles west of Rodriques when it was sighted—some four days sailing. A new departure was taken.

All through the voyage this westerly error is present in the positions logged. Gross as these errors seem to us, they are insignificant when compared to other observations of historical record. Just how much of this can be attributed to faulty navigation by the various captains is hard to ascertain. The great number of errors in the almanacs of the period could well be a very significant factor.

It is interesting to note that as the little vessel neared home waters and fell in with other ships Boit's positions varied greatly with theirs. When one considers that these craft were just a few days out, one would expect more accurate positions. This was not the case. When working out the positions back from the landfall it was found that *Union*'s positions were much the better.

One might well consider the practical use of lunar navigation to have begun about the time of or soon after Captain James Cook's first voyage of 1769-71. The captain's enthusiasm for the system left him a bit dubious about the first chronometer he was to have on the second voyage.

Within a few years this vastly improved system of navigation was to be relatively well known to progressive mariners in America and working "lunars" was to become the mark of accomplishment in Yankee ships.

It is difficult to believe that ships blundered about the distant oceans of the world with nothing in the way of charts and information.

Log entries and Remarks of the *Union*'s voyage indicate that Captain Boit was well supplied with charts for the voyage. Most of these would have been the published charts of the better known portions of the globe. Atlases of recent voyages of exploration had become available by the time of the voyage and would have contained needed information on the Northwest Coast and the islands of the Pacific.

In addition to these readily available materials there is mention in other accounts of manuscript materials. Logs and journals of other voyages were consulted and needed data copied longhand. Chart materials were laboriously traced.

Some of this material was shared and was soon to be incorporated into new or revised charts for general sail. Other material was regarded as "secret" by the ship owners and their masters and we can assume that it was only for the eyes of those in that particular commercial venture. The instructions to the masters taking out ships in the fur trade support this conclusion.

The chart of Bulfinch Sound in the Log of the *Union* was done for the sloop's own use and information as were other drawings of anchorages and local harbors. The chart of the Falkland Islands (*see* p. 22) is another matter. When the time spent in that region is considered along with the labor of provisioning, wooding and watering the ship it becomes quite obvious that Boit did not have time for such a detailed survey. An examination of that chart shows an array of detail and place names, indicating that in all likelihood this was copied or traced from a chart more up-to-date and detailed than the one in his possession—perhaps from the whaler that was there at the time. It is possible that it was traced from a chart on board the whaler he fell in with there. Boit's positive identification of the Jasons Isles necessitated a pilot or sailing directions of some sort.

Captain Robert Gray of the ship *Columbia Rediviva* compiled charts of various anchorages frequented by his vessel and of Gray's Harbor and the Columbia River. These latter were made available to Captain Vancouver of the *Discovery* and were copied for his use. It is only reasonable to presume that Captain Gray was provided with like material and information from Captain Vancouver's notes and surveys, as most cordial relations existed between the two captains. The owners must have provided Captain Boit with manuscript copies of these.

The discovery and naming of Hatch's Isle, the statement that it had not been previously discovered, and his exact position for a point of departure are evidence of a reasonably complete chart of the Sandwich Islands at hand. Vancouver's detailed chart of the islands was not published until 1798 so the content of the chart had to date from Captain Cook and subsequent visitors.

Much the same observations can be made about the approach to China. The evidence of charts and a pilot of sorts is there. Trade with China had long been established with the English, Dutch and French and charts and pilots were published and available from these sources. The new part of the route was the approach from the reaches of the broad Pacific.

By the time the *Union* was making its voyage there was a wealth of published material on the oceans of the world and copies of pertinent sections could easily have been available to mariners—manuscript copies if nothing else. The world chart in the atlas of Cook's third voyage to the Northwest Coast is clear and detailed in the octavo edition. The much larger quarto edition and its atlas were even more detailed.

The journals and atlas of Captain Cook's third voyage had been published in 1784, and Meares's account had come out in London in 1790 and would have been known to those involved in the venture. Nathaniel Portlock and George Dixon had been shipmates with Captain Cook and were back on the Northwest Coast with their respective ventures in 1786-87 and at least some of the details of these voyages were probably known to the American traders.

While Captain Cook's observations of many remote regions would have been of little practical value at the time, the account of the route down the South China Sea is most informative. It indicates that it was only an expansion and remarks based on earlier data.

The gross errors of navigation reported were all too common but this does not of necessity imply that the observations and calculations were at fault. The lack of information on currents and seasonal variations in wind and weather are major factors. Being set away from one's objective by stress of weather or other cause remained a condition beyond control until the end of the sailing era.

A great number of these passage-making problems were not strictly deficiencies in navigation but were rather an adverse condition of wind and sea that prevented the desired landfall being made, or if made, thwarted every effort to proceed. We might cite the situation of the *Union* off the Columbia River; the navigation was correct but the prevailing conditions prevented the entering the river.

Method of Keeping a Journal at Sea

[Extracted from Nathaniel Bowditch, *The American Practical Navigation* (1808)]

The daily occurances on board a ship are marked on a large board or slate, called the "log-board" or "log-slate," kept in the steerage for that purpose. This log is usually divided into seven columns: the first contains the hours from noon to noon, being marked by some every two hours, but by others for every single hour; in the second and third columns are the knots and fathoms the ship is found to run per hour, set against the hours when the log was hove (some navigators do not divide the knot into ten fathoms, but into half knots only, marking the third column H.K.); the fourth column contains the courses steered by compass; the fifth, the winds; the sixth, the lee-way, and the seventh, the alteration of the sails, the business done a-board, and what other remarks the officer of the watch thinks proper to insert. It should be observed that it is usual to divide the ship's company into two parts, called the starboard and larboard watches, who do the duty of the ship for four hours and four hours, alternately, except from 4 to 8 P.M., which is divided into two watches. The remarks made on the log-board are daily copied into a book called the log-book, which is ruled like the log-board. This book contains an authentic record of the ship's transactions, and the persons who keep a reckoning, transcribe them into their journals, and then make the necessary deductions relative to the ship's place, every day at noon, which operation is called working a "day's work." While a ship is in port, the remarks entered in the log-book are called "harbour work," or "harbour journals," and the day is then estimated according to the civil computation as on shore, that is from mid-night to midnight. But at sea the day's work ending at noon is dated the same as the civil day, so that the day's work marked Monday began on Sunday noon, and ended on Monday at noon; the day thus marked is called a "nautical day"; the first 12 hours being marked P.M. and the latter A.M. There are various ways of keeping journals at sea, according to the different tastes of navigators. Some keep only an abstract of each day's transactions, specifying the weather, what ships or lands were seen, accidents on boards, the latitude, longitude, course, and run; these particulars being drawn from the ship's log-book. Others keep a full copy of the log-book, and the deductions drawn therefrom, arranged in proper columns; the latter is the most satisfactory to those who may have occasion to inspect the journal.

When a ship is about losing sight of land, the bearing of some noted place (whose latitude and longitude is known) must be observed, and its distance estimated and marked on the log-book; this is called "taking a departure." In working this first day's work, the calculation is made in the same manner as if the ship had sailed that distance from that place upon a course opposite to that bearing, and that course and distance are to be entered accordingly into the traverse table, after allowing for the variation.

Canoes

The only artists to portray the canoes of the Queen Charlotte Islands were George Davidson and Robert Haswell who were with Captain Robert Gray. Davidson was a competent observer and his drawings include a great amount of detail. One must discount the contemporary conventions of the American folk art of the period in some of his settings. Haswell was not as accomplished a draftsman, but his details are in close agreement.

The George Dixon and Nathaniel Portlock material has not been gone over as time was limited on this project. Some of the coastal profiles and information that came out of these ventures is of high quality.

Some of the Spanish illustrations of 1792 show canoes that do not fit the details of the Nootkan and "head" canoes, and it is quite certain that there was a much greater variety along the coast than these two distinctive types.

Paul Kane, in his drawings made half a century later, depicts both of these types in detail and includes other variations of the 'great canoes' of the period. These craft show the development of design and decoration brought about by the introduction of steel tools and the prosperity of the coastal Indian culture.

Colophon

Goudy Old Style and Goudy Thirty are the typefaces used in *The Log of the Union*. Both were crafted by Frederic W. Goudy, arguably the greatest American designer of type. The text was set in Goudy Old Style; Goudy designed the Old Style capitals after letterforms produced in the sixteenth century by Hans Holbein the Younger. Goudy felt that this 1915 design was "almost" as great an innovation as his earlier Kennerley face. Goudy Thirty (the display typography in this volume) is an extraordinary face, a pen-drawn calligraphic roman; Goudy stated that he took a roman face and "gothicized" it. First drawn in 1942, Thirty has often been misrepresented as the designer's last typeface; Goudy had merely requested that it not be issued until after his death, for he wanted it to be "the last word in type design," a face on which his reputation would rest.

The display typography was produced by Spartan Typography of Oakland, California. The text was set by Irish Setter and printed by Durham & Downey, both Portland firms. The book is printed on warm-white 80# felt-finish Teton Text, and the paperbound copies are bound in companion 80# cover stock. The clothbound books are covered with Holliston Sail Cloth.

Visual life has been given to *The Log of the Union* by Hewitt Jackson's striking color frontispiece, six evocative wash drawings, the many precise line plans, cross sections and profiles of the *Union*, and by his maps, all specially commissioned for this volume.

The Log of the Union was designed by Bruce Taylor Hamilton.